WOODCARVING Country Folk

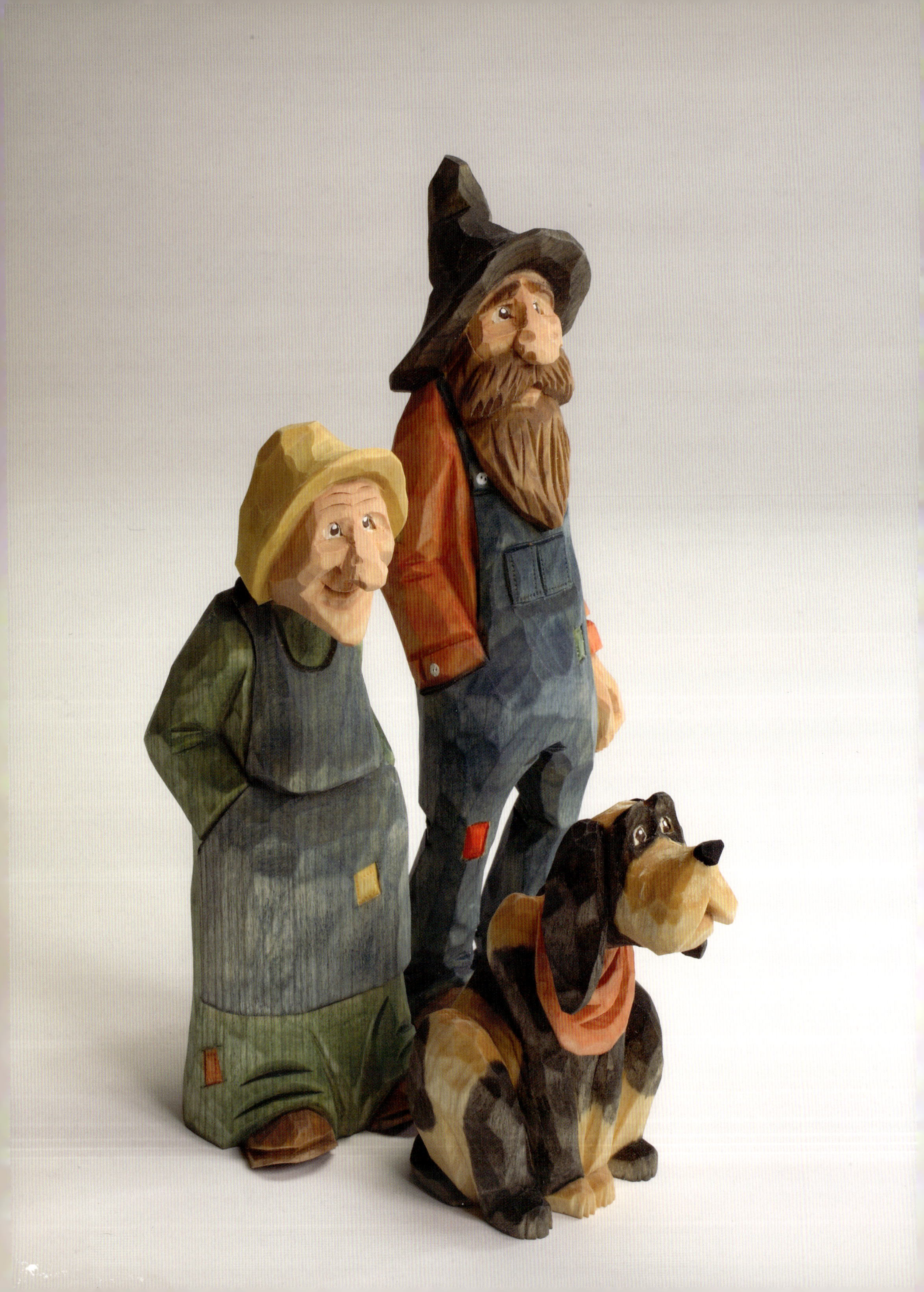

WOODCARVING Country Folk

By Mike Shipley

Fox Chapel Publishing
1970 Broad Street • East Petersburg, PA 17520
www.FoxChapelPublishing.com

Acknowledgements
Thanks to Sherry, my wife and partner.

Alan Giagnocavo
Publisher

Peg Couch
Acquisition Editor

Gretchen Bacon
Editor

Troy Thorne
Cover Design

Linda Eberly
Layout

Bob Fleming
Photography

Jack Kochan
Pattern Illustration

ISBN-13: 978–1–56523–286–0
ISBN-10: 1–56523–286–0

Publisher's Cataloging-in-Publication Data

Shipley, Mike.

Woodcarving country folk / by Mike Shipley. -- East Petersburg, PA :
Fox Chapel Publishing, c2006.

p. ; cm.

ISBN-13: 978-1-56523-286-0
ISBN-10: 1-56523-286-0

1. Wood-carving--Technique. 2. Wood-carving--Patterns.
3. Ozarkers in art. 4. Mountain people in art. 5. Country life-- Anecdotes.
I. Title.

TT199.7 .S55 2006
736/.4--dc22 0605

To learn more about the other great books from
Fox Chapel Publishing, or to find a retailer near you,
call toll-free 1-800-457-9112 or visit us at *www.FoxChapelPublishing.com*.

Note to Authors: We are always looking for talented
authors to write new books in our area of woodworking, design,
and related crafts. Please send a brief letter describing your idea to
Peg Couch, Acquisition Editor, 1970 Broad Street, East Petersburg, PA 17520.

Printed in China
10 9 8 7 6 5 4 3 2 1

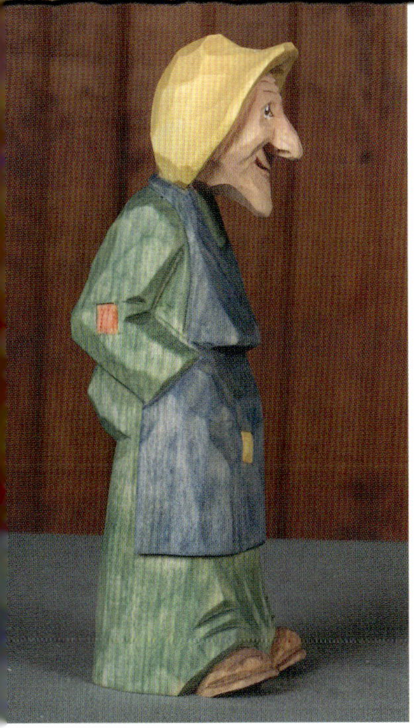

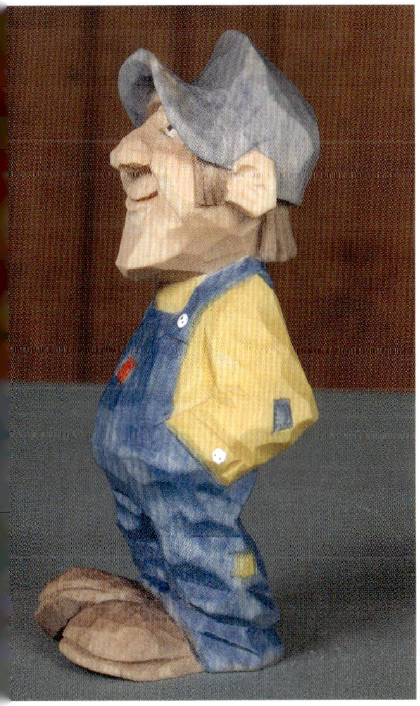

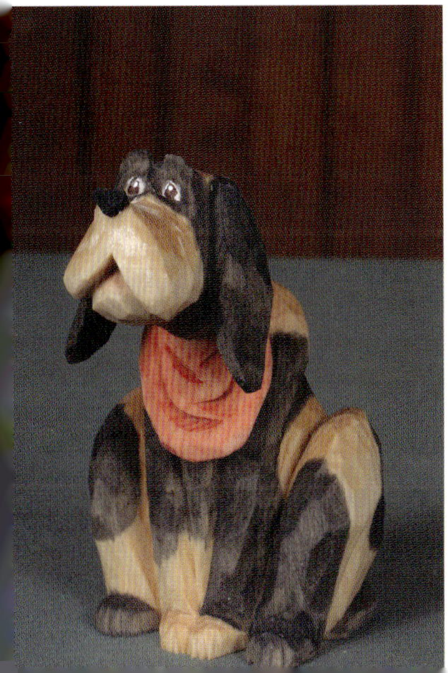

Contents

About the Author

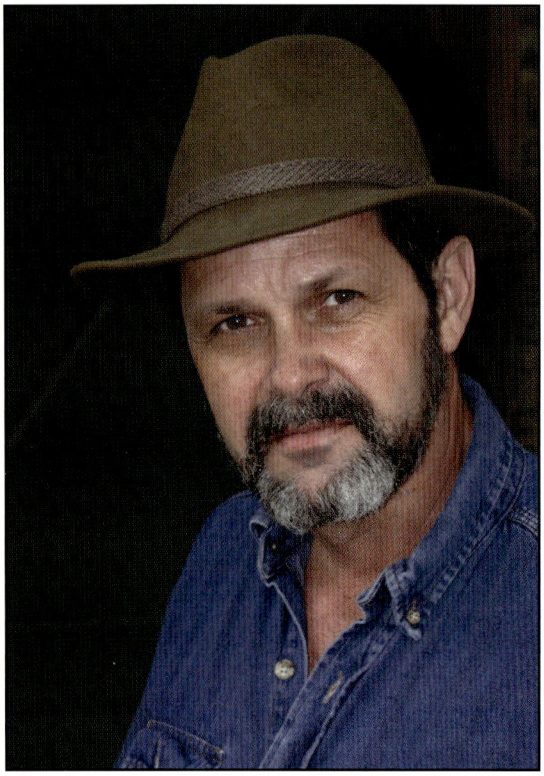

Mike Shipley is a full-time professional woodcarver and teacher with more than 30 years of carving experience. A self-taught carver, he is well known for his distinctive clean-cut style of carving and for his Santa figurines. Mike is also a production carver and has created as many as 100 carvings per month, entirely by hand, and finished with his own homemade stain. His carvings are sold at woodcraft shows, online, and from his studio in the Ozark Mountains.

Woodcarving Country Folk is Mike Shipley's fifth book. Other titles include *Carving Ozark County Characters* (out of print), *Whittling the Old Sea Captain, Handcarving Santas and Snowmen,* and *Woodcarving the Country Bear and His Friends,* which were all published by Fox Chapel Publishing. He has also been featured in *Wood Carving Illustrated* magazine.

Introducing Country Folk,

by a Country Folk Hisself

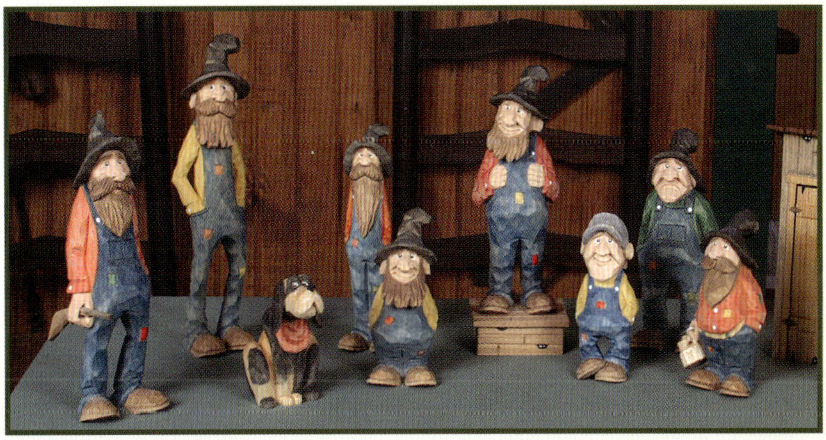

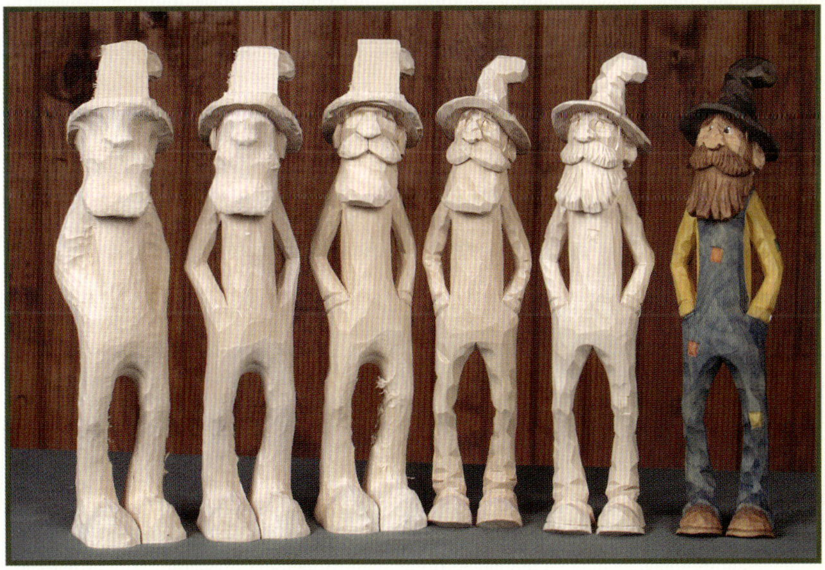

Welcome to the Ozarks! Most everybody has heard of the Ozark Mountains. I was born and raised in the heart of the Ozark Mountains in Ozark County, Missouri. This book is dedicated to those famous and fabled characters of the Ozarks, otherwise known as hill folk or hillbillies. I can poke a little fun at these folks because I'm pretty much one of them.

When thinking of hill folk, we all know the first image that comes to mind is someone who's laid back and simple minded, or maybe a little on the ornery side, with only one concern in life—makin' moonshine. But to be honest, the opposite is true. You won't find harder-working, more honest, or trustworthier people than the folks in the Ozarks. I created the characters in this book to take us back for a visit to the time when these guys might have been seen walking down an old back road (and, by the way, we still have those back roads!).

I'm not a historian, but I'm sure that, in this part of the country, woodcarving came about out of necessity: When folks here needed something, they made it. If what they needed was wooden, then some type of carving was required. As times have changed, woodcarving has evolved into a more pleasurable pastime, not only here in the Ozarks, but also across the country.

Times were simple back in the old days. For the most part, the only form of entertainment was homegrown music. My whole family played music. I can still remember going to those Saturday night music parties. My late brother, Kenny, was a fiddler; while still in his teenage years, he won many local fiddler contests. My Great-Grandpa Alec was also a fiddler. I'm told he would play alone or to groups and tell jokes while he played. He also was the blacksmith in the tiny village of Dawt, Missouri. It was told that one day Alec was in the blacksmith shop, when in walked this character that Alec was not too fond of. It seemed this man was having

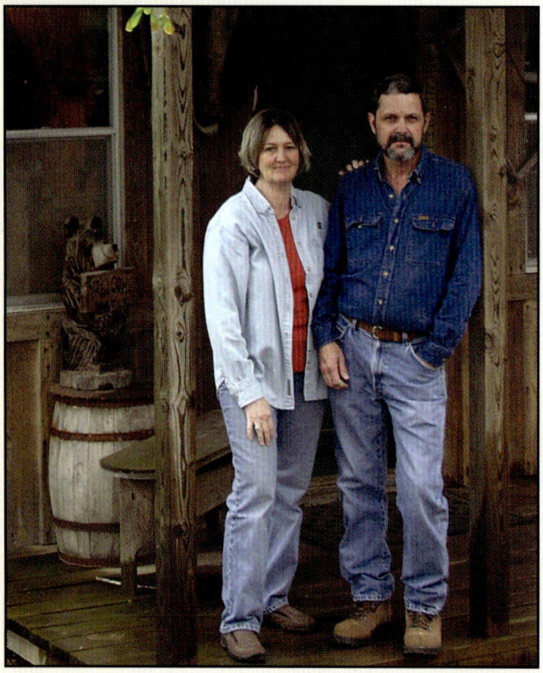

trouble with his rifle and asked Alec to fix it. Alec said that he would take a look at it when he had time. About a week later this guy came back for his gun and said, "Alec, did you fix my gun?" Alec said, "Yeah, all it needs is a good brushin'." The guy said, "What do you mean, 'It needs a good brushin'?" So Alec picked the gun up, walked over to the door, and flung the gun out into the brush. "Like I said, all it needs is a good brushin'," Alec told him.

My Grandma Lizzy was quite a character, too. She was always canning vegetables, fruit, and just about anything that you could stuff into a jar. I asked her why she canned all of this stuff, and she said, "we almost starved once, but we won't starve again." We usually tried to be hanging around Grandma's about dinnertime. I can remember asking her, "What's for dinner?" and she would always say, "Cornbread pone. Them that don't like it can leave it alone." I could go on with the old stories, but I don't want to bore you.

Of course, these characters from my life aren't the least bit boring to me. In fact, I am very excited about this book and the characters that we are about to carve because they take me back to the things I grew up on. As I mentioned earlier, my family played music. I am the only one who didn't play, but I am the only one who is a woodcarver, so I figure we came out just about even. Any jokes or humor about these hill folk is all in fun; I grew up around these wonderful people, and I wouldn't want to live anywhere else in the world. So I'll dedicate this book to the legend of the hillbilly. Times may have changed, but I believe that the hillbilly is still alive and well.

—Mike Shipley

If you have any comments or questions, please feel free to contact me. I sell blanks and rough-outs for all of the projects in this book and offer carving classes. You-uns, come see us.

Mike Shipley, Shipley Wood Carving
Rt. 1 Box 4490
Dora, Missouri 65637
(417) 284-3416
shiplfam@townsqr.com
www.ozarkcountycharacters.com

How to Talk Ozark

Every area in the country has its own way of talking and pronouncing words. The Ozarks is no different. Here are a few of the more interesting words that are altered just a little to fit the needs of the Ozark lifestyle.

Ozark talk	The other way to talk
Shore am tard.	I am really tired.
That's a goodin'.	That is a good one.
Yunt to?	Do you want to?
You-uns	All of you
Tamar	Tomorrow
Pone	Cornbread
Brushin'	To throw away
Hollar or Holler	Valley
Drekly	Directly
We got a right smart rain.	We got a good rain.
She's sprangin'.	She's pregnant.

Ozark talk	The other way to talk
Littlin'	Kid
Cifer'en	Figuring it out
Hisn	It's his.
Yourn	It's yours.
Tators	What hill folk eat three or four times a day
Wretch	Reach
Aimen	Intend to
This sevnin	This evening
Hey. Geet yit?	Hey, did you eat yet?
Toad strangler	A good rain
Nary one	Neither one

Getting Started

I know you're anxious to get started carving the projects in this book, but you'll need to spend a few minutes getting your tools and materials in order. Let's take a look at the tools and type of wood that I recommend for these projects.

Tools

Of course, carving starts with tools, and turning out a nice, finished carving doesn't require a huge investment in tools. Carving figures like these actually requires only a few basic hand tools. If I had to go with the fewest possible tools, I would choose a knife with a hefty two-inch blade, a detail knife, a 4 mm V-tool, and an 8 mm V-tool. These four tools are my favorites and are a must for my type of carving. Of course, there are a lot of good-quality tools available, and they will all get the job done. Choose the tools that you are most comfortable using. However, I don't recommend that you buy tools in a set because there will be tools in the set you will never use.

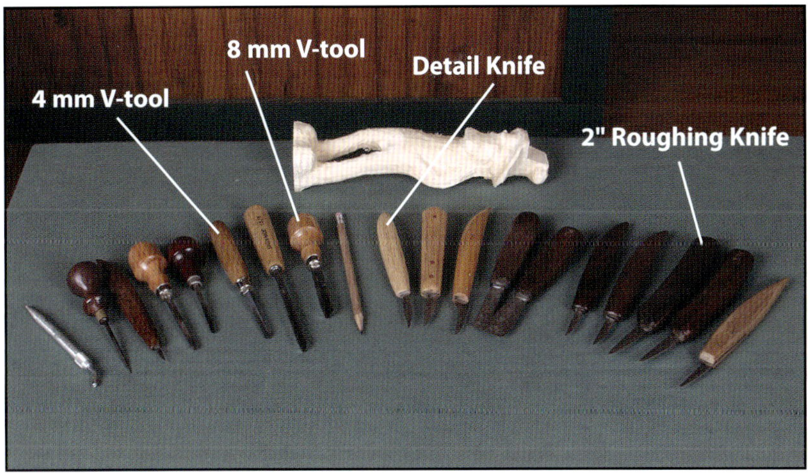

A number of tools can be used to carve the figures in this book. If you're just beginning, the tools you'll really need are a knife with a hefty two-inch blade, a knife with a smaller detail blade, a 4 mm V-tool, and an 8 mm V-tool.

Sharpening

On my workbench, I keep several of the same knives and gouges; when one gets dull, I just pick up another one. When I have a few dull tools accumulated, I'll sharpen several tools instead of one at a time. This saves a lot of carving time. As I said earlier, it all starts with the tools, but they have to be sharp.

I've found out that there are all kinds of edges you can put on a tool. I never stop experimenting with my tool sharpening, but one thing I always do is grind my knife blade flat. I don't want a bevel on the blade. Currently, I use a vertical 2-inch-by-72-inch belt sander with a 180-grit belt. I lay the blade flat on the belt and grind the blade down to a wedge shape without any bevel.

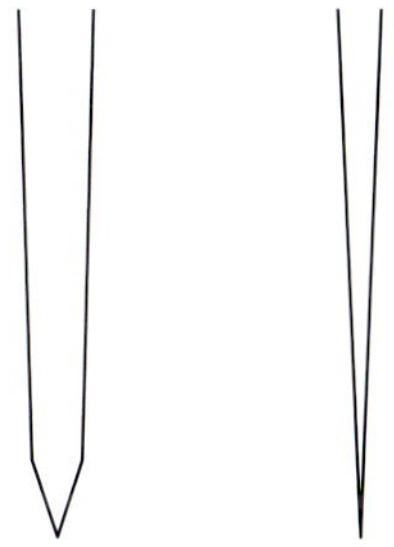

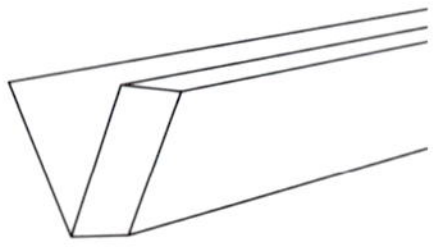

V-tool bevel before lengthening the bevel

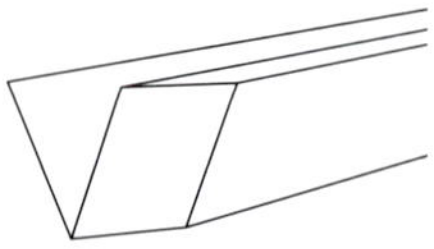

V-tool bevel after lengthening the bevel

Gouges and V-tools have their own natural bevel. I try to lengthen that bevel and take care to grind it flat with the belt sander. The main things are to keep the bevel flat on the belt and don't let the bevel become rounded. I sharpen my tools freehand, but a holding device can help if you find it necessary.

After grinding the tool—whether it's a knife, a gouge, or a chisel—on the belt, I buff the edge with a cotton buffing wheel coated with jeweler's rouge. The buffing will round the edge slightly each time it is buffed, but I can buff several times before I have to reshape the edge.

Wood

All of the projects in this book are carved from northern basswood. I've experimented with many types of wood, but my favorite is always basswood. I like the close grain and the softness of basswood. It also takes detail well.

Basswood is readily available from any carving supply store and some art supply stores. Choose a block of wood that's light in color and light in weight. Avoid using any basswood blocks that show dark streaks, knots, or other surface imperfections.

Basswood is a close-grained, soft wood that takes detail well. It should not have any dark streaks, knots, or other surface imperfections.

Transferring a pattern

Transferring a pattern to the block of wood can easily be done with a piece of carbon paper and a stylus or a pounce wheel. Simply place the carbon paper between the wood and the pattern, carbon side down, and trace over the outline of the pattern. You'll notice that the front view pattern and one of the side view patterns in this book are outlined with a dashed line. This line indicates the band saw cut line. A disc sander can be used to remove excess wood from the band sawed blank.

I prefer using carbon paper to transfer the pattern onto a thicker paper, such as poster board, then cutting out the silhouette with scissors. The silhouette is all that I need when band sawing the pattern.

If you are fortunate enough to have sketching or drawing abilities, they will be a big plus in your carving as you pencil in the various areas of the piece. Before I start any carving, I have all of the features and details of the piece in mind, and, of course, having a well-designed pattern in front of you will only help.

When I transfer the pattern to the wood, I concentrate on well-proportioned side and front view silhouettes. Then, I carve the details to fit the proportions that I've sawed with the band saw. Correct beginning proportions are critical: A good finished piece comes from a well-proportioned blank.

It is possible to finish a piece from a blank with a few distinctive features sawed in with the band saw, and you could even start with a square blank of wood, but you will need to do a lot of extra work to remove the excess wood. Removing too much excess wood is distracting, and it's hard work. Be sure to follow the band saw lines on the patterns and remove the right amount of wood to save time and effort.

Safety

We all know that sharp tools are a must for woodcarving, and along with that comes the risk of cutting yourself. It is always a good idea to wear some type of carving glove to protect the hand that is holding the carving. I am right-handed, so I always wear a glove on my left hand. In the step-by-step section, you will notice that I am wearing a leather glove. I prefer this type of glove over a cut-resistant glove because I can grip the wood better, which allows me to do faster production carving. It also creates less hand fatigue. You'll, of course, want to choose a safety glove based on your personal preferences, but always be sure to wear a glove.

Another safety practice is to always know your cut—know where the cut is going and where it is going to stop. I do this by always being aware of the pressure on the tool, never just cutting free-hand, and always having a means of stopping the cut by using stop cuts. Because I'm right-handed, I like to use my left thumb to push or hold back on the tool. With a little practice, you will know where the cut is going, and this awareness will improve your safety as well as your carving ability.

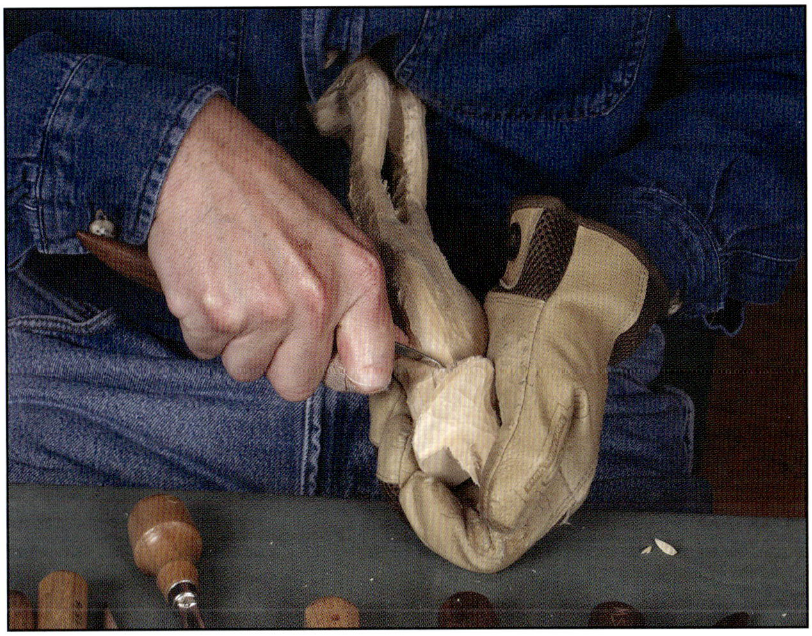

Always wear some type of glove on the hand that is holding the carving. I use a leather glove because it grips the wood well.

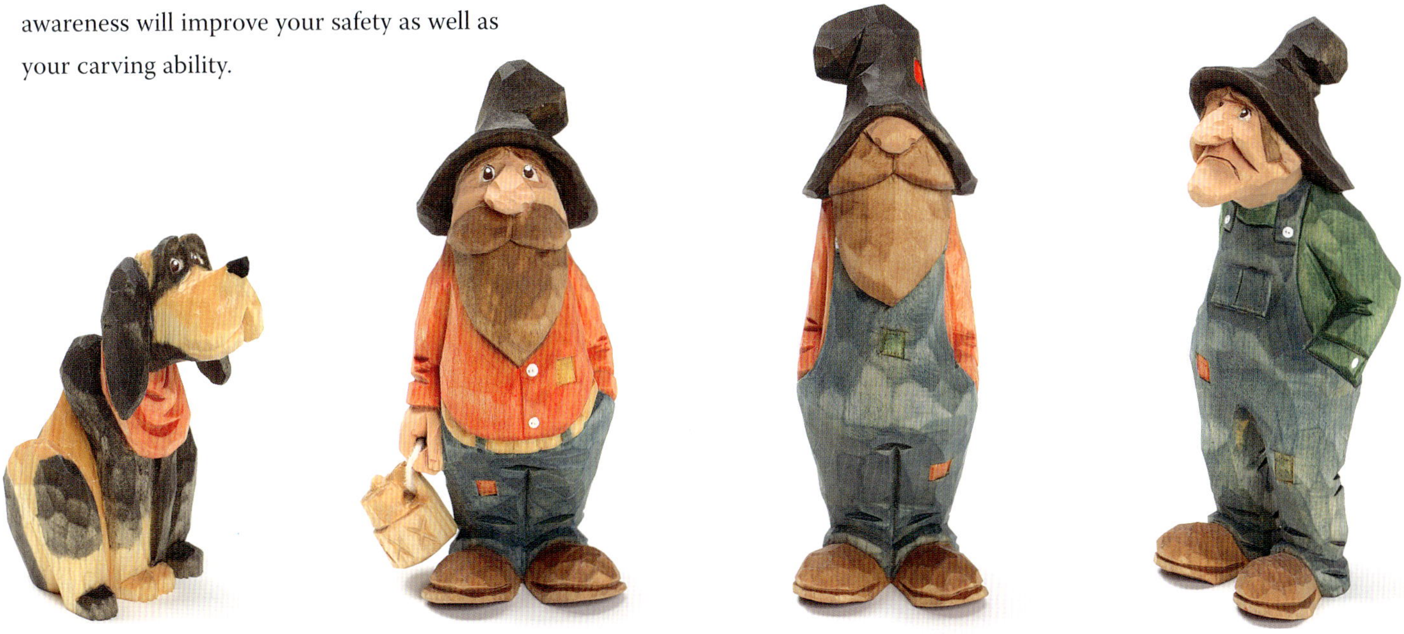

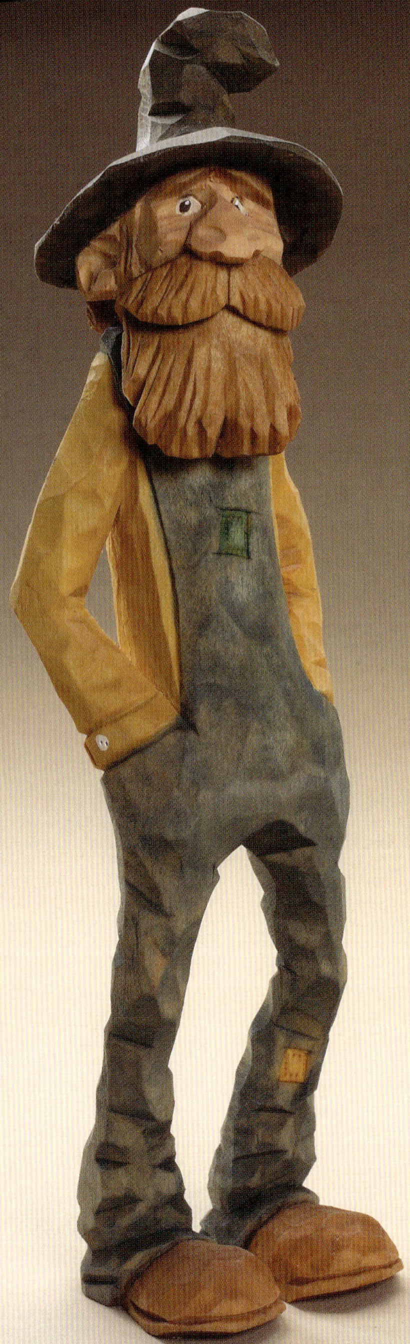

Creating Delmer
Step-by-Step

Our step-by-step project will be old Delmer. He's long, lanky, and fun to carve. I have placed his hands in his pockets; but Delmer has some action, and the carving process flows nicely for a step-by-step demonstration.

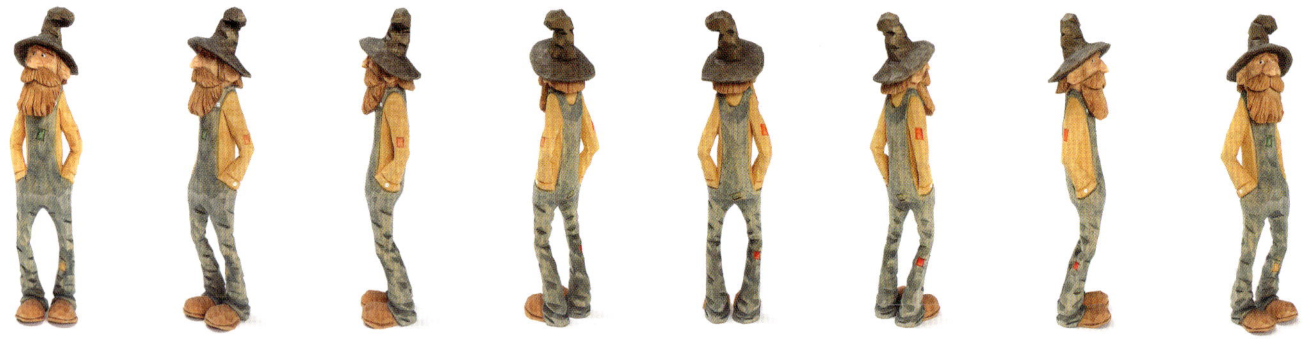

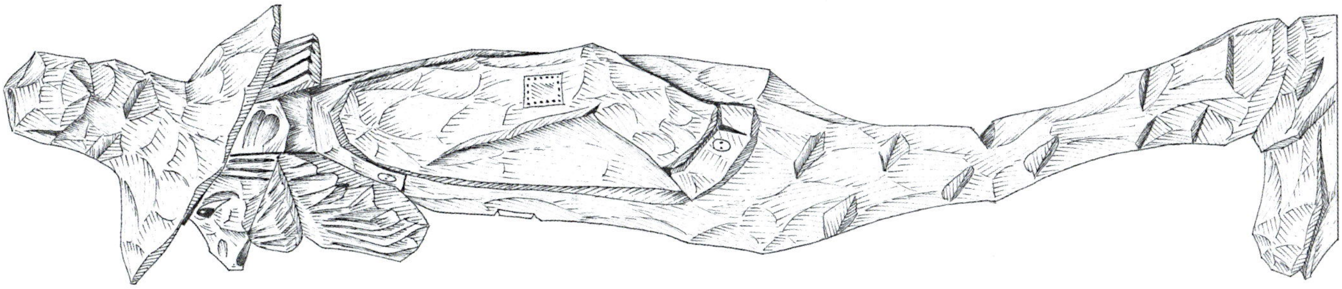

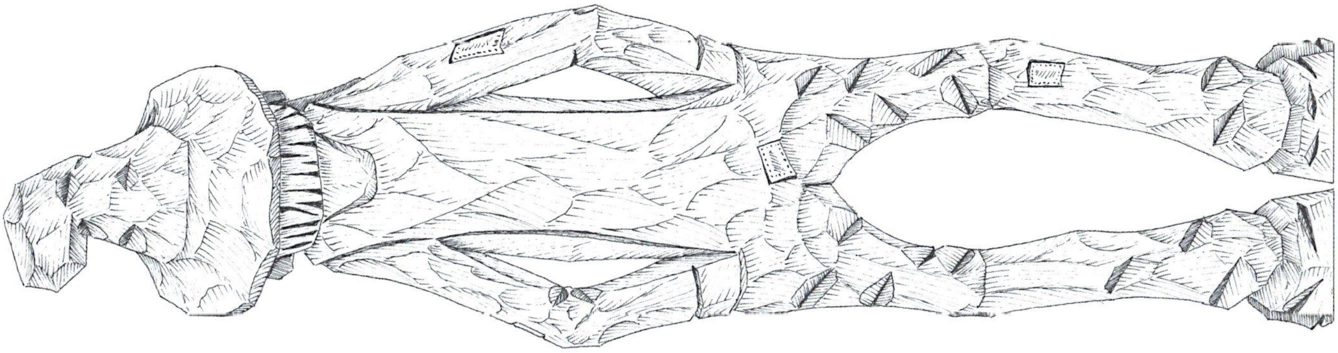

Enlarge pattern 133%

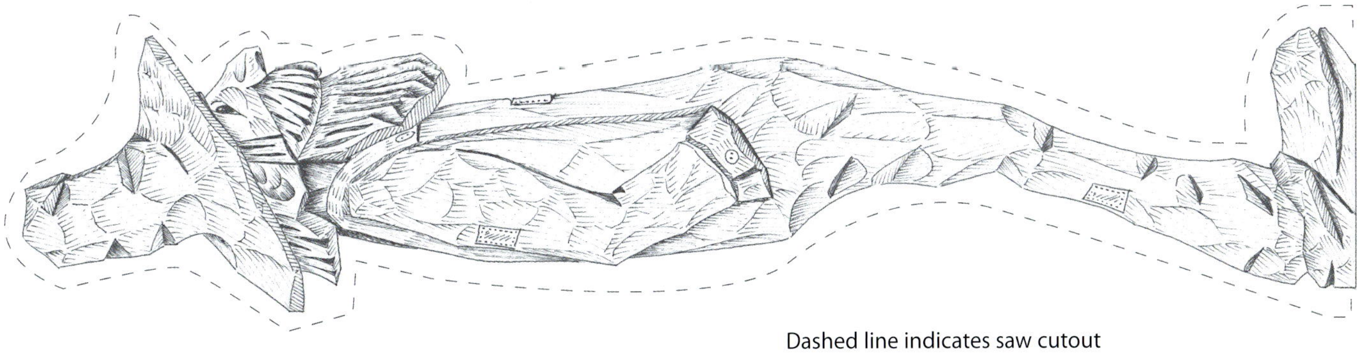

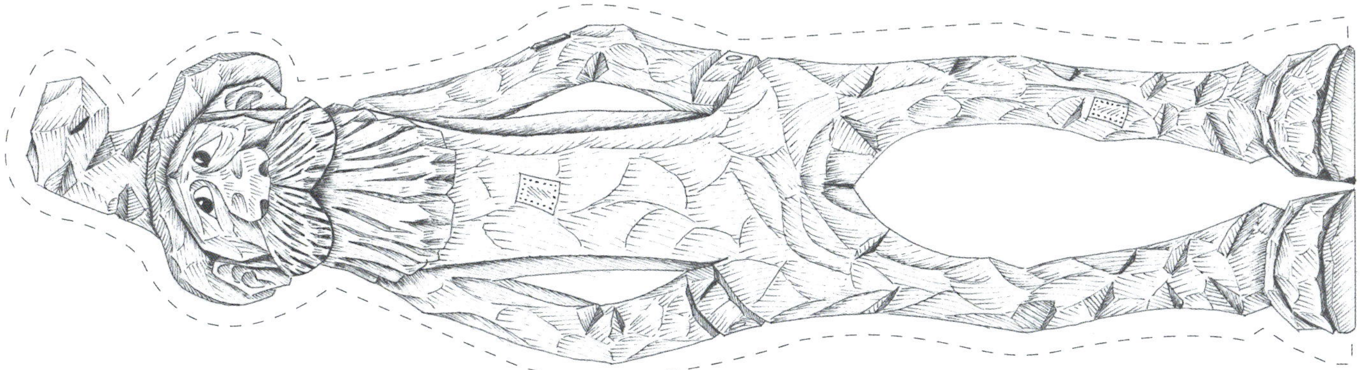

Dashed line indicates saw cutout

Carving

In this step-by-step section, I will be showing you how to carve Delmer from a band saw blank. As you are carving Delmer, use the photos of the finished project on pages 26 and 27 and the patterns on page 5 as a reference to help you visualize the end result.

In the finished piece, you can see that Delmer's head is slightly turned. This turn of the head adds more character, but it is difficult to get without carving the head and the body separately. As you can see from my pattern and blank, I carved Delmer in one piece. If you want to have even more of a turned head, carve the head and the body in two pieces. Start by simply tracing the head pattern and the body pattern separately. Add a ½" square neck stem about 1" long to the head, and then drill a ½"-diameter hole for the neck stem on the shoulders of the blank. Follow the carving steps for the one-piece blank; then, carve the neck stem to fit the neck hole. Both the one-piece blank and the two-piece blank will result in a nice finished piece, so let's get started!

Tools and Materials

- Basswood block 2¼" x 2½" x 10"
- Band saw
- Disc sander
- Pencil
- Carving glove
- 1" flat shallow gouge
- ¾" shallow gouge
- 3 mm U-gouge
- 3 mm deep gouge
- Detail knife
- Knife with 2" blade
- 8 mm V-tool
- 6 mm V-tool
- 4 mm V-tool
- 220-grit sandpaper

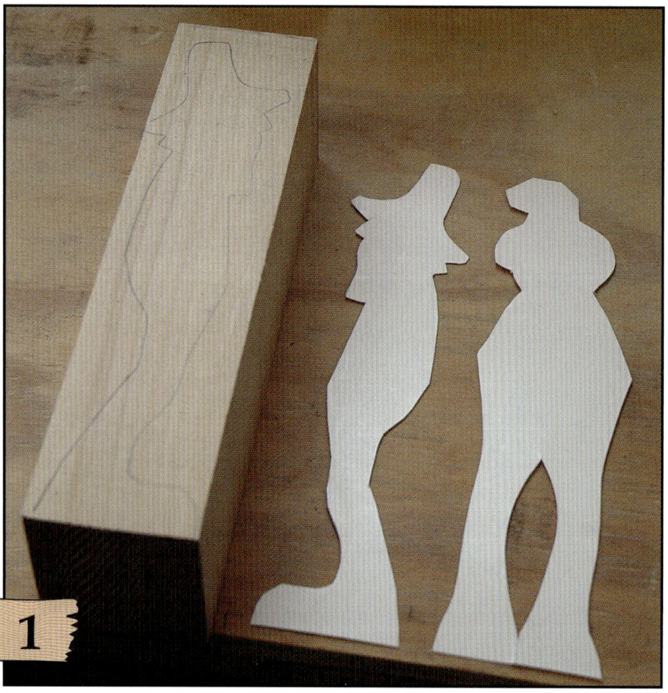

1

Start by tracing the band saw pattern onto some kind of heavy paper, such as poster board. Don't use cardboard; it is a bit too thick. You can see that all I need is the side view and the front view. I always start with the side view, and here I have traced the side view onto the basswood block.

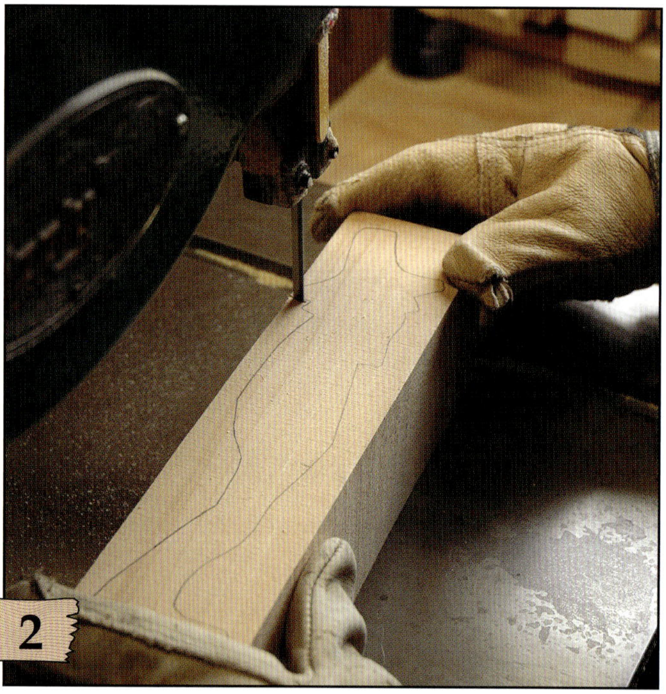

2

On the back side, make the cuts in from the pattern line first—cut under the hat brim and under the hair. Back out of each of these cuts, and then continue cutting the profile.

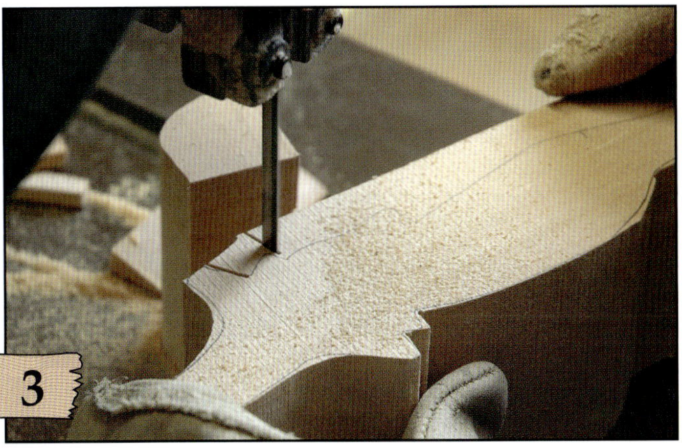

3

All of the cuts in the rear are complete. Now cut the front of the side view.

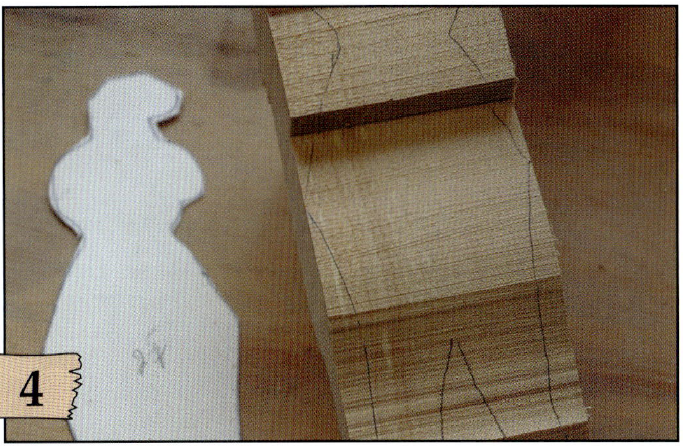

4

With the side profile cut, trace the pattern on the front. You won't have a flat surface due to the peaks and valleys of the previous cuts, but trace the pattern lines as close to the pattern as possible.

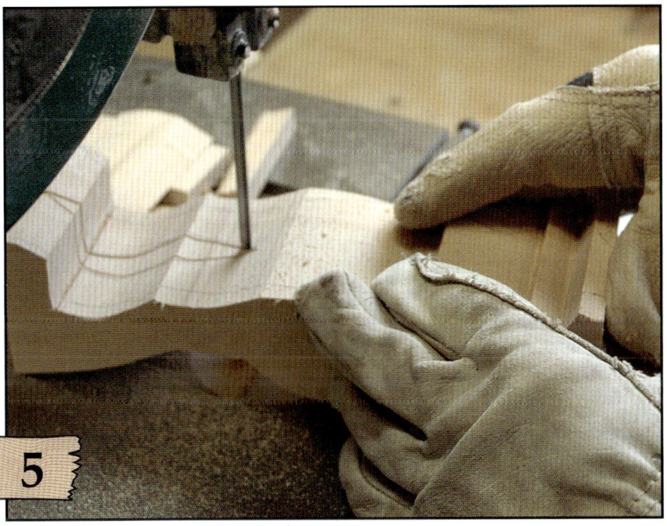

5

Here I am separating the legs. Notice that, because the heel and the rear hat brim are the same height, the blank lies level on the saw table. Stay as close as possible to the lines so that you'll spend less time removing waste wood during the carving process.

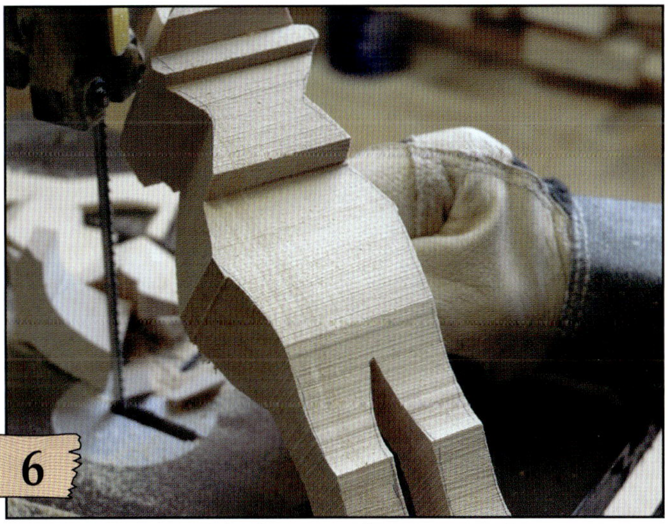

6

Here's our finished blank. Notice that the main features are evident—you need to be able to recognize enough features to steer you through the carving steps.

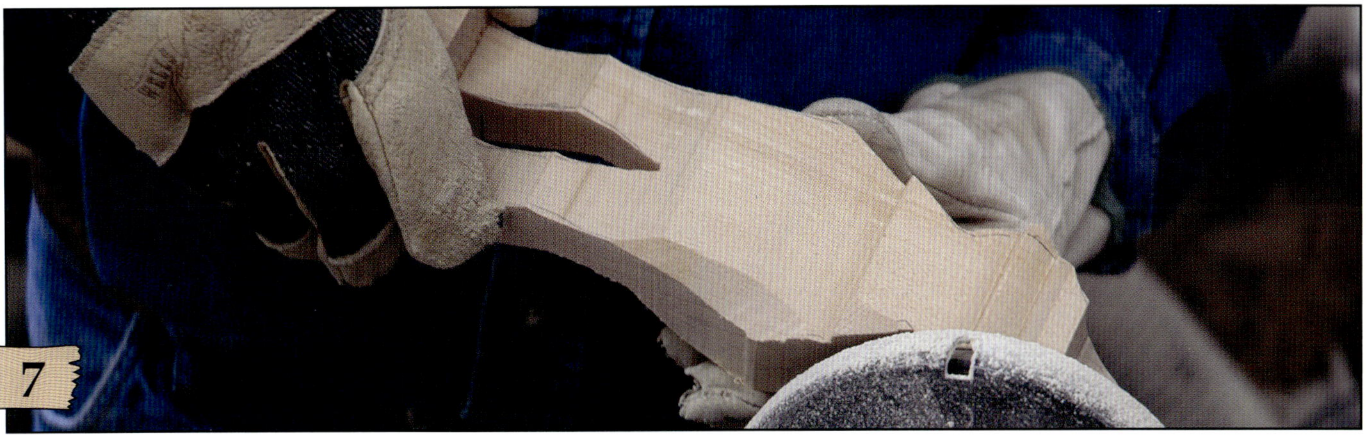

7

If you have a disc sander, use it to round off the blank. Before you begin, take some time to study the pattern so that you don't sand away too much wood. Here I'm using a disc sander with an 80-grit disc to round any obvious square edges.

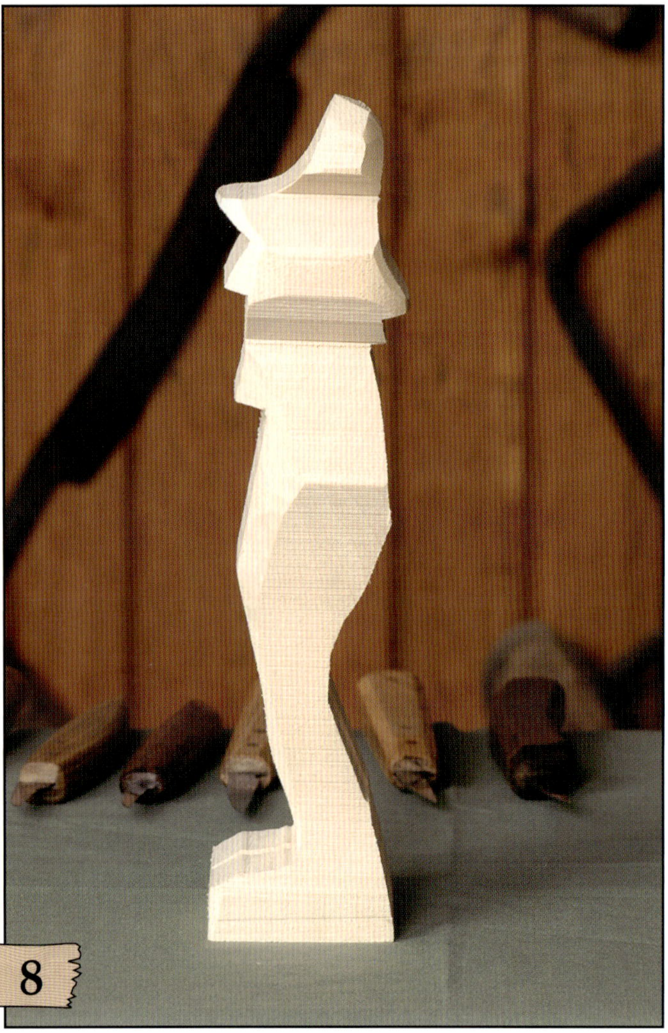

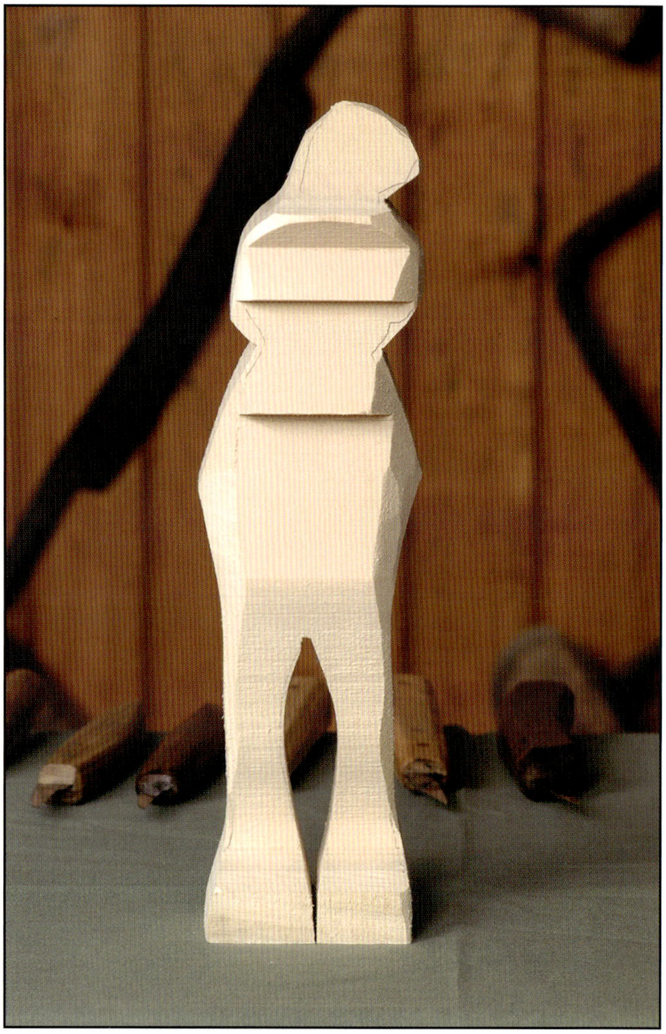

8

Here are the side and front views of the band saw blank after sanding. You can see how I've rounded the body in the front of the arms and the hat. I haven't really taken away that much wood, but you will be surprised how much carving time removing this little bit of wood will save.

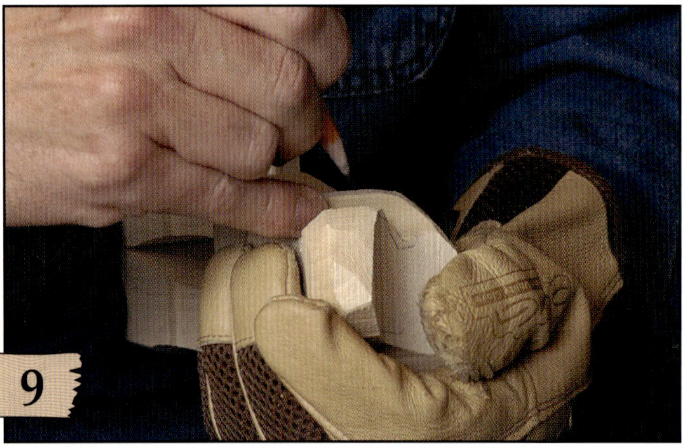

9

With most any piece, I start by roughing in the head or hat. We'll start under the hat brim. Pencil a line between the front and back hat brim.

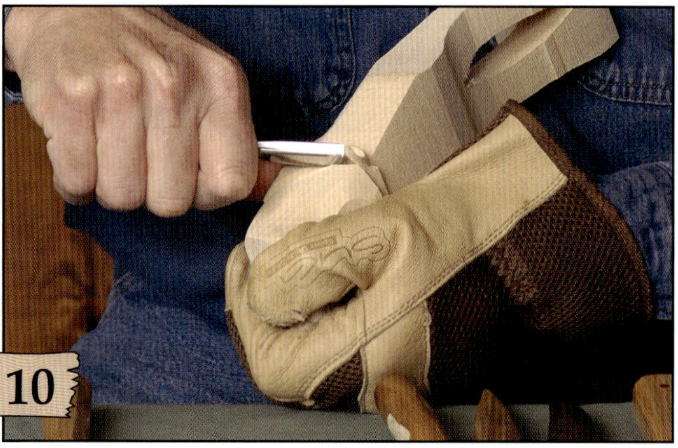

10

With an 8 mm V-tool, cut the pencil line under the hat brim. Make several passes to deepen this cut.

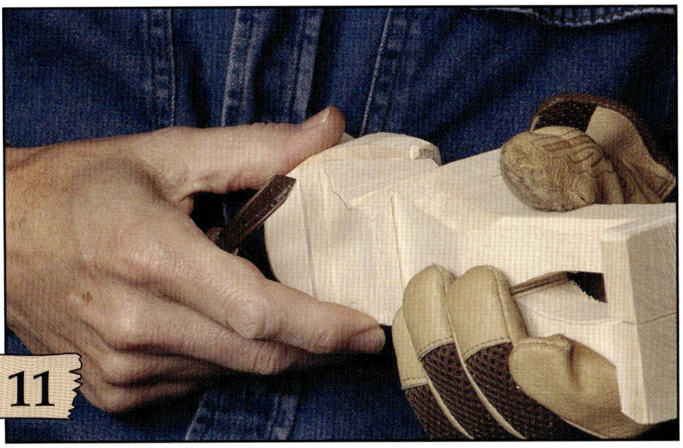

Make the V-tool cut on both sides of the head. Here I've made several passes with the 8 mm V-tool.

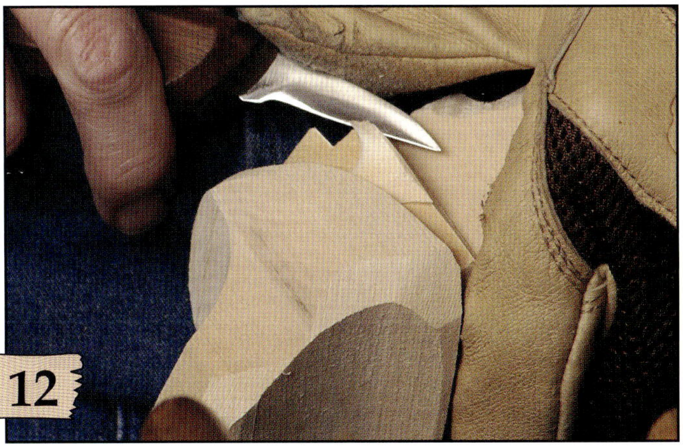

After making the V-tool cuts, use a roughing knife to remove wood on each side of the head up to the hat brim.

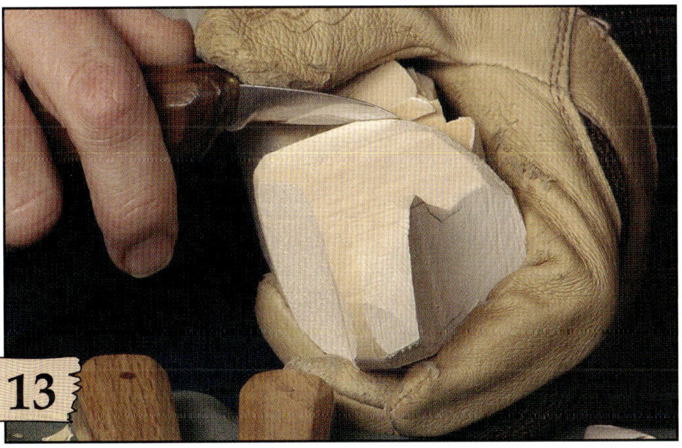

Remove wood on both sides of the head, checking the head proportions to make sure both sides are even.

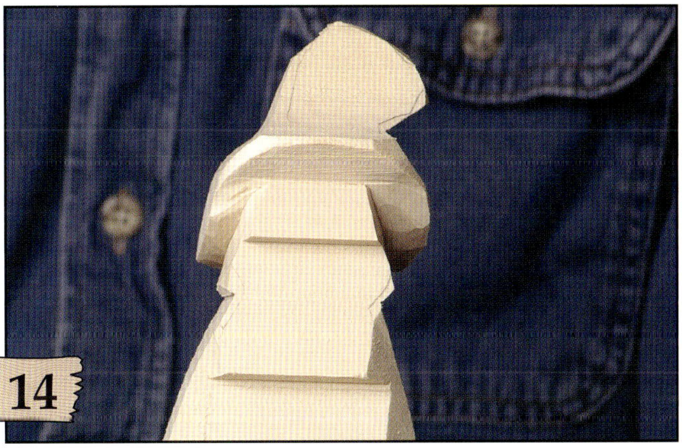

Notice the depth on both sides of the head. This width is about what we need at this point.

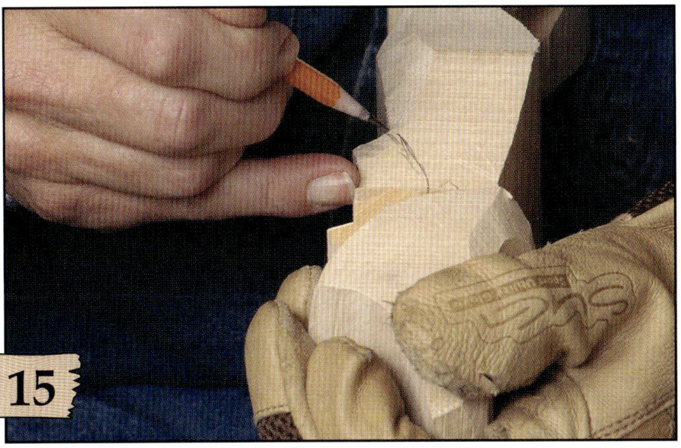

Use the back of the hair as a guide to pencil on the ears because there will be hair behind the ears. Draw a rough, oversized ear; it can be a rough square at this point. Pencil in the beard line, which will come up to the bottom front corner of the ear.

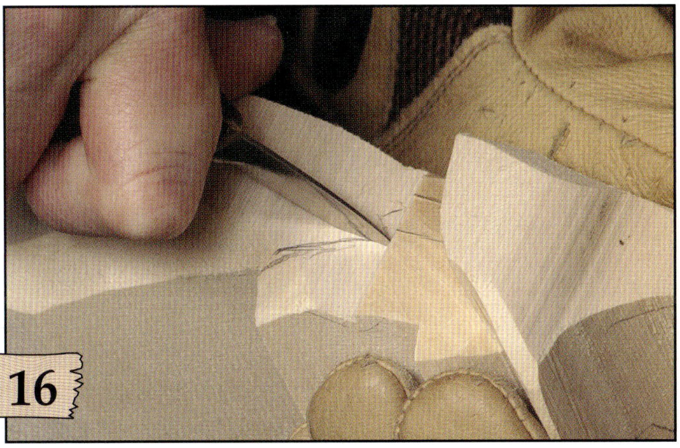

With the 2" roughing knife, cut straight into the pencil lines to outline the ear and the beard.

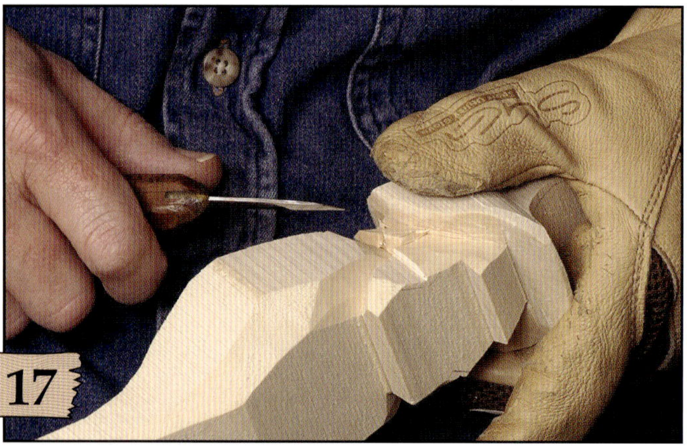

17

Use the knife to remove wood behind and in front of the ear to raise it out from the head. The ears will be oversized and comical and will protrude from the head. Also make an undercut under the beard.

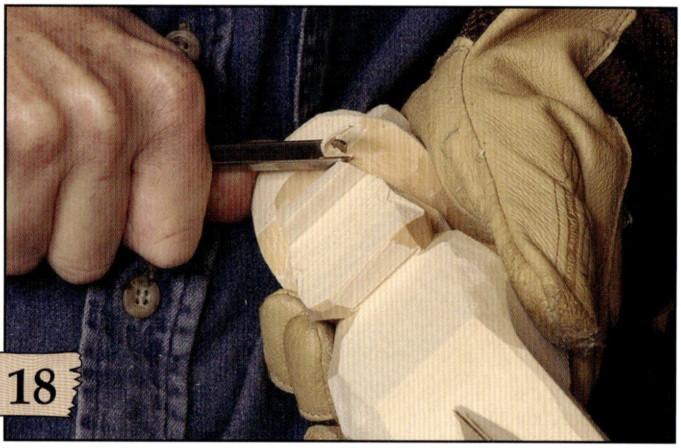

18

After roughing in both ears, use the 4 mm V-tool to make a cut under the hat brim and above the nose. This will be the beginning of the eyebrow and separates the brow from the hat.

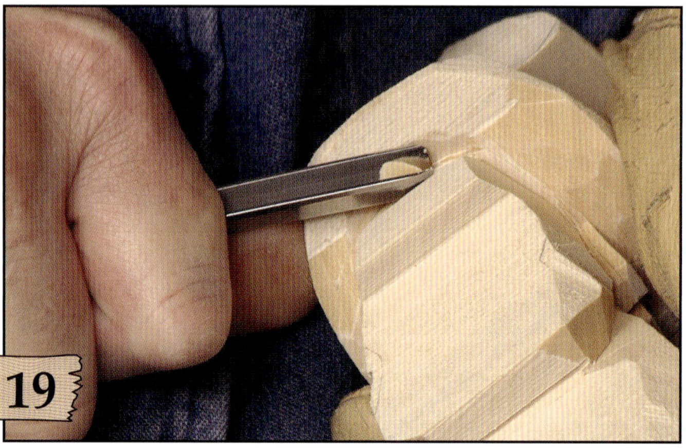

19

Drop down slightly and make another cut across the face above the nose to further form the eyebrow. Deepen the cut above each eye socket, but lessen the cut across the bridge of the nose. The eye sockets will be sunken while the bridge of the nose will protrude to separate the eye sockets.

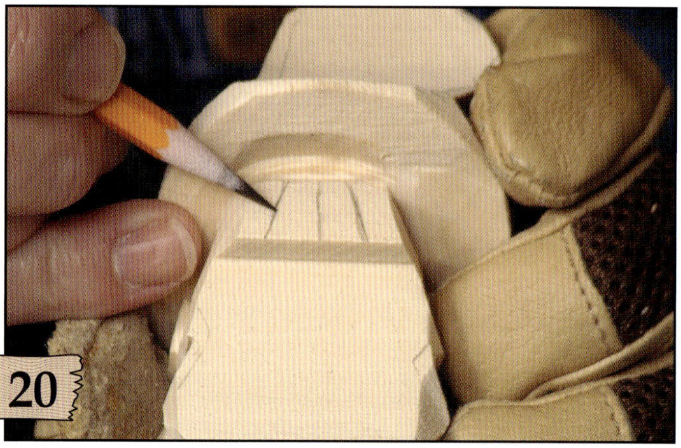

20

Here you can see the two V-tool cuts that formed the eyebrow. Pencil on the nose by making a centerline and then drawing a large triangle-shaped nose.

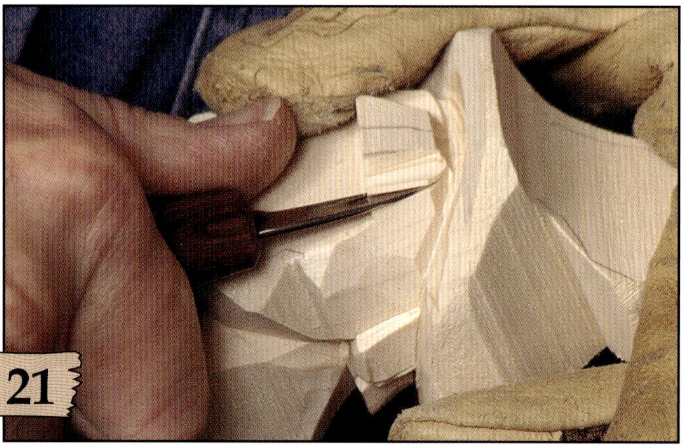

21

Notice the rough ear—wood is removed in back and in front of the ear, and the front and back bottom corners of the ear are cut. We'll finish the ear later. With a detail knife, cut straight into the nose lines to make a stop cut. Remove wood on both sides of the nose to bring it out.

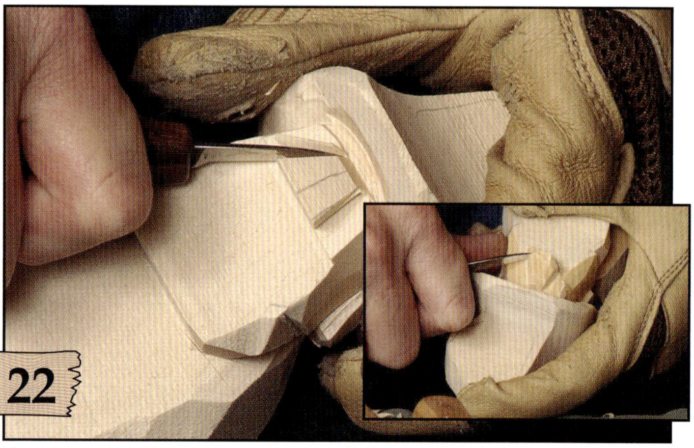

22

The nose is taking shape. Cut off the bottom corner on each side of the nose; then, clean and shape the nose.

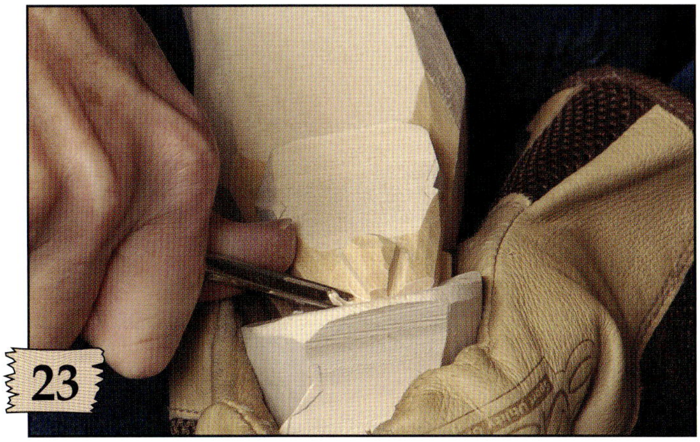

Here's the nose shape at this point, after cleaning and shaping the nose and cheeks. Use the 4 mm V-tool to cut across under the eyebrow again.

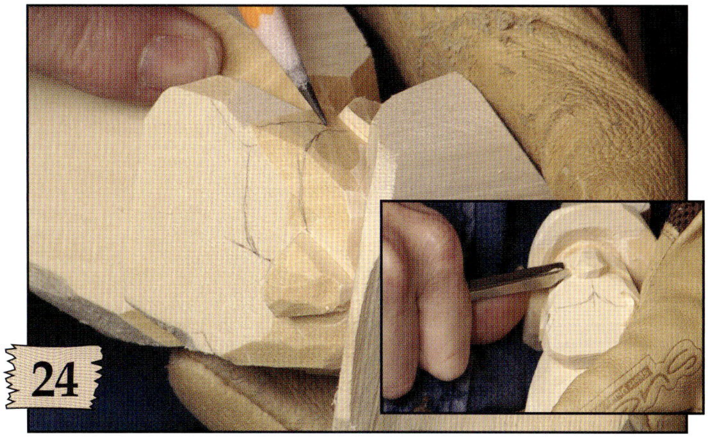

Pencil on the mustache. The tip will come to the bottom corner of the ear. The size and shape of the mustache can be whatever you prefer. Cut the pencil lines to outline the mustache with the 4 mm V-tool.

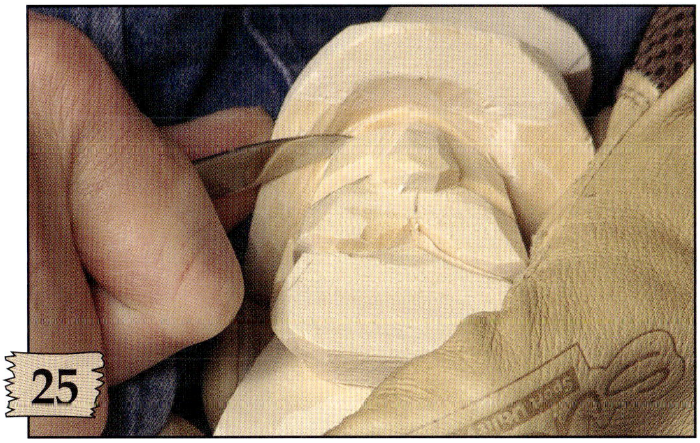

The mustache is roughed in. Use the detail knife to make straight cuts along the V-tool cuts, on both sides of the nose, and under the eyebrow. These stop cuts separate the areas more clearly. Clean cuts will help to lessen the bleeding of paint from one area to another during the painting process.

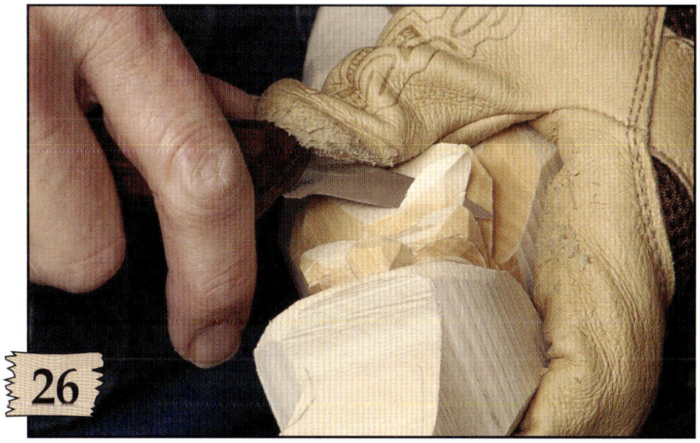

Clean the beard up to the stop cut under the mustache. Notice the nice, clean separation as the cleaning cut meets the stop cut. Now start shaping the mustache.

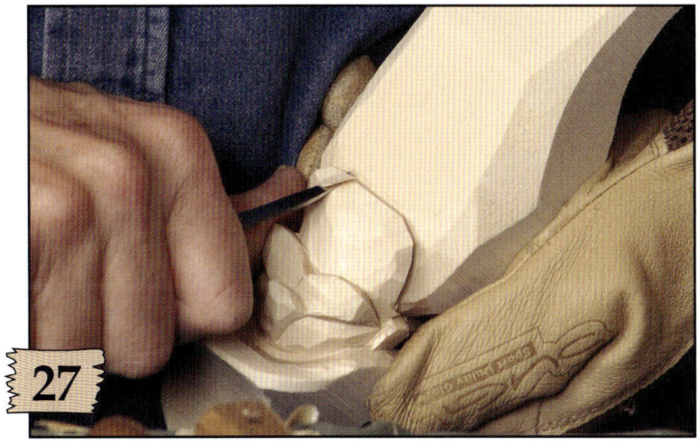

Notice the clean separation where all of the areas of the face meet. The stop cuts around all of the facial features will help to achieve a cleaner face. Finish shaping the beard and mustache.

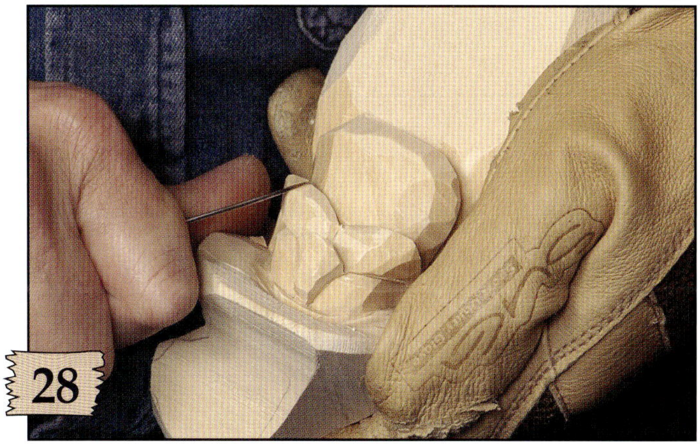

The mustache and beard are sized, so now we'll clean up a little.

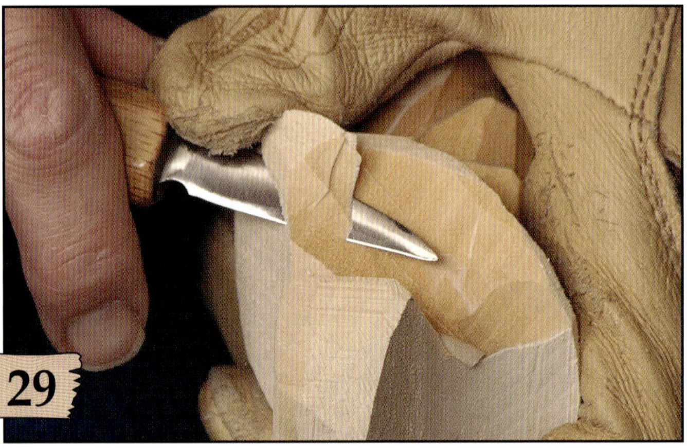

29

We'll leave the head and face at this point. Use the roughing knife to rough in the hat.

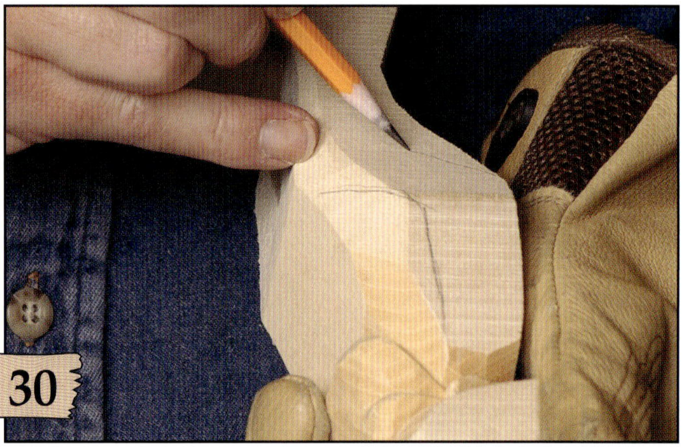

30

Pencil the arm lines on the body.

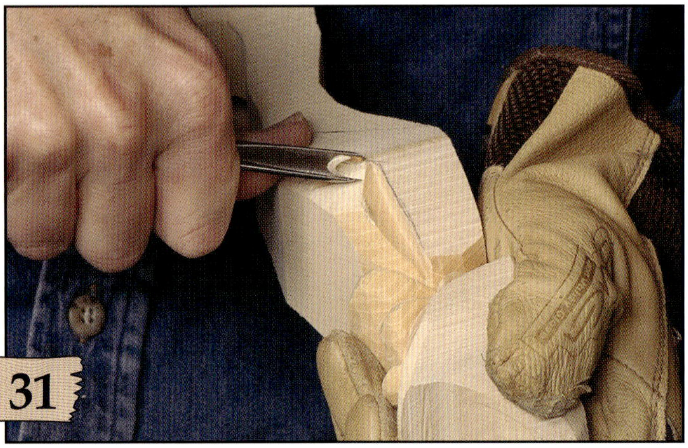

31

Cut along the lines with the 8 mm V-tool. Make several passes and deepen the cuts. In an area like this, I will use the sides of the V-tool much like a knife. There is a lot of excess wood to remove on the side of the body, so just work it down.

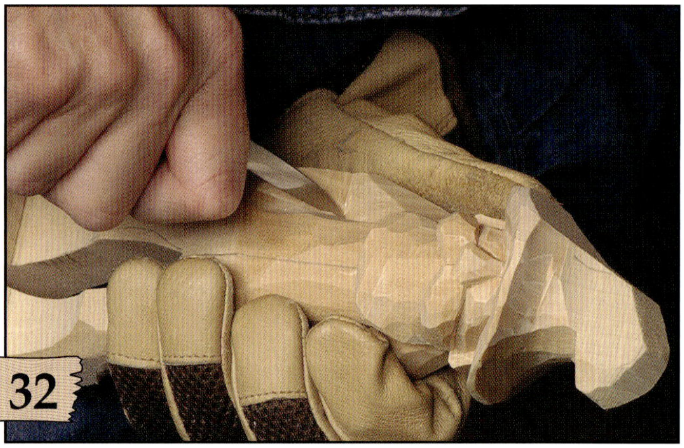

32

Draw the centerline on the body, and use it to get the skinny body correctly proportioned. You can see the depth and width of the arm; now make deep cuts between the body and arm with the roughing knife. Straight-in, deep cuts will help to work out the area between the body and the arm.

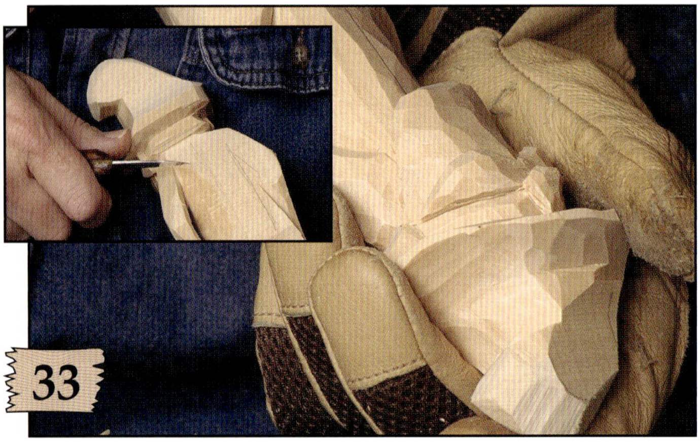

33

Continue working from the front and the back until the arm is separated from the body at the crook of the elbow. A knife tip works well to clean the area between the hand and the side. Here you can see the arm is worked down to a finished size. The inset shows the rear view of the arm.

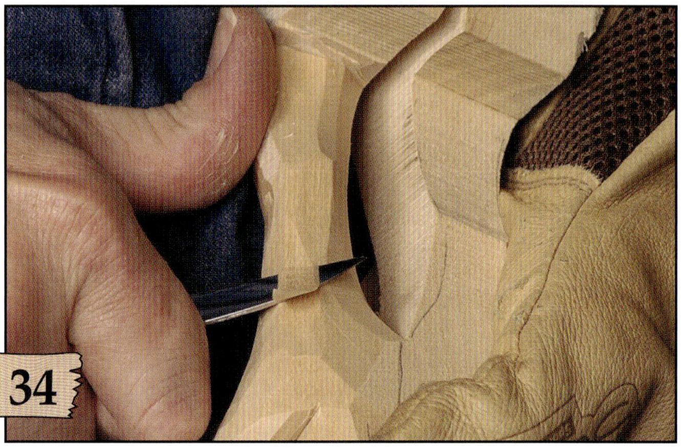

34

Both arms will be in equal proportion, so work both arms out in the same manner. Next, move to the lower body. Use a 6 mm V-tool to clean the area where the hand enters the pocket. Then, rough in the upper legs close to their finished size. Round the rough edges of the lower legs and shoes. Just rough them in at this point; we'll finish them later on.

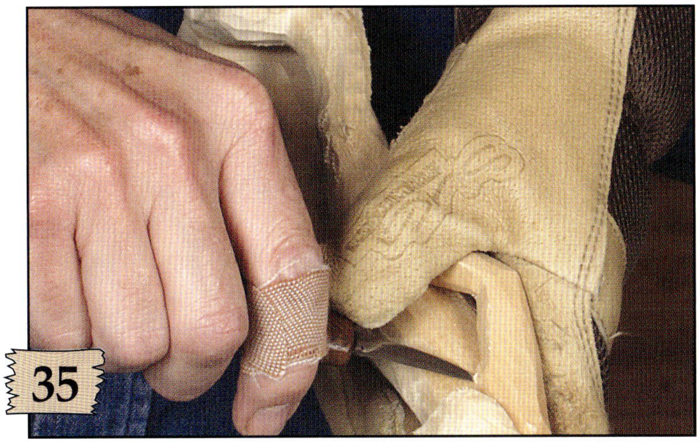

Now clean up the chest and upper body so that the finished arms and shoulders will flow up to the beard and head.

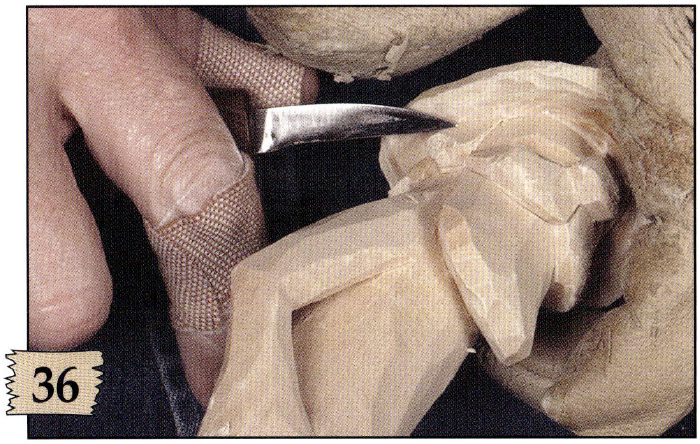

In the beginning, we roughed in the ears; now shape and clean up the ears. Notice I've trimmed and shaped the front of the ear. The ears need to be oversized and sticking out from the head. Gently trim the corners and clean up the ear.

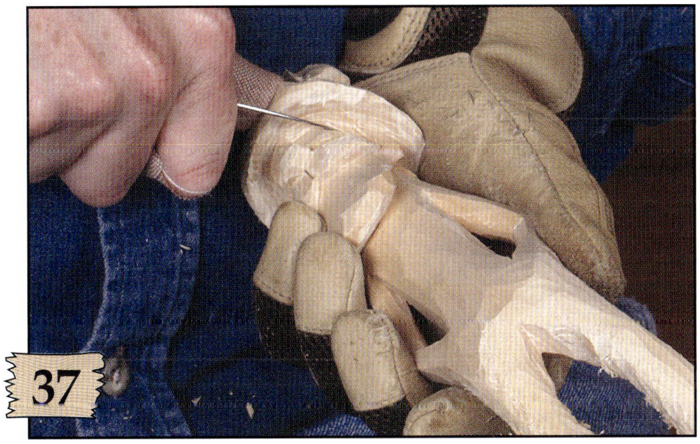

After shaping the ears, clean and shape the face. A thin hairline or sideburns will come down from under the hat and will disappear under the mustache.

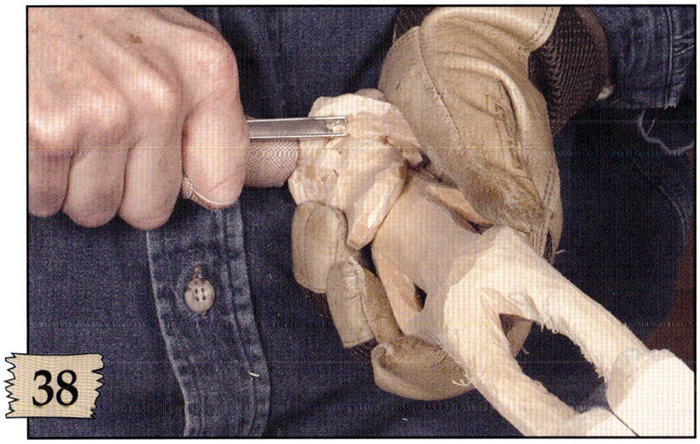

With the 4 mm V-tool, gently cut on top of the eyebrow between the eyebrow and the hat to clean and separate the two areas. You can also use the detail knife tip for this step.

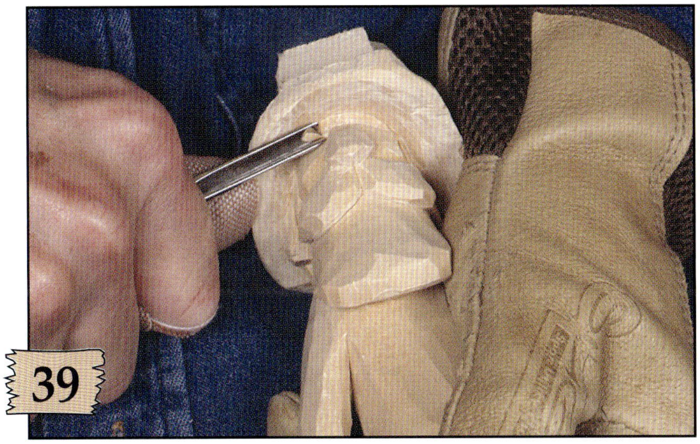

With the same V-tool, clean below the eyebrow. Remember to leave the bridge of the nose raised higher than the eye socket area.

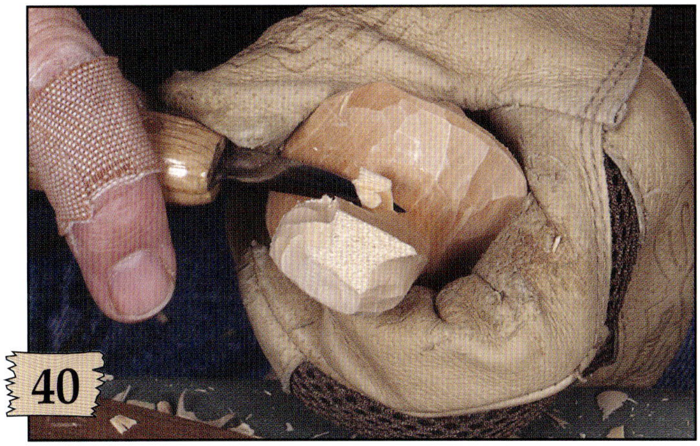

Now finish shaping the hat with a detail knife.

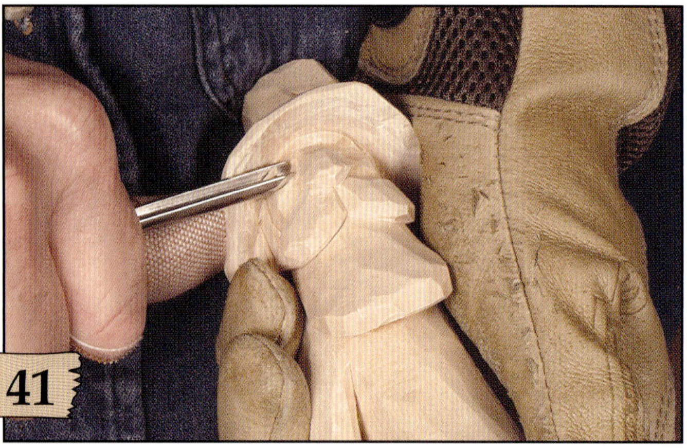

41

Now that I have the face and beard cleaned up to a finished point, it's time for the eyes. Use a 3 mm deep gouge to scoop shallow eye sockets—not too deep though. Compare and make them match.

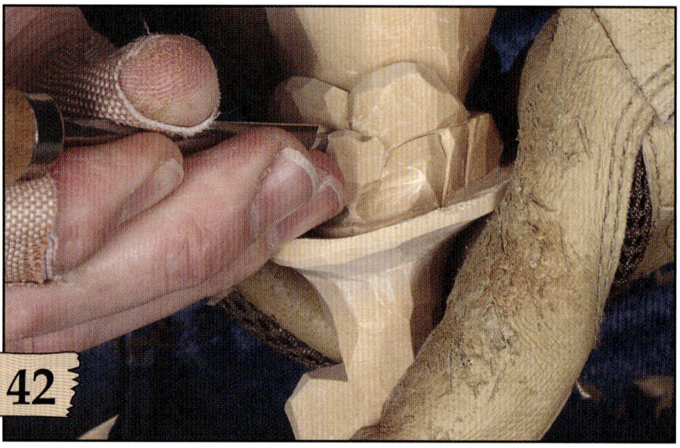

42

While I have the deep gouge in my hand, I'll scoop out the nostrils on the nose. Notice how I'm holding the gouge like a pencil. Make a small shallow scoop to form the nostrils on the bottom of the nose.

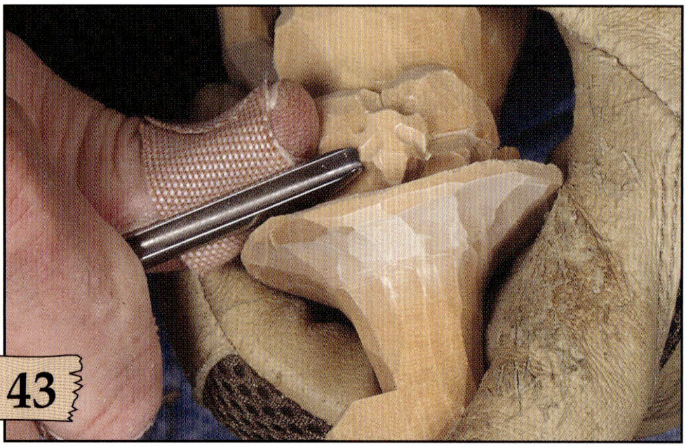

43

Now scoop out the indentations on top of the nose on each side of the nose.

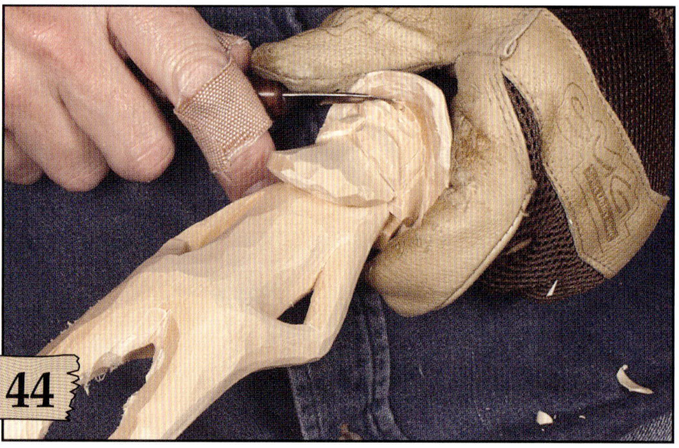

44

With the detail knife tip, make small cuts to separate the eyebrow just above the bridge of the nose. This requires just two simple cuts starting in the center of the brow and angling out toward the eye.

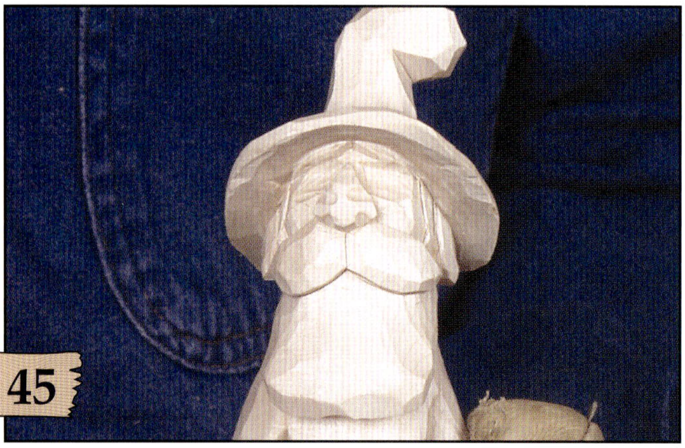

45

Now we have the face ready for eyes. We won't be carving the mouth because it is covered by the wide mustache.

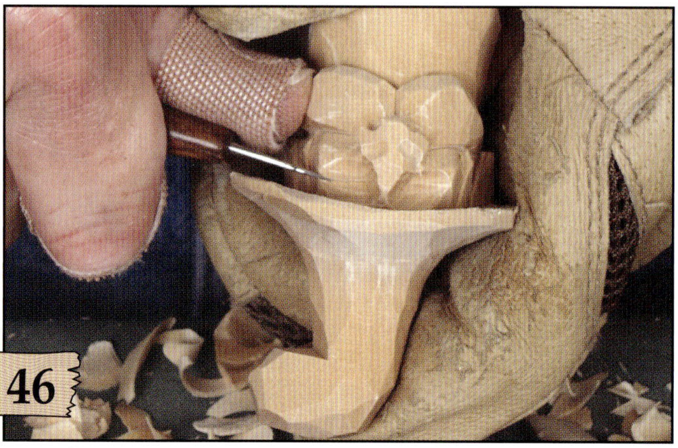

46

We will make a simple, basic eye. Use the knife tip to cut a horizontal line on each side. This will be the lower lid.

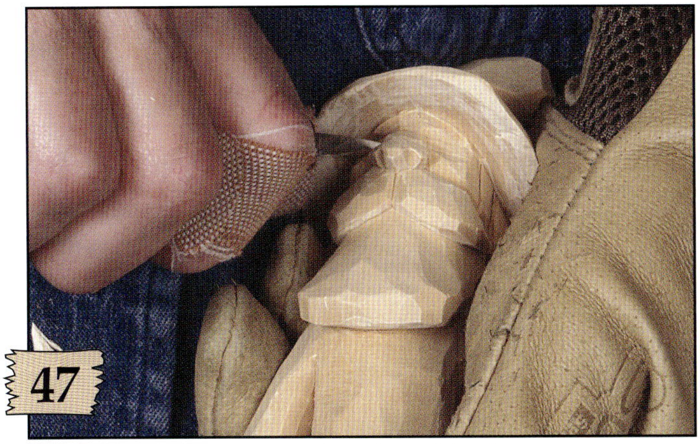

Don't cut all of the way to the edge of the face; cut just far enough to make the width of the eye. I can't give you an exact measurement, but try eyeballing it based on the pattern and the photograph of the finished piece.

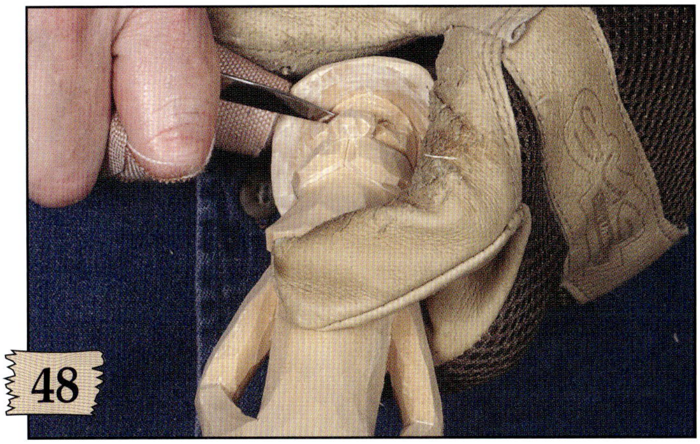

I'm afraid I didn't get a real shot of finishing the eyes. With the lower eyelid cut in place, cut a half-moon on top of that cut to form the eye. Size is not critical, but the eye should be a little larger than what would seem natural to keep with the comical style of the project. (See Step 82 for a close-up of the eyes.)

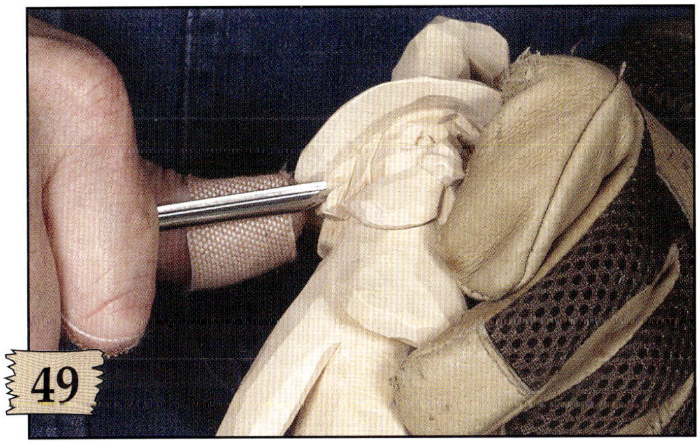

Here's a shot of the half-moon cut on top of the lower lid. Use the detail knife tip to trim the outside edges of the eyeball to slightly round the edges. Then, with the 3 mm deep gouge, scoop out the ears.

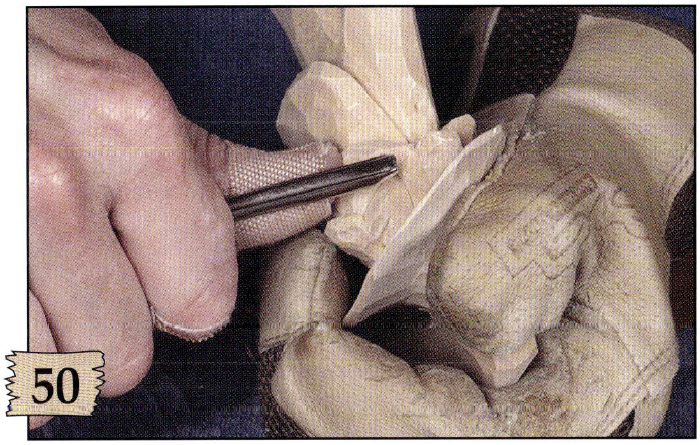

Make a scoop cut above each earlobe. This cut will slightly raise the lobe. Notice how I cut straight, then angled down toward the bottom of the ear.

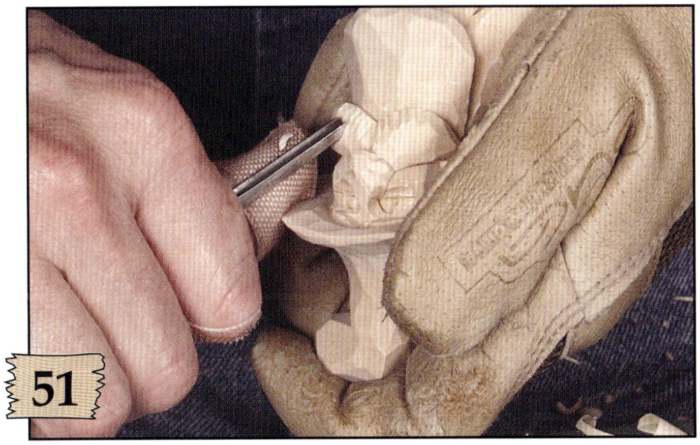

After finishing the eyes and ears, use a small V-tool to cut the whisker lines in the mustache.

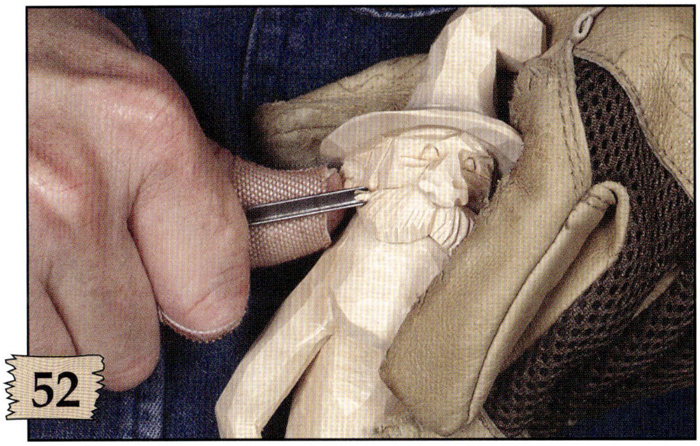

Finish cutting the whisker lines on both sides of the mustache.

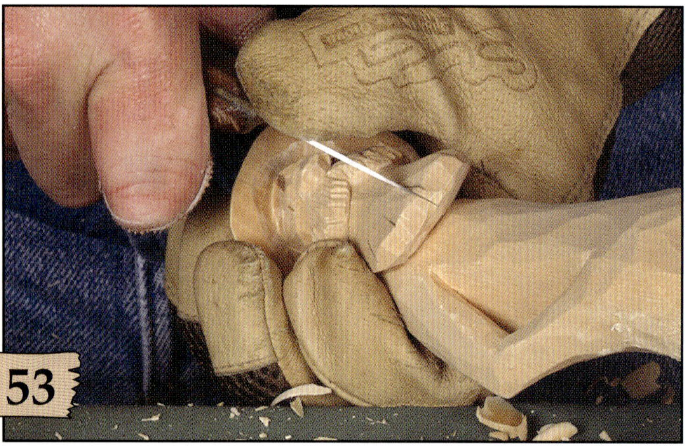

53

Here I have penciled some random lines on the beard and am using the 2" knife to cut a V at each of these lines. This will give the beard some character and the appearance of locks.

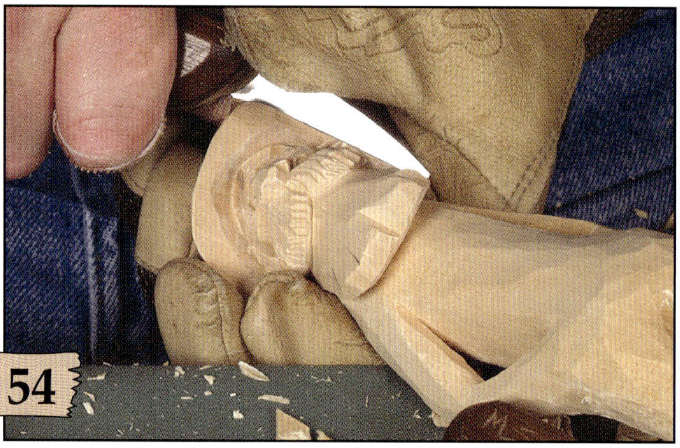

54

Again, just simple V-shaped cuts form the locks in the beard.

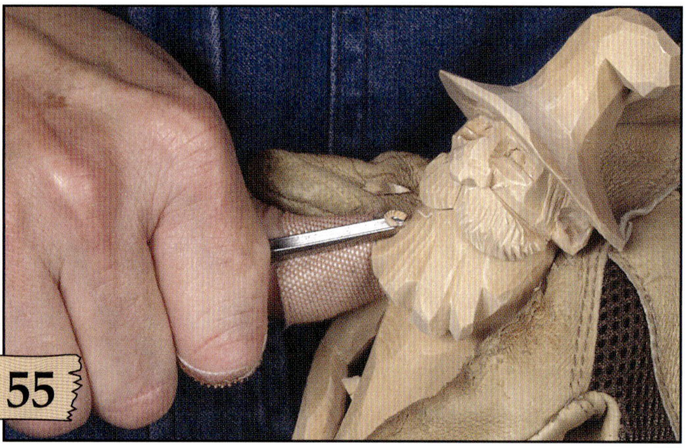

55

Use the small 2 mm V-tool to cut the whiskers in the beard. Make random cuts with some deeper than others to give the appearance of flowing whiskers.

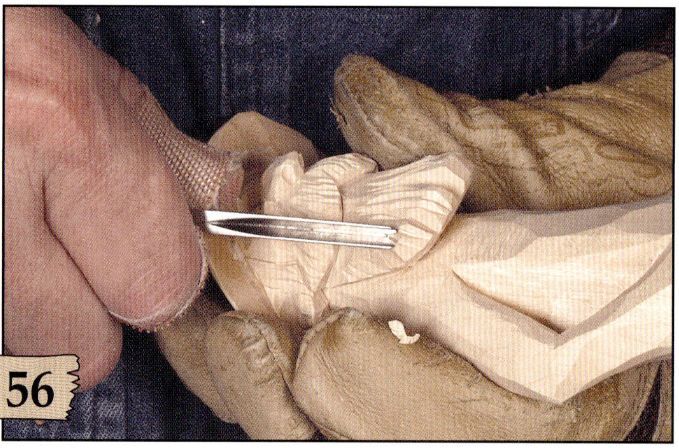

56

Now the beard is pretty much finished.

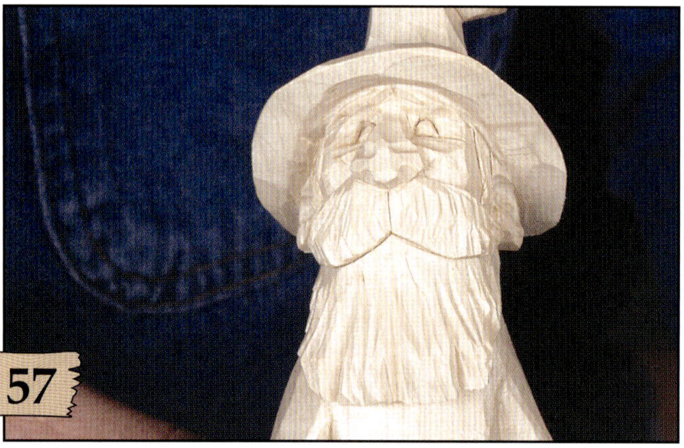

57

Stop here to check your progress. Is the hat shaped the way you want it to be? Are the face, beard, and mustache to your liking? Is there enough space between the arms and the body?

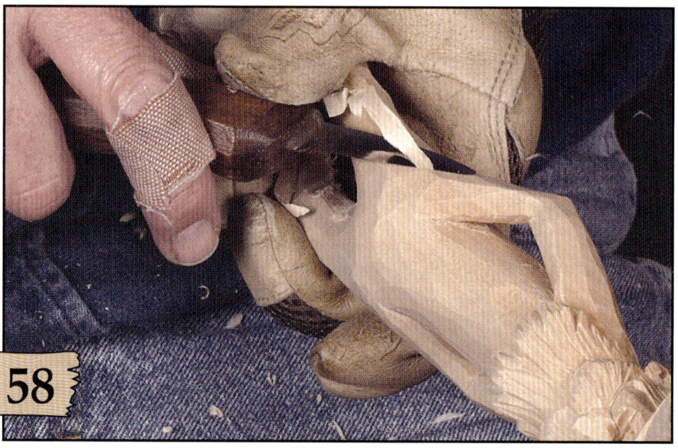

58

With the head and upper body finished, start rounding and cleaning up the legs. Like the skinny arms, the legs will be very thin by the time we are finished cleaning them up. So take care to remove just a little wood.

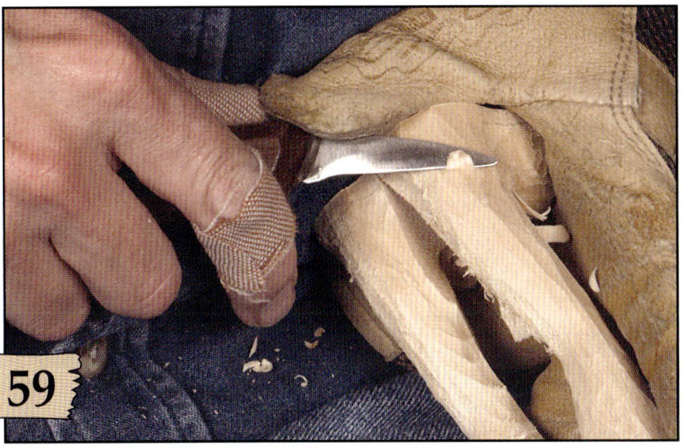

59

Clean the pant legs up to the bend of the knee. Be careful at the knee; there is not much wood left in this area. Use extra care at the bend of the knee because the grain changes directions.

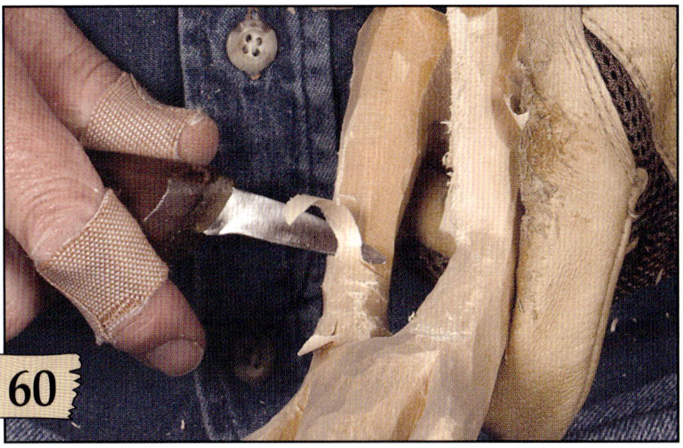

60

Here I'm cleaning the back of the upper leg.

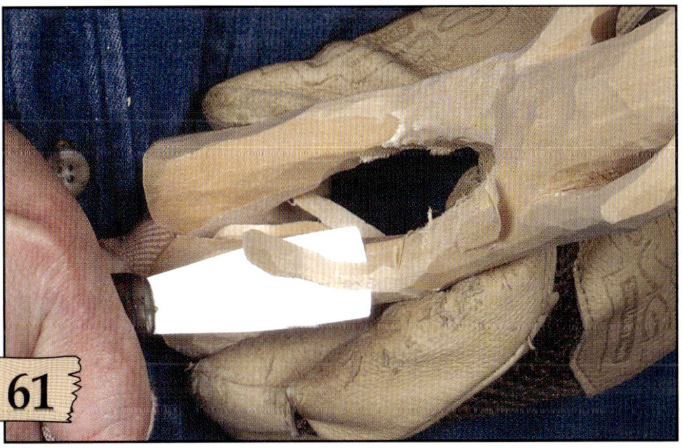

61

I can also use a 1" flat shallow gouge to do some cleaning cuts.

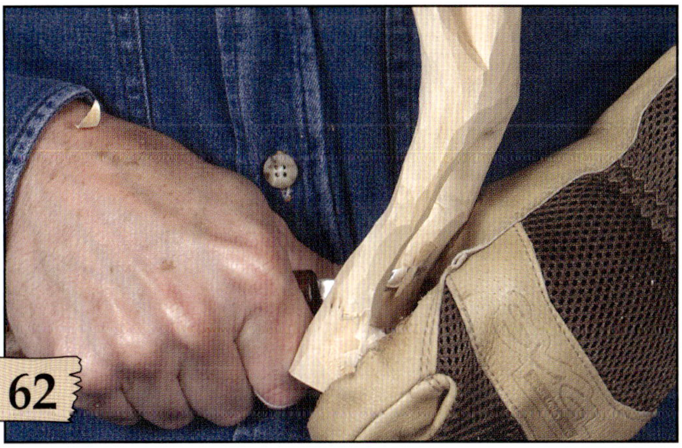

62

Clean the inside of the pant legs with the 2" knife.

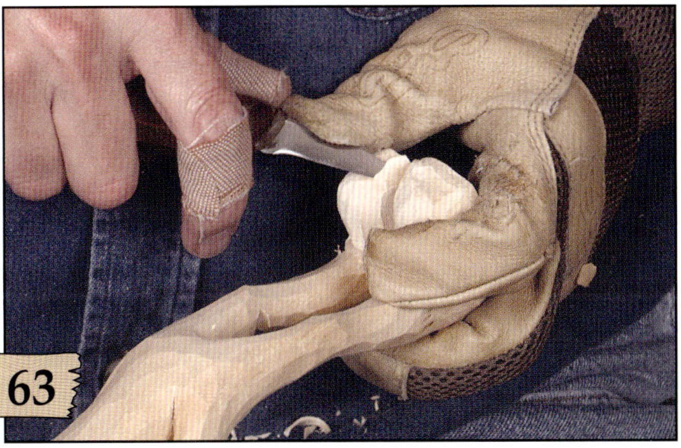

63

Here the pants are cleaned to their finished size. Now start rounding and shaping the shoes. The pant legs will come all the way down and cover the heel of the shoe. Remember, the legs are thin and fragile.

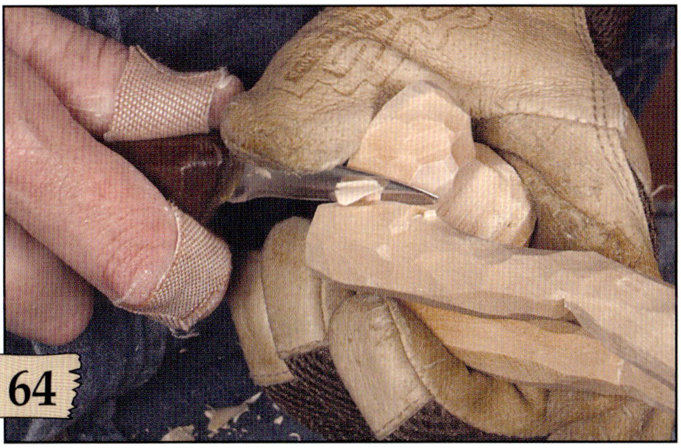

64

After the shoes are roughed in, cut the pant legs to cover the heels of the shoes.

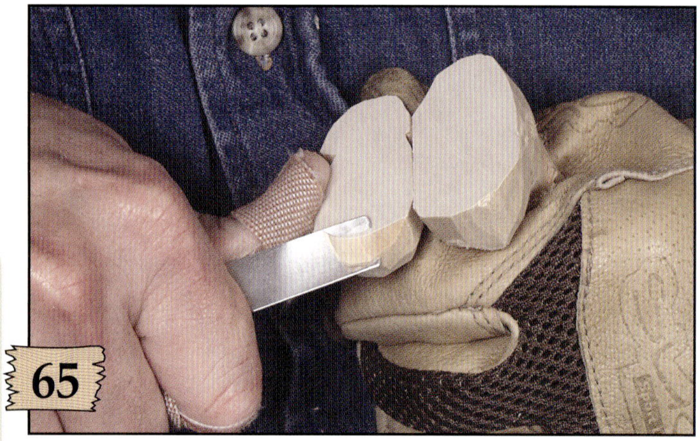

With a ¾" shallow gouge, cut across the underside of each boot toe to slightly turn up the toes.

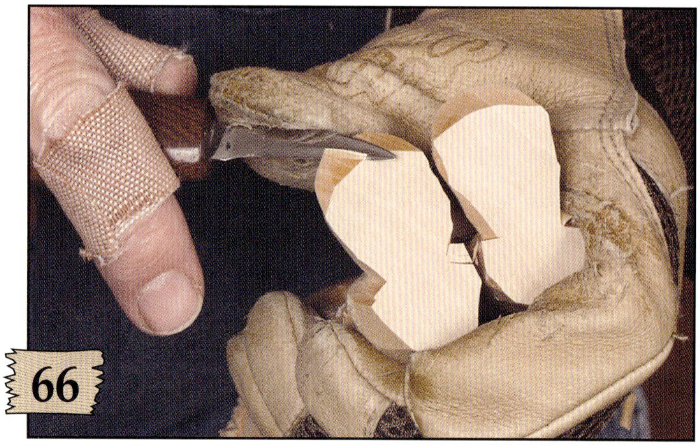

You can also use the knife on the underside of the boot toes.

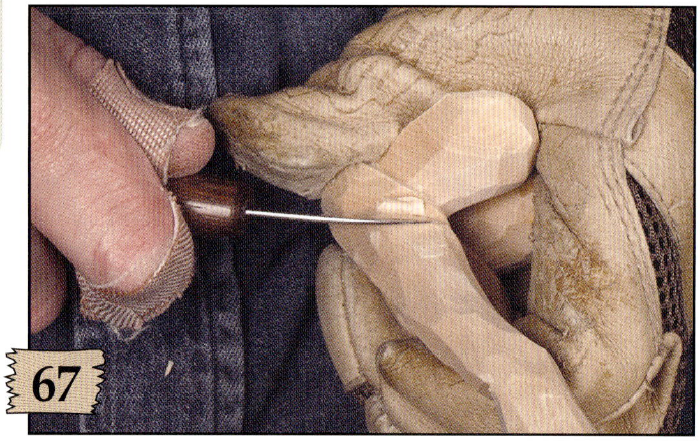

After finishing the boots, use the knife to cut the pant leg hems. These cuts are shallow, in-and-out cleaning cuts that leave a V-shaped indentation.

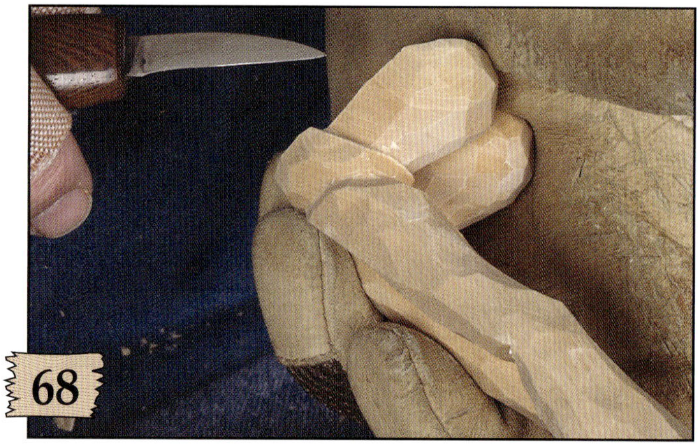

Notice how the cleaning cuts are roughly V shaped. We will use this same cut in the next step to put wrinkles in the pant legs.

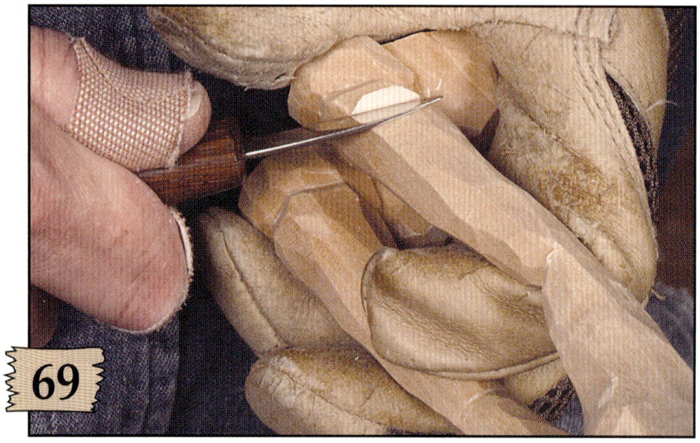

With the hems in place, use the V-shaped cleaning cuts to make wrinkles in the pant legs.

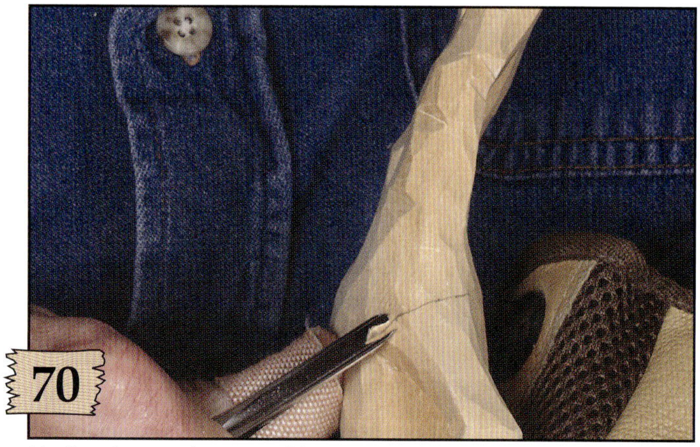

Notice the random wrinkle cuts on the leg. Use the 4 mm V-tool to cut the pocket lines.

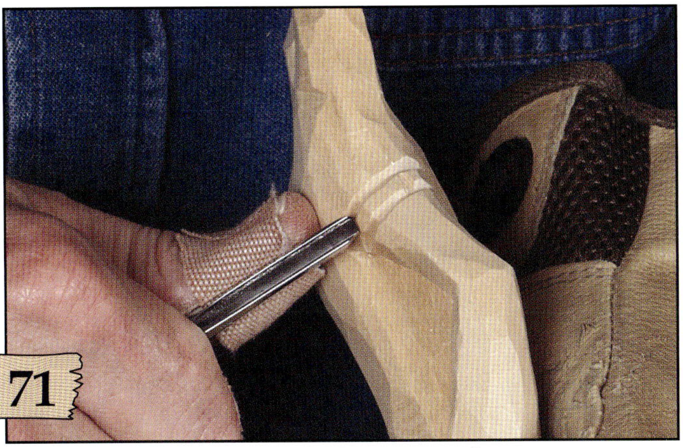

Cut the shirtsleeve cuffs with the same tool.

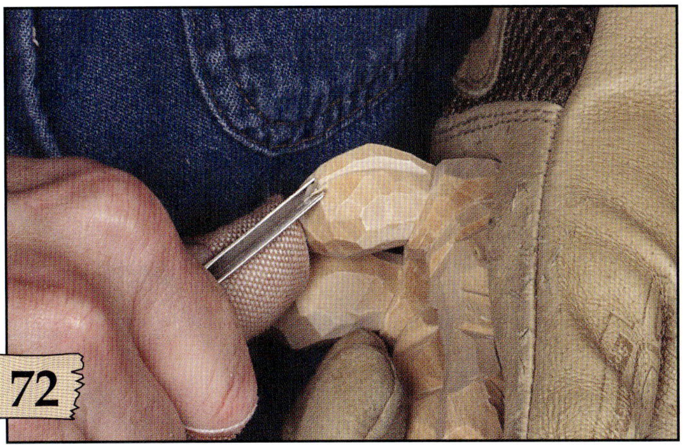

Continue to use the same V-tool to cut the soles of the shoes.

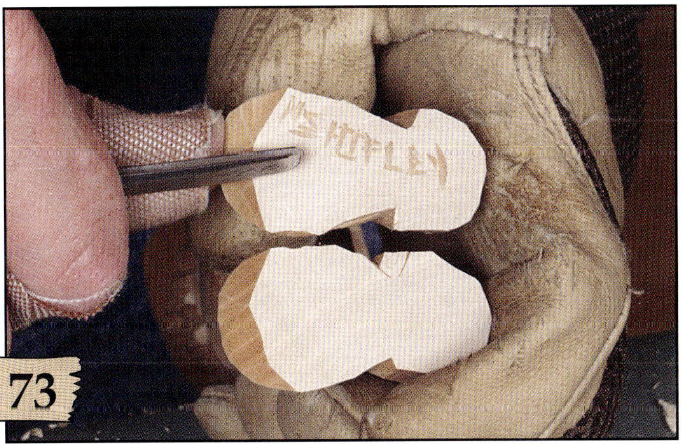

While you have the V-tool in your hand, sign the bottom of the boot sole.

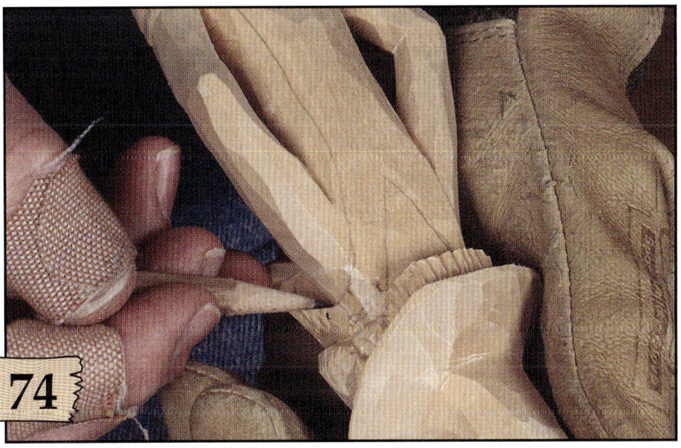

Pencil on the overalls, front and back.

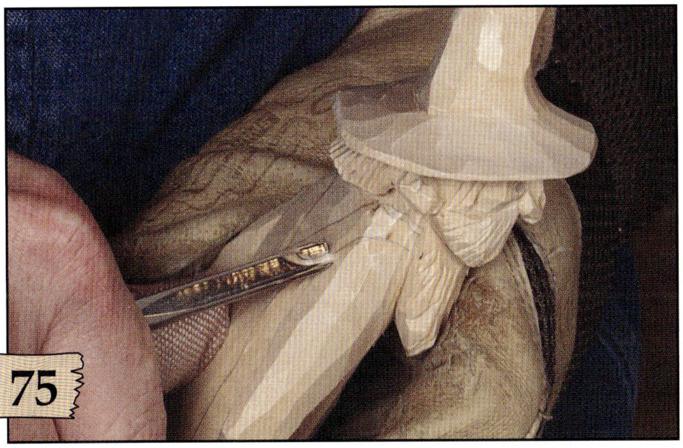

Cut the lines of the overalls with the 4 mm V-tool.

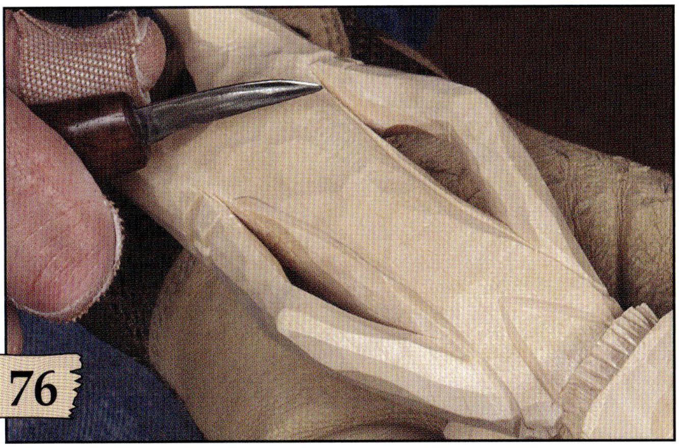

Here all of the lines are cut in. (Notice the detailing on the hair that sticks out of the back of his hat.)

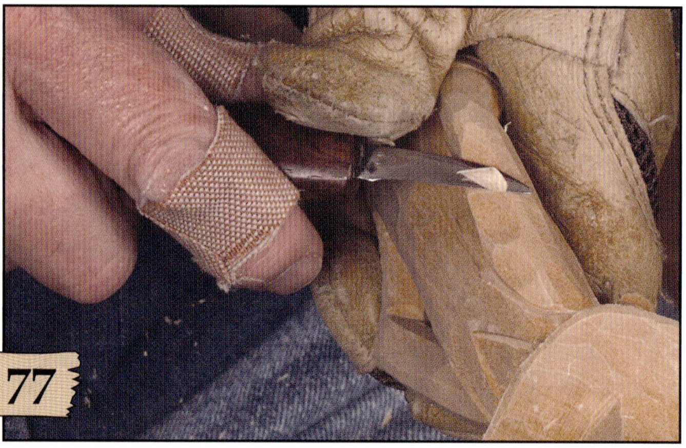

77

Now add some wrinkles to the shirtsleeves. Some of these cuts can just be simple scoop cuts made with the detail knife.

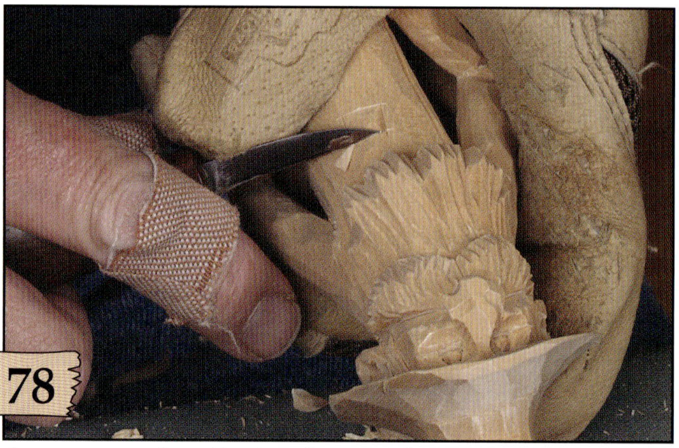

78

Cut some patches. Use just four simple cuts to form a square, and then trim the edge of the patch.

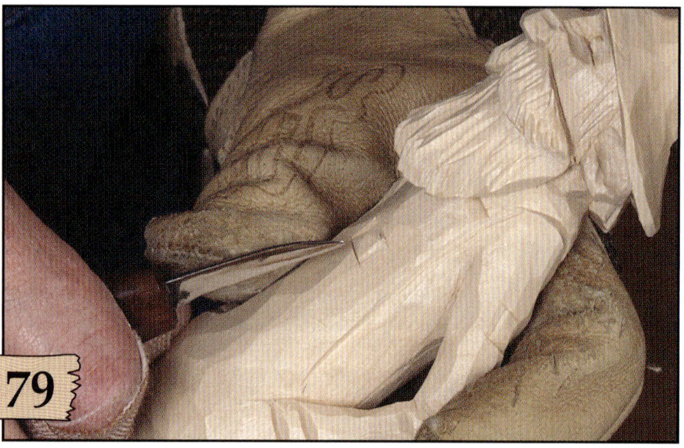

79

Now we have a finished patch. Add as many as you like in various places. You can also see the front of the finished overalls in this picture.

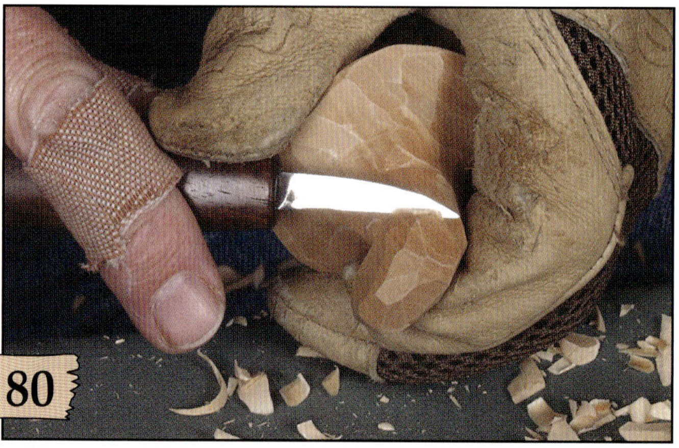

80

Add some wrinkles on the hat.

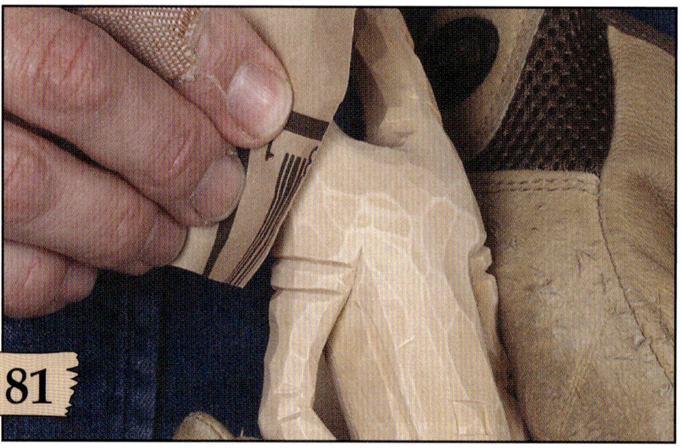

81

Look over the figure for any needed adjustments and any leftover fuzzies. Then, lightly sand with 220-grit sandpaper. I'm not trying to remove any wood; I just want to give the piece a worn look.

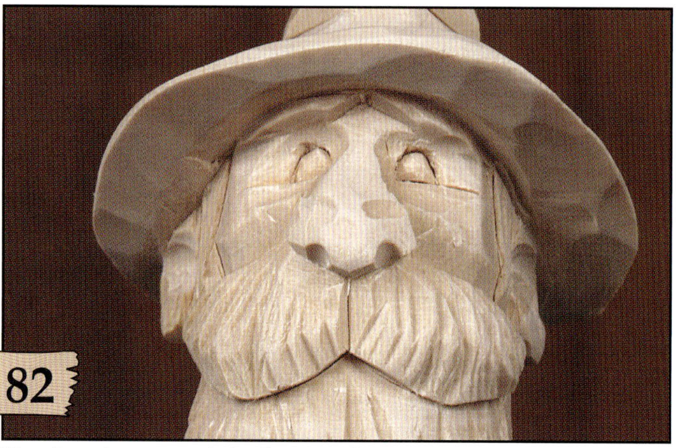

82

Here's a close-up of the face. Make sure you get rid of all of the fuzzies before you paint.

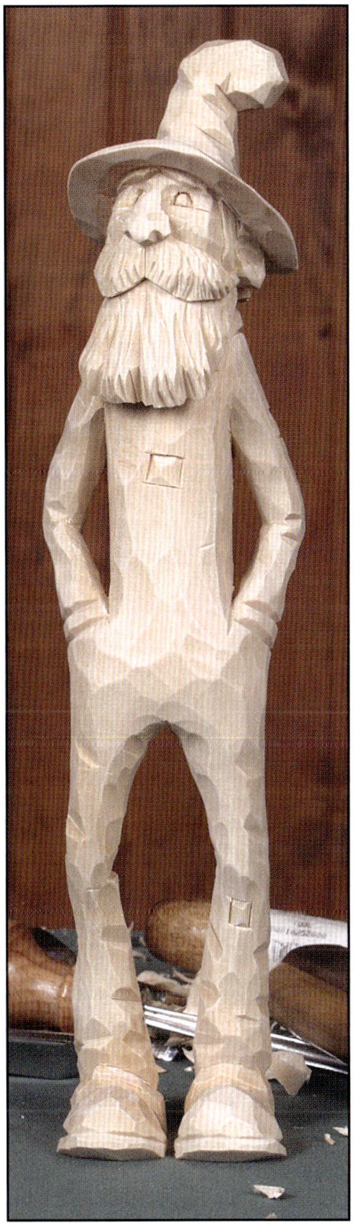

Here's our finished piece.

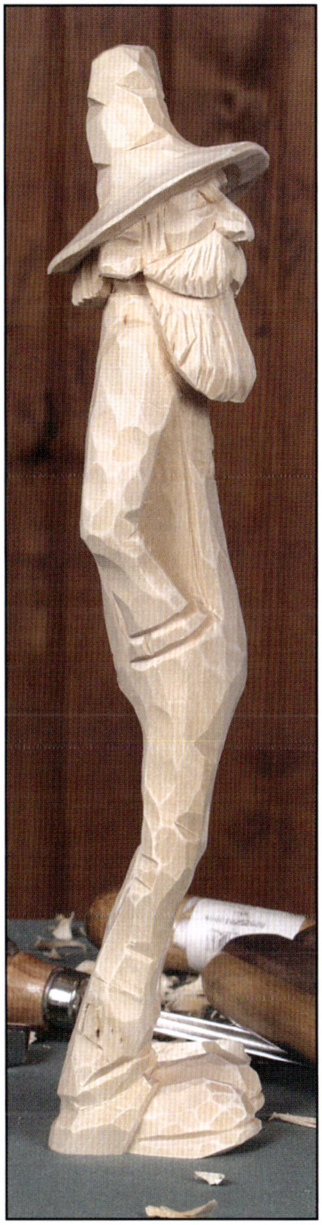

And here he is from the side. I just love those skinny legs!

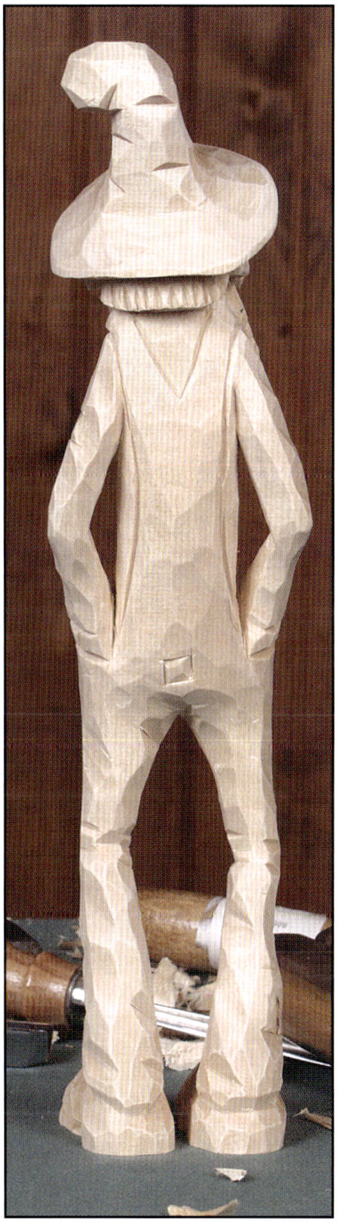

Notice the wrinkles and the scoop cuts on the view of the back.

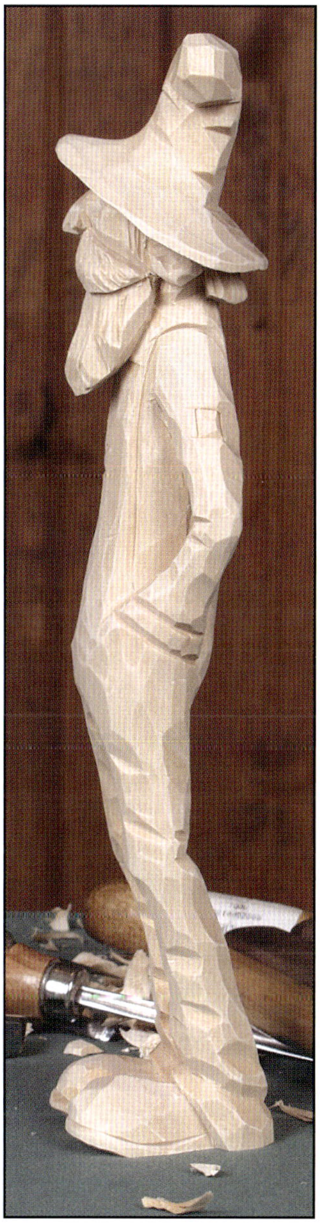

The left side is similar to the right because this piece is symmetrical. Carving this guy was so much fun, I hate to stop; but it's time to paint.

Painting

Now let's trade the tools for paintbrushes. I use good sable brushes because they don't fray on the ends like the cheaper brushes. Also the stiffer, cheaper brushes tend to flip or spray paint at the end of a brush stroke. However, I do use the cheaper acrylic paints because I find that they work just as well as more expensive paints, and they are readily available in art supply and department stores. Acrylics have several advantages: They can be easily mixed, they can be thinned to any shade that you want, they dry quickly, and they clean up easily with water. When painting, I mix about 25% paint to about 75% water. This ratio will give you a nice wash that allows the grain of the wood to show through. I store the mixed paint in small bottles. The mixed paint will store indefinitely as long as the bottle is sealed. Also, I clean the brushes well after each use according to the manufacturer's directions.

Tools and Materials
#2 shader brush
#4 shader brush
#6 shader brush
4/0 spotter brush
Paper towels
Ponce wheel
Awl
Toothpick

Acrylic Paints
White
Coffee bean brown
Flesh
Black
Navy blue
Straw (yellow)
Various colors for the patches
Burnt umber

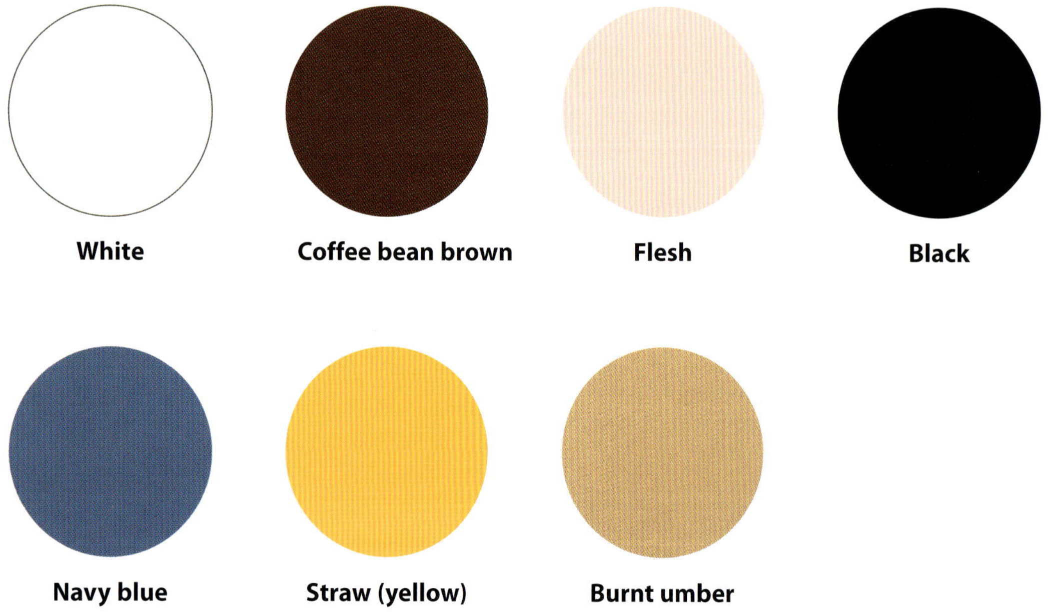

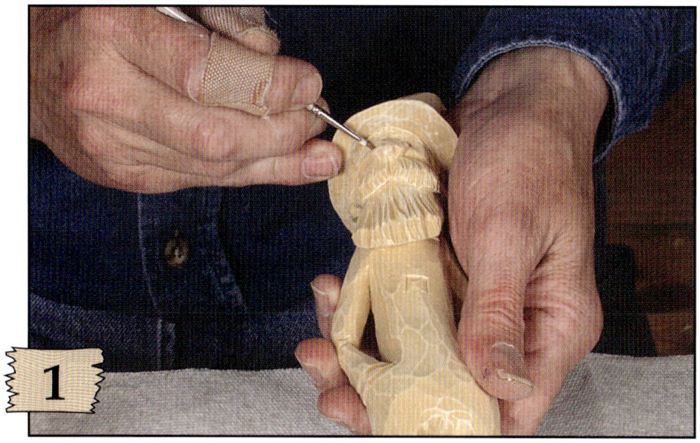

Use the 4/0 spotter brush to paint the eyeballs—just the eyeballs—white. Notice I have my little finger planted to steady my hand.

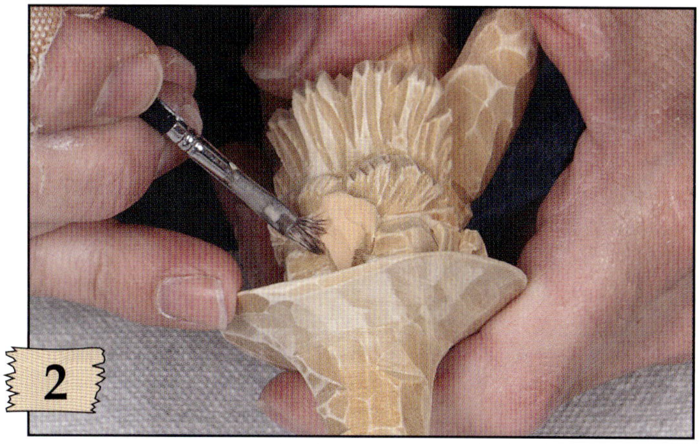

Paint the face and ears flesh. Use the #2 shader brush. Again, notice how I'm using my finger to help keep the brush stable.

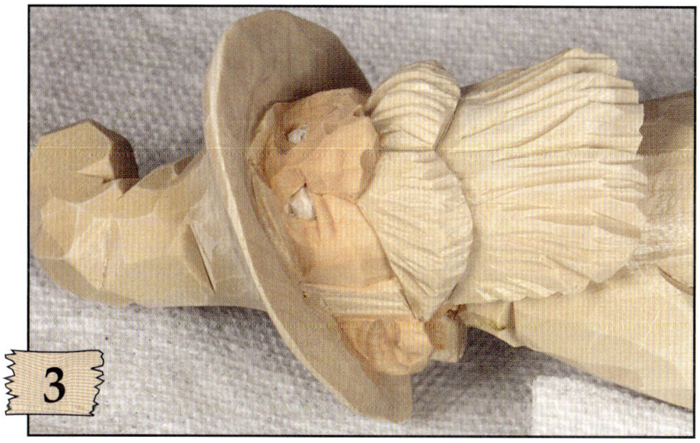

The face and the whites of the eyes are done.

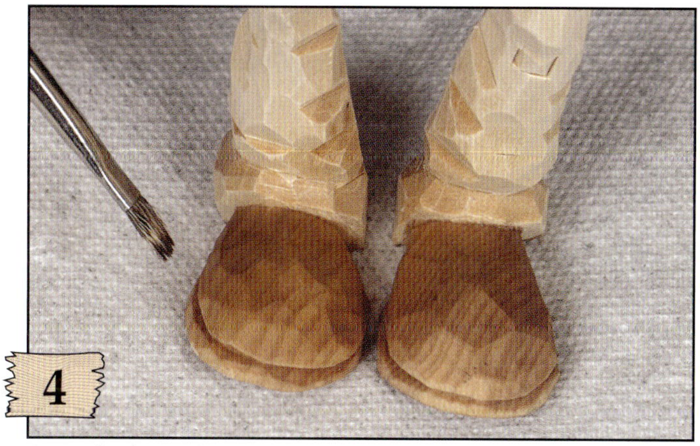

Paint the boots burnt umber using a #6 shader brush.

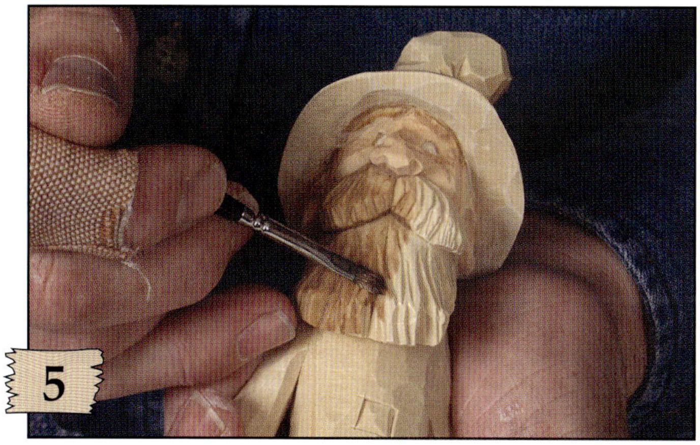

Use coffee bean brown for the beard, hair, and eyebrows. Use the #2 shader brush for the beard and hair and the spotter brush for the eyebrows.

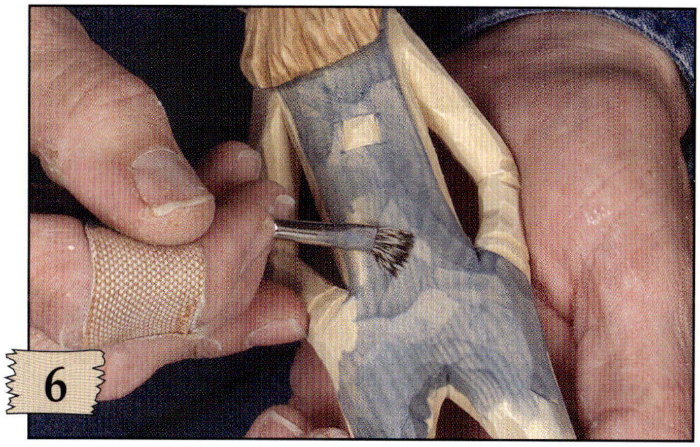

Paint the overalls with navy blue and a #4 shader brush. On a large area like this, use circular blending strokes. If you let the paint edge dry, the acrylics will not blend well. Just move along quickly and do not let the painting edge dry. This is especially important with darker colors.

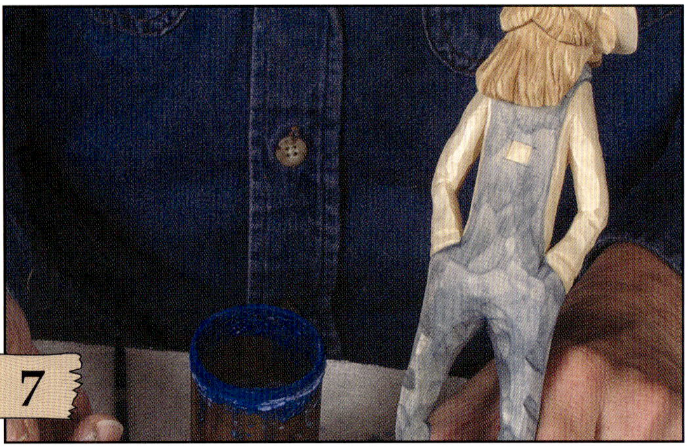

Finish the overalls, front and back, but do not paint the patches.

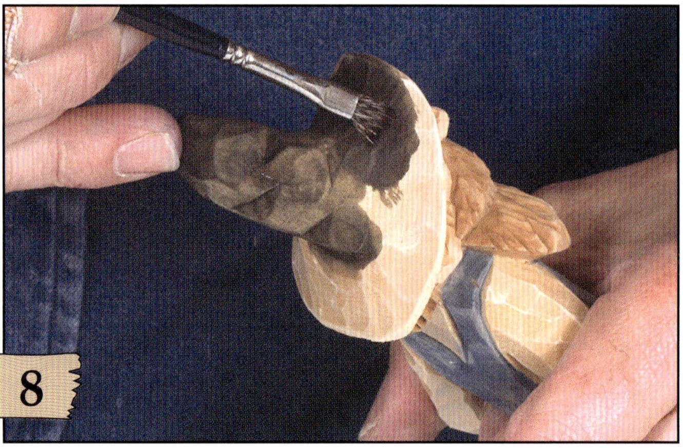

Paint the hat black, using the #4 shader. Black is another darker color that has to be blended with the circular strokes to avoid streaking.

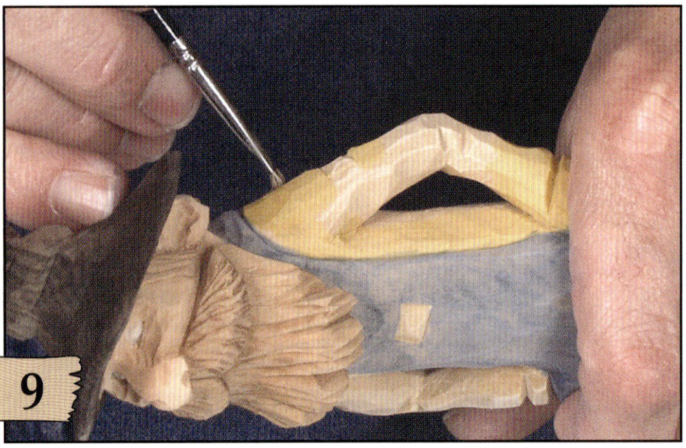

Paint the shirt straw. Use the #4 shader. Take care while painting around the patches.

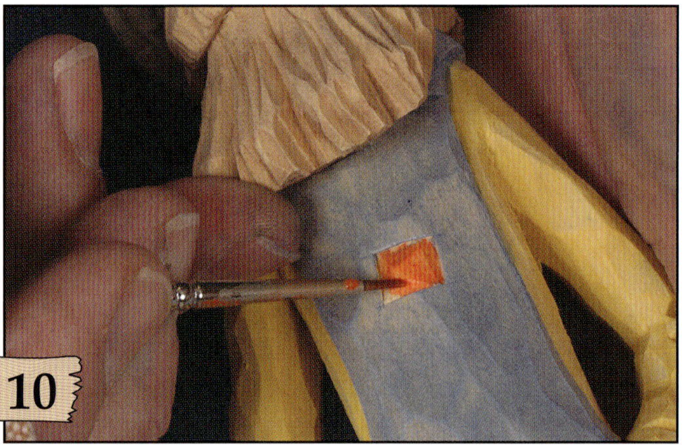

Now paint the patches various colors. Use the spotter brush for these areas.

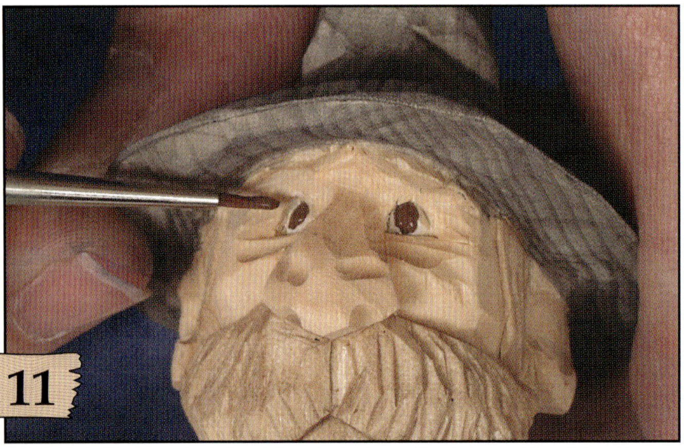

Paint the eyeballs using coffee bean brown straight from the bottle. Using the spotter, load the tip of the brush with paint, carefully dot the eyeball, and then gently expand the dot until you have a natural-size eye. Place the dot in the left corner of each eye so the figure appears to be looking in that direction.

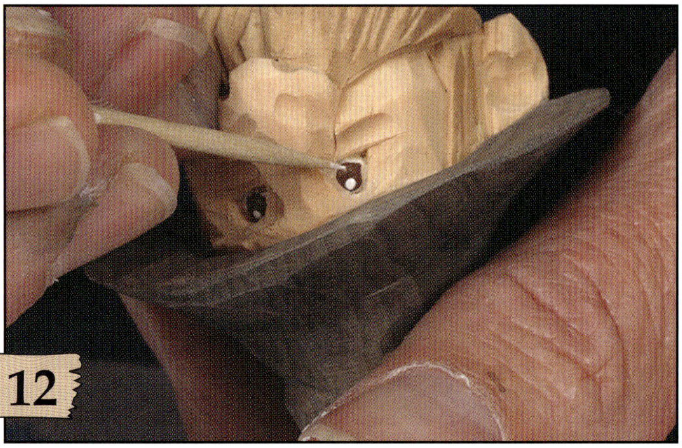

Let the brown dry for approximately 10 minutes; then, use a toothpick and white paint straight from the bottle to place a small dot on each eyeball. I like the dot to be on the top of the eyeball; notice how this placement highlights the eye.

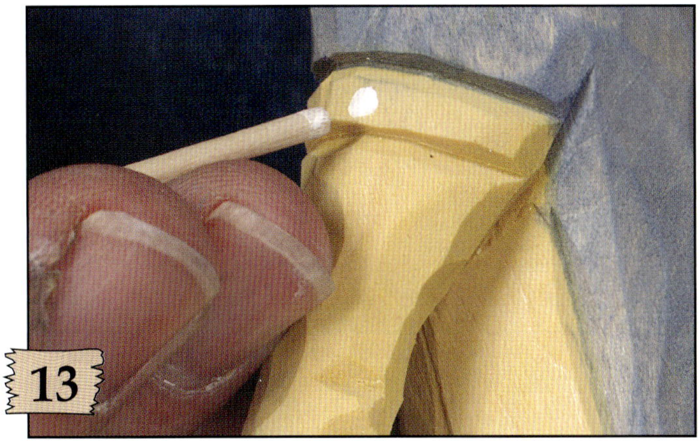

Now cut off the end of the toothpick and dot white buttons on the shirtsleeve cuffs. Buttons can be carved, but, in this case, we'll just dot on some simple buttons.

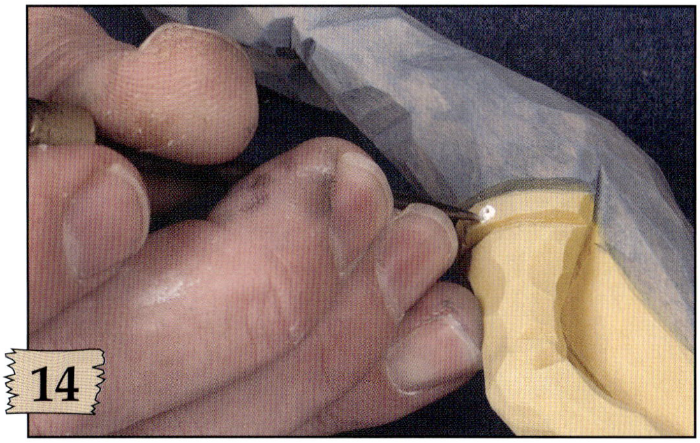

Let the buttons dry for approximately five minutes; then, punch two thread holes in the buttons with the awl.

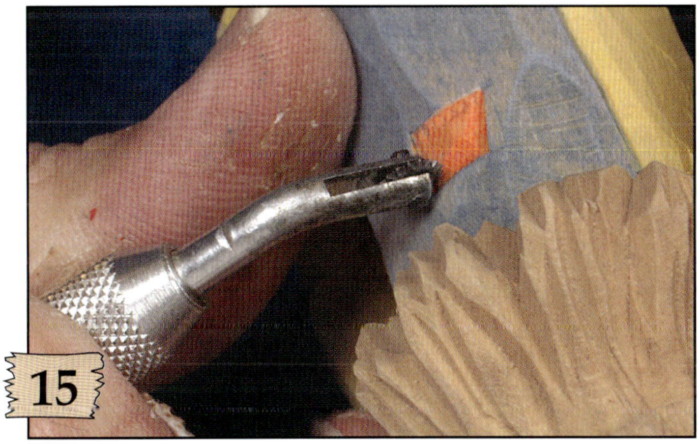

Once the patches have dried, which takes about a minute, use the ponce wheel to roll stitches on the outside edge of each patch.

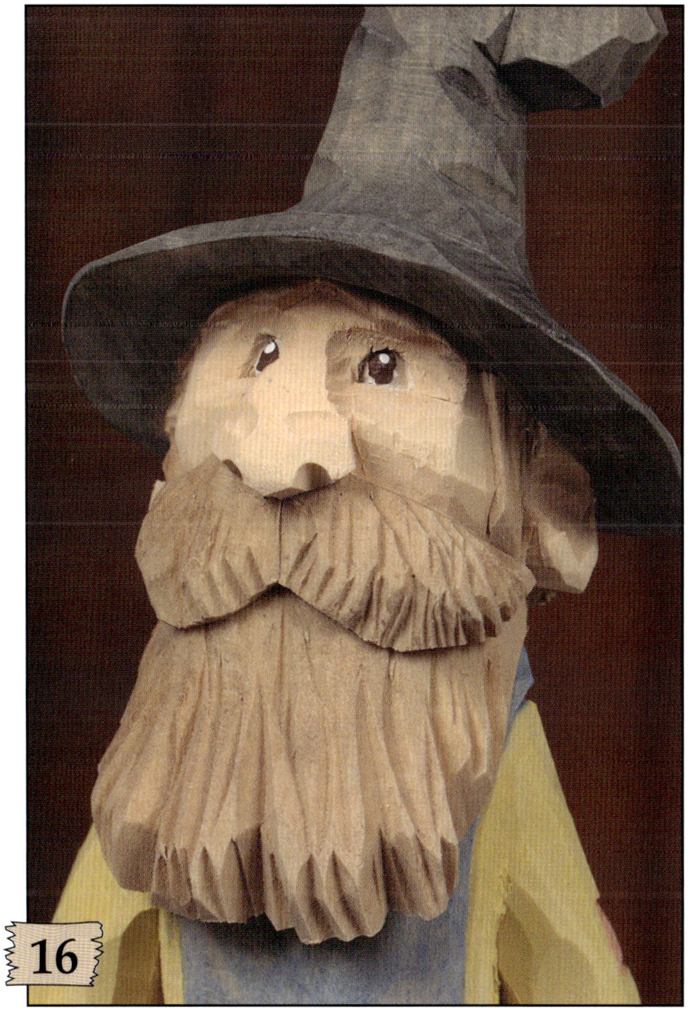

The painting is completed on the head.

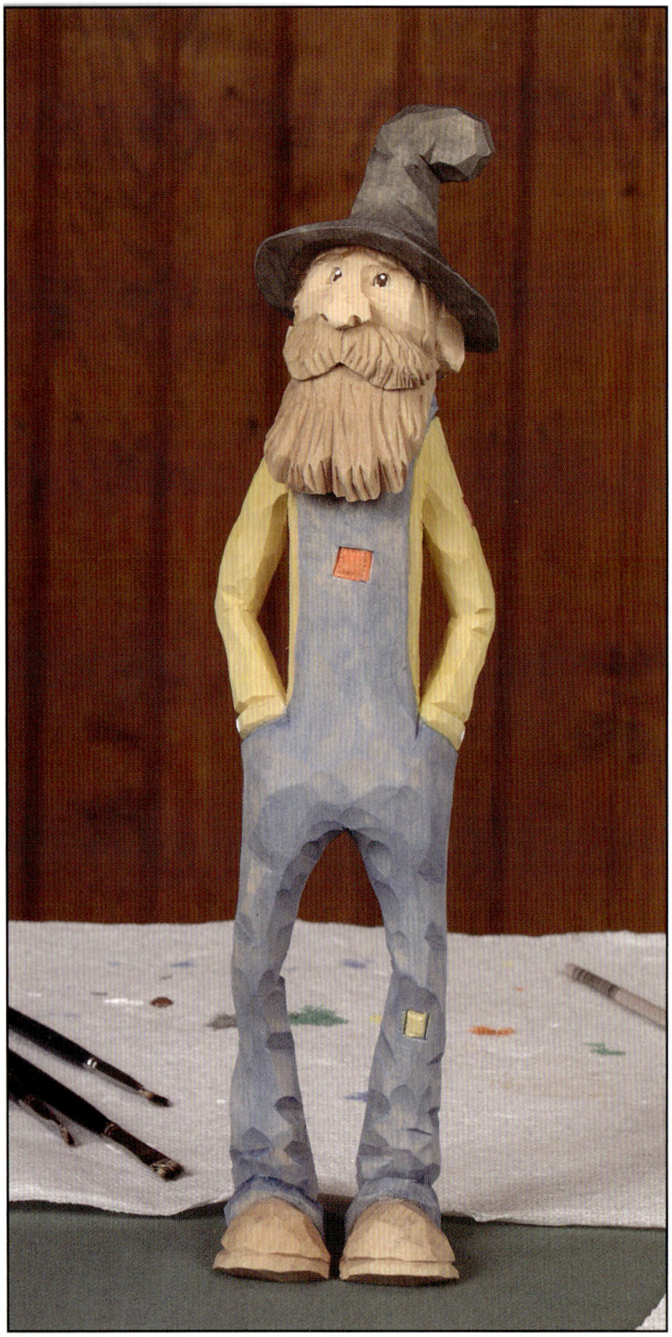

Here's our finished piece. Check over it for any painting miscues. Let the piece dry for about one hour before staining.

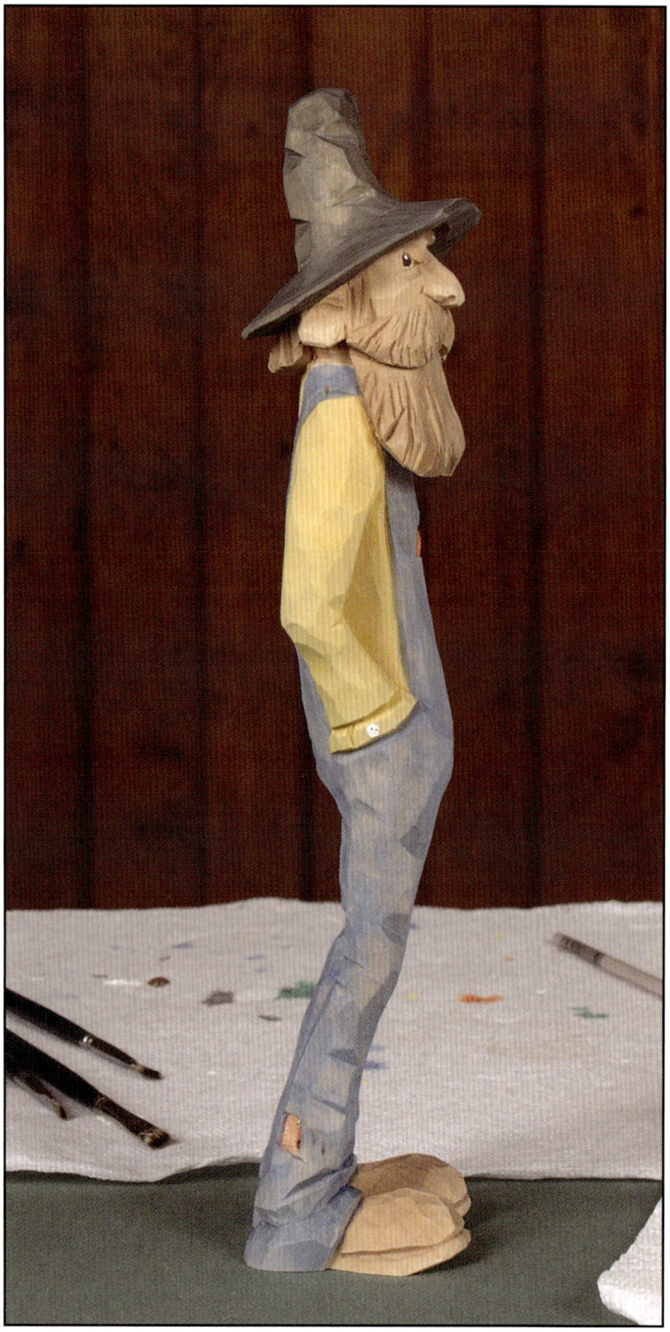

A view from the side shows how the figure's hands are tucked in his pockets and how his pant legs cover the backs of his boots.

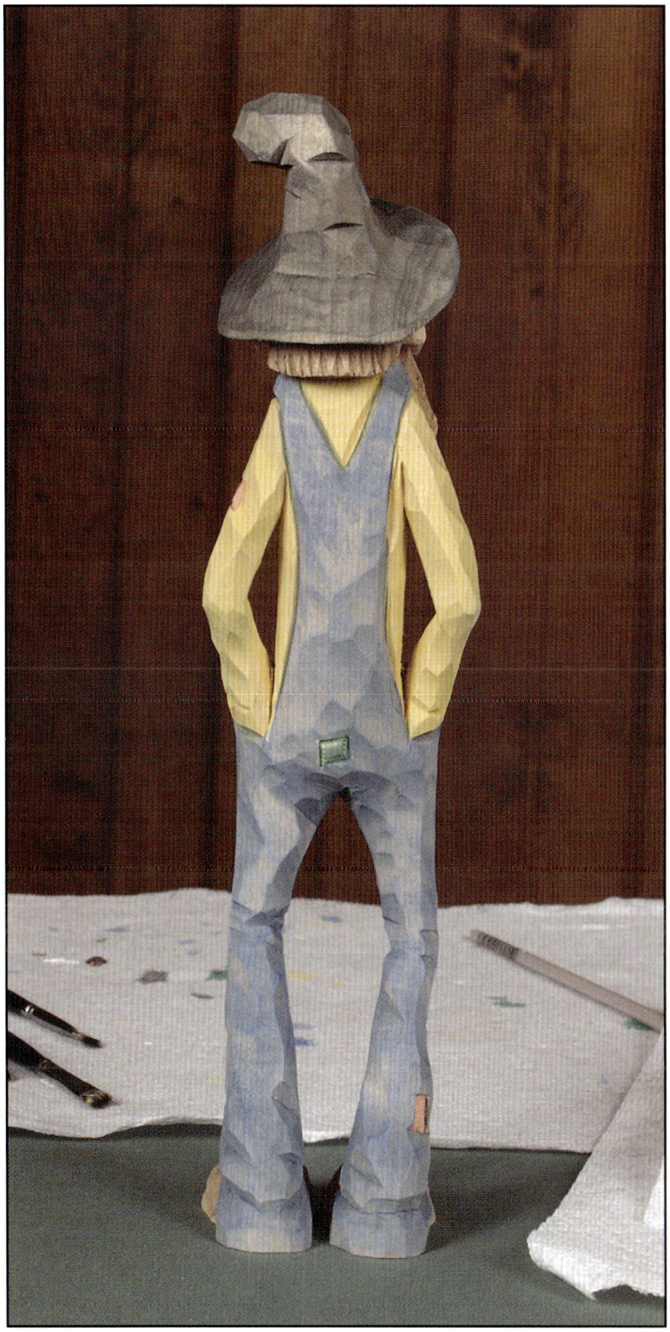

Notice how the knife cuts create highlights and lowlights, giving the paint some added dimension.

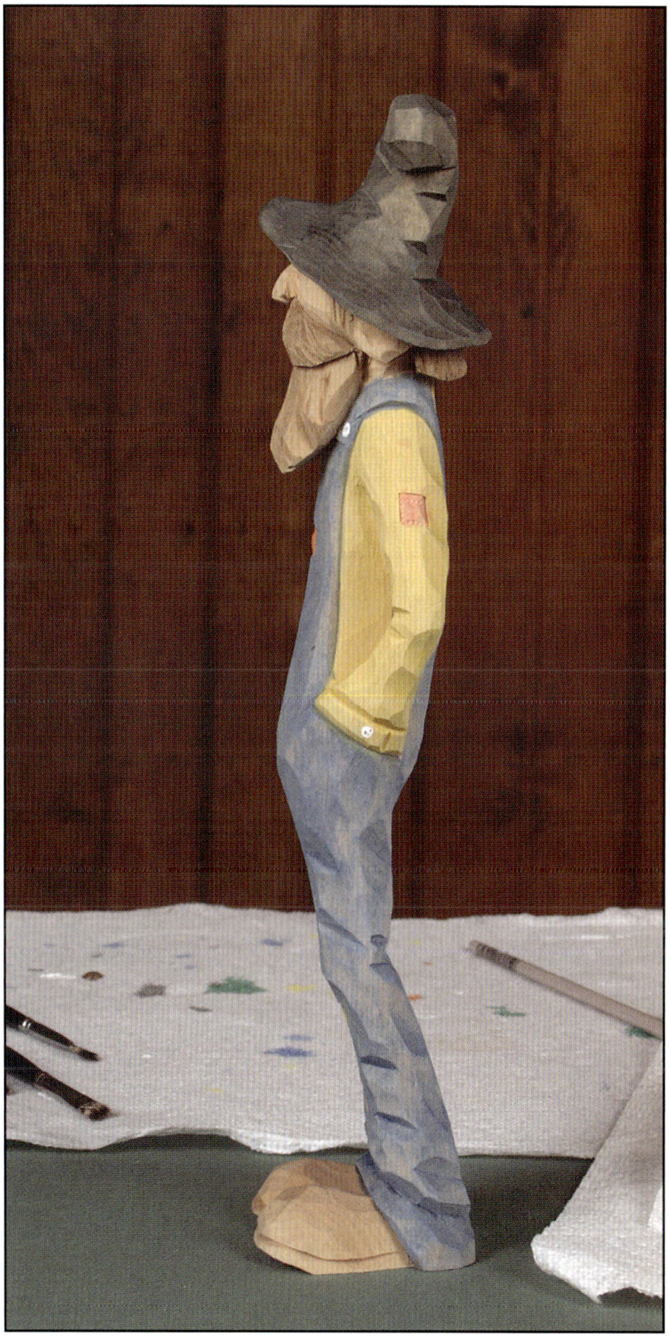

All we have to do now is dip this guy in some stain, and then he can be on his way.

Staining

The stain that I use is boiled linseed oil with a small amount of raw umber oil paint and mineral spirits. The mixture starts with one quart of boiled linseed oil; into that, squeeze approximately 1/2" raw umber oil paint from the tube, add 25% mineral spirits, and mix well. The first time I mix the stain I use a kitchen blender. Stirring is enough in later uses. Dispose of the oil-soaked towels properly; they can combust. Check on trash disposal for this type of item in your area, but do not store any oil-soaked materials indoors.

Tools and Materials
Boiled linseed oil
Raw umber oil paint
Mineral spirits
Paper towels

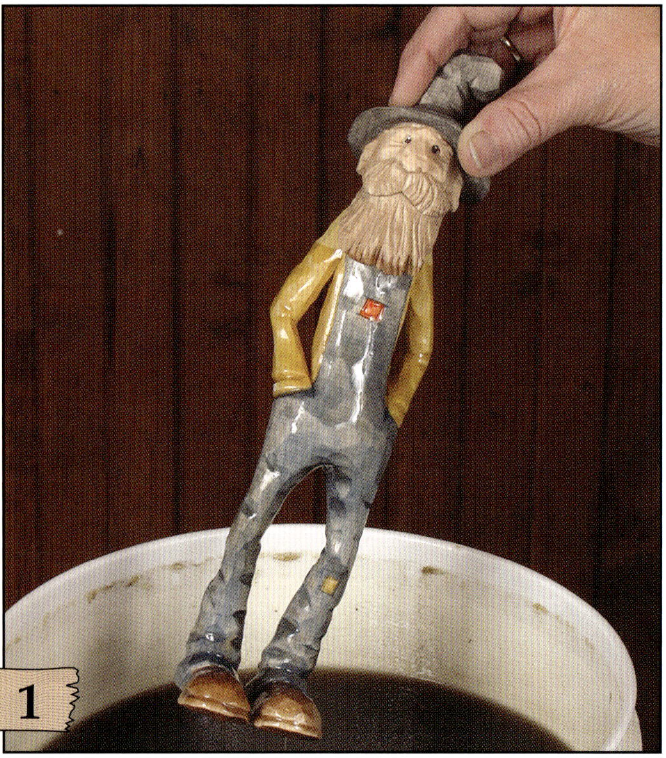

1 Simply dip half of the piece into the stain and let it drip for a short time.

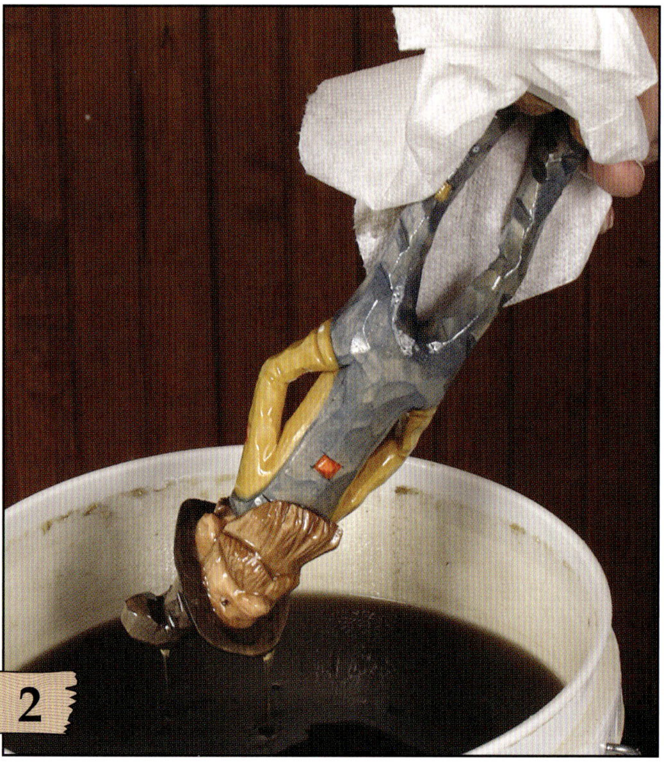

2 Now dip the other half and let the excess drip for a minute.

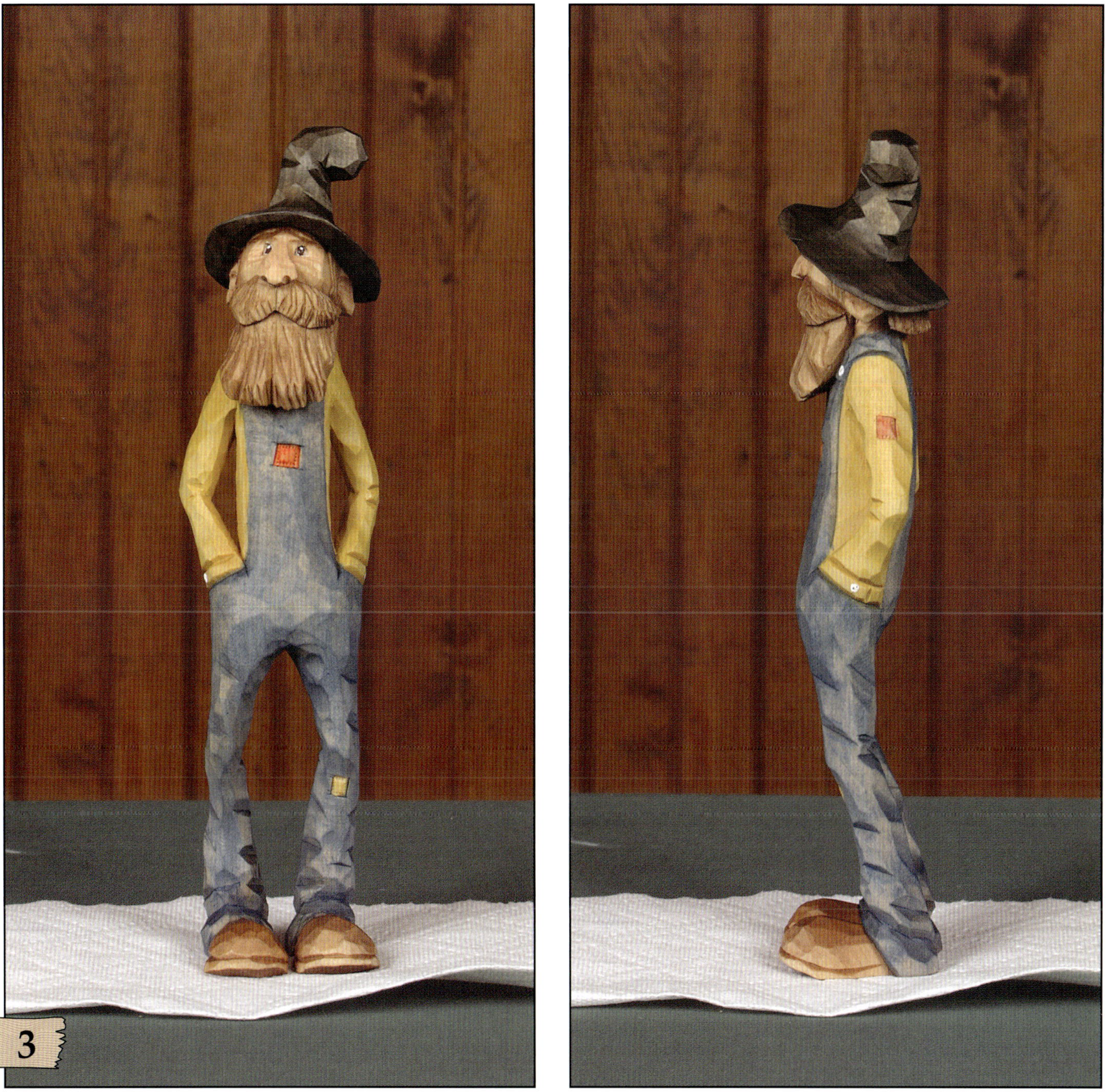

3

Towel the piece dry with paper towels. You won't be able to completely dry the piece, but you can dry the visible oil away. Complete drying will take about 24 hours. The odor will also pretty much disappear overnight. Now let's just "set back" and enjoy our finished piece.

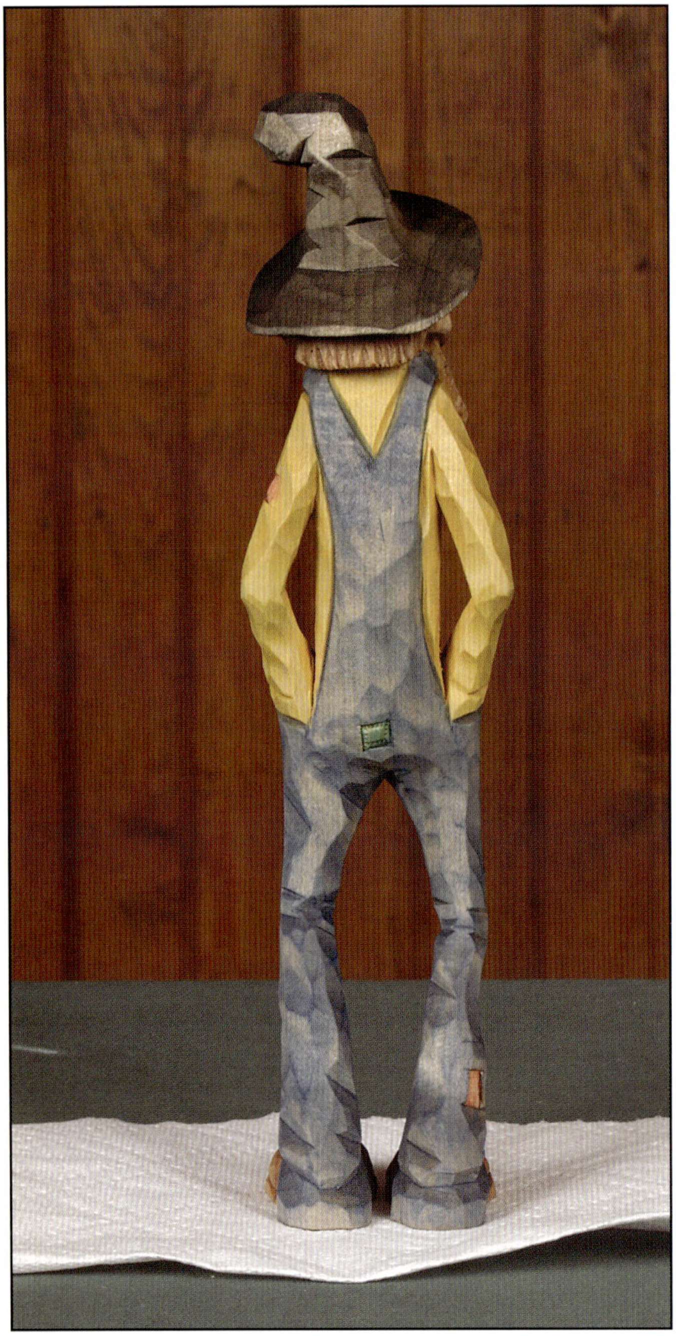

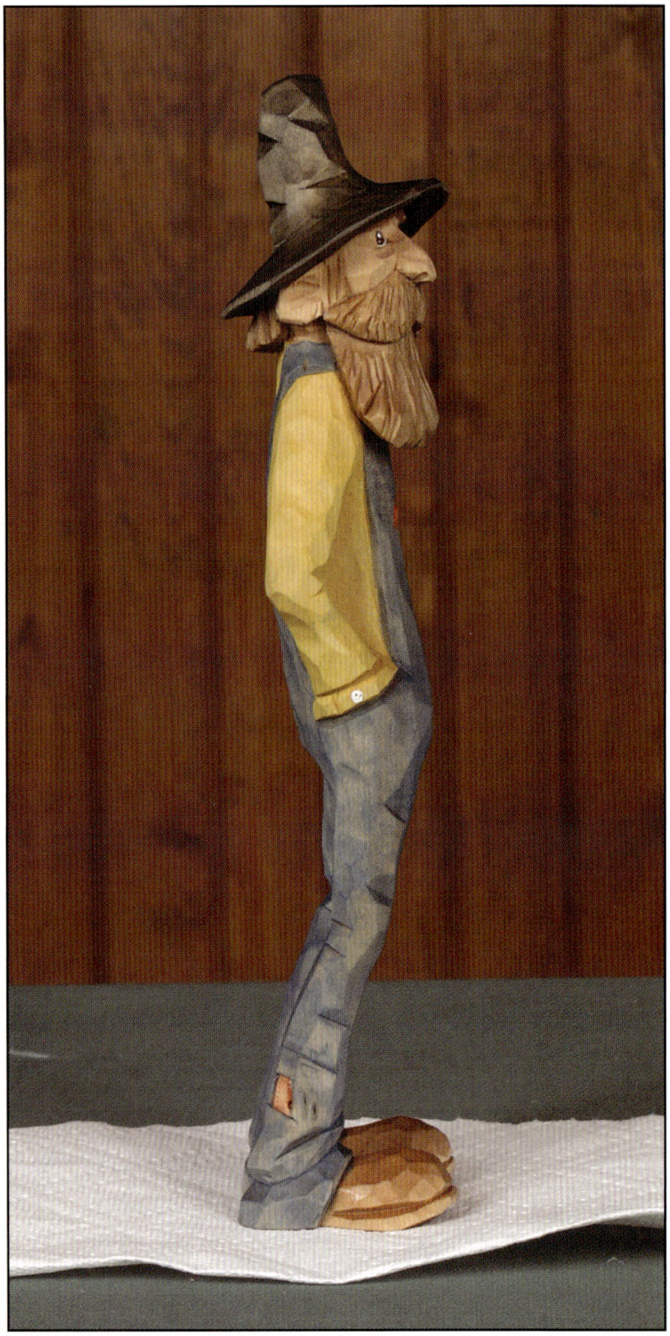

Projects

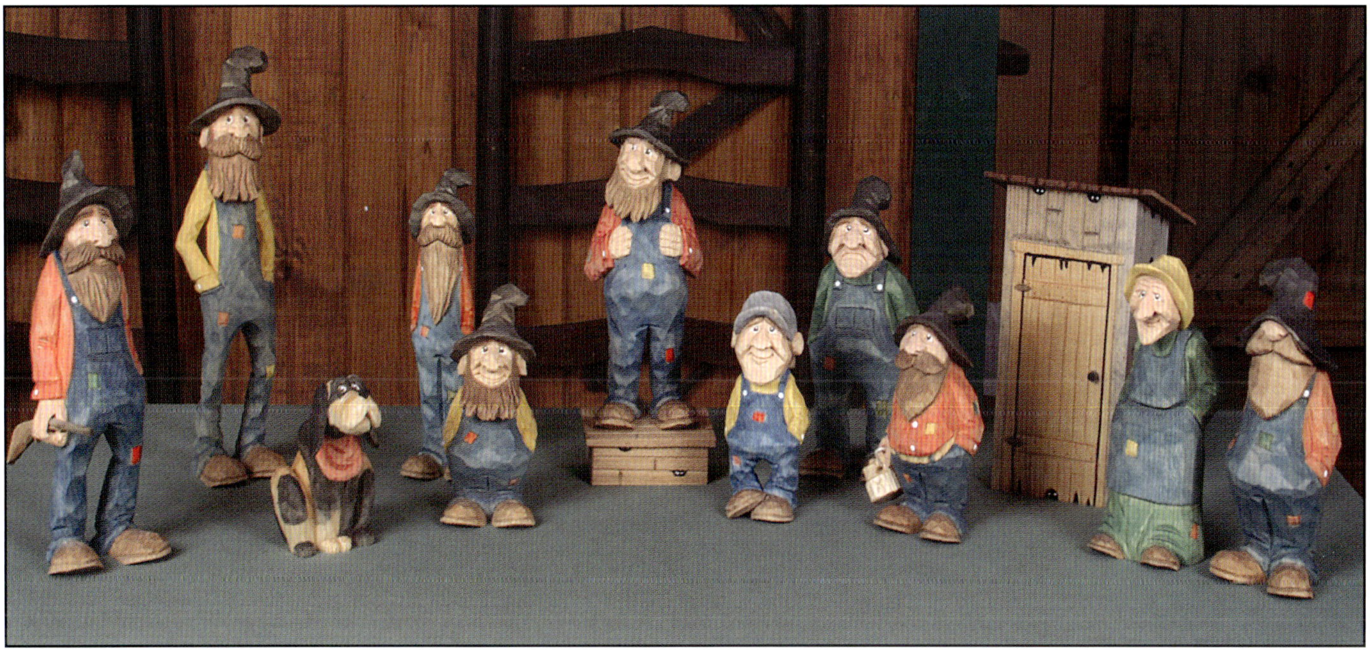

Here's the rest of the family. Most of these other projects are similar in design and carving style, but I've added enough variety to make it fun. Each project can easily be altered if you want to make a change here and there. All of these projects were carved using the same tools and materials that were used to complete the step-by-step project (see page 4).

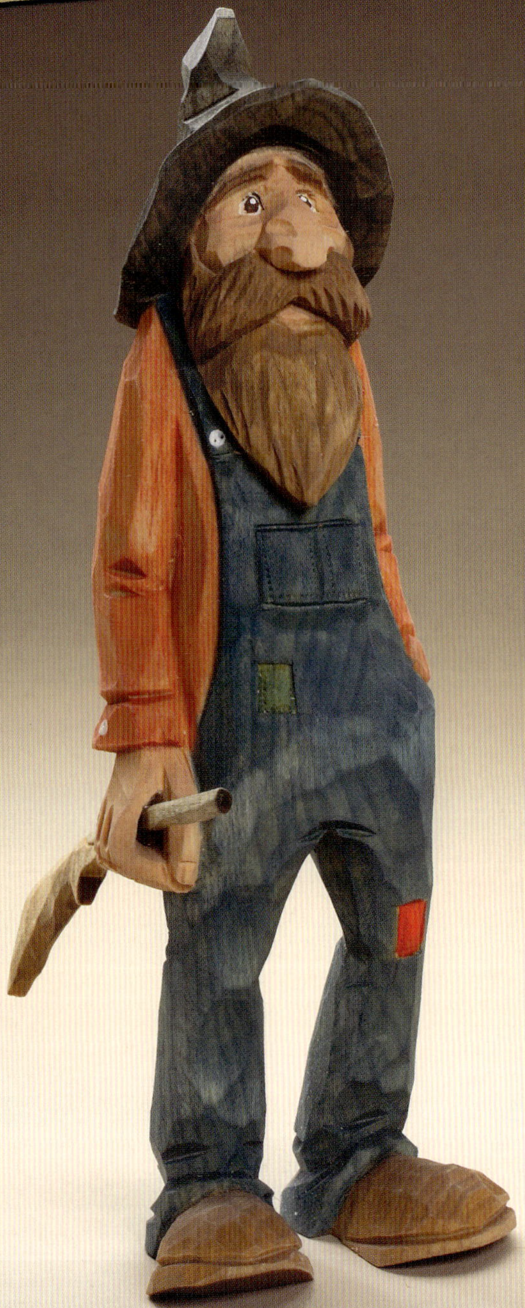

Frank

Frank's favorite pastime is possum hunting with his trusty dog, Beau. Frank avoids the honey-do chores around the house by sneaking off for a good hunt. Actually, he's not too good at sneaking; he's good at kind of just melting away into the woods. Frank would walk a mile to tree a good fat possum if it weren't for walking that mile. That's where cousin Delmer comes in handy. His long legs can cover a mile in nothin' flat. All Frank has to do is point Delmer in the direction of Beau's treeing bark and turn him loose. It's probably just a matter of time before you see these two hunting legends on one of those outdoor channels.

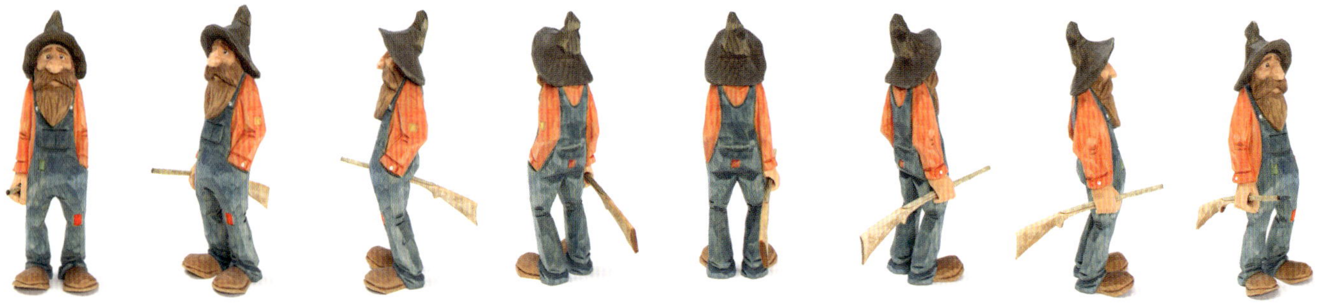

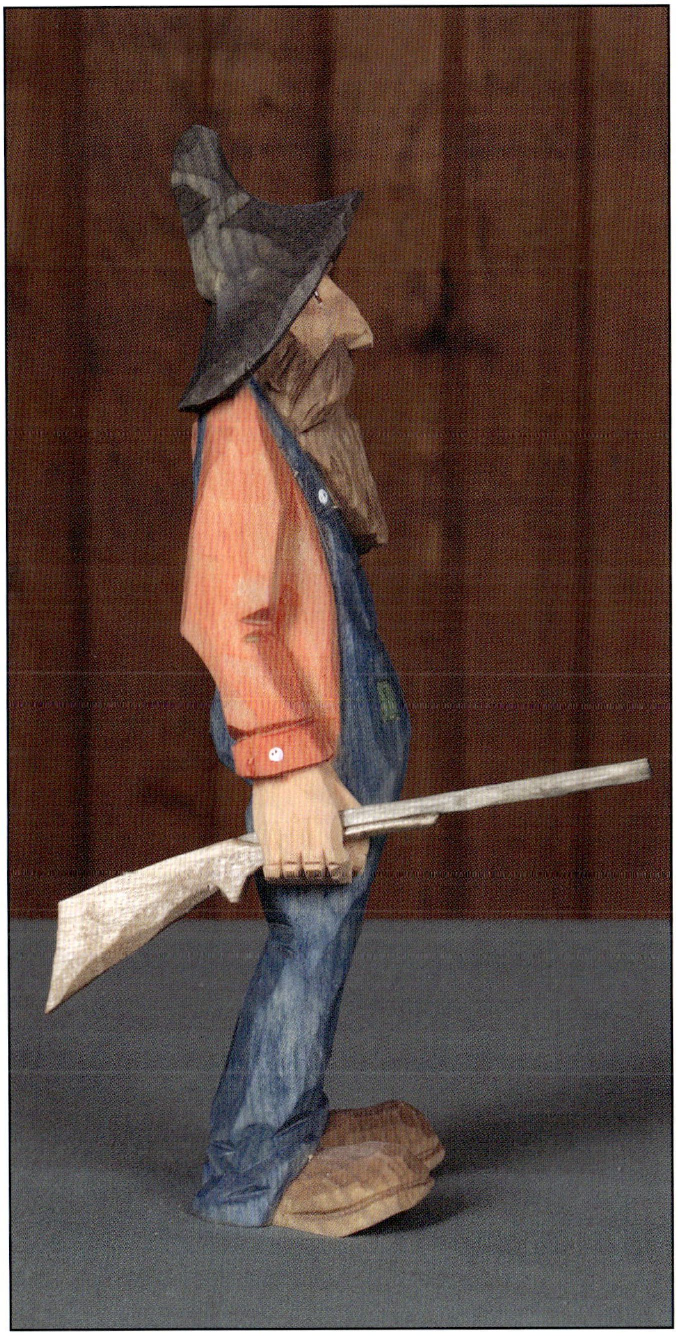

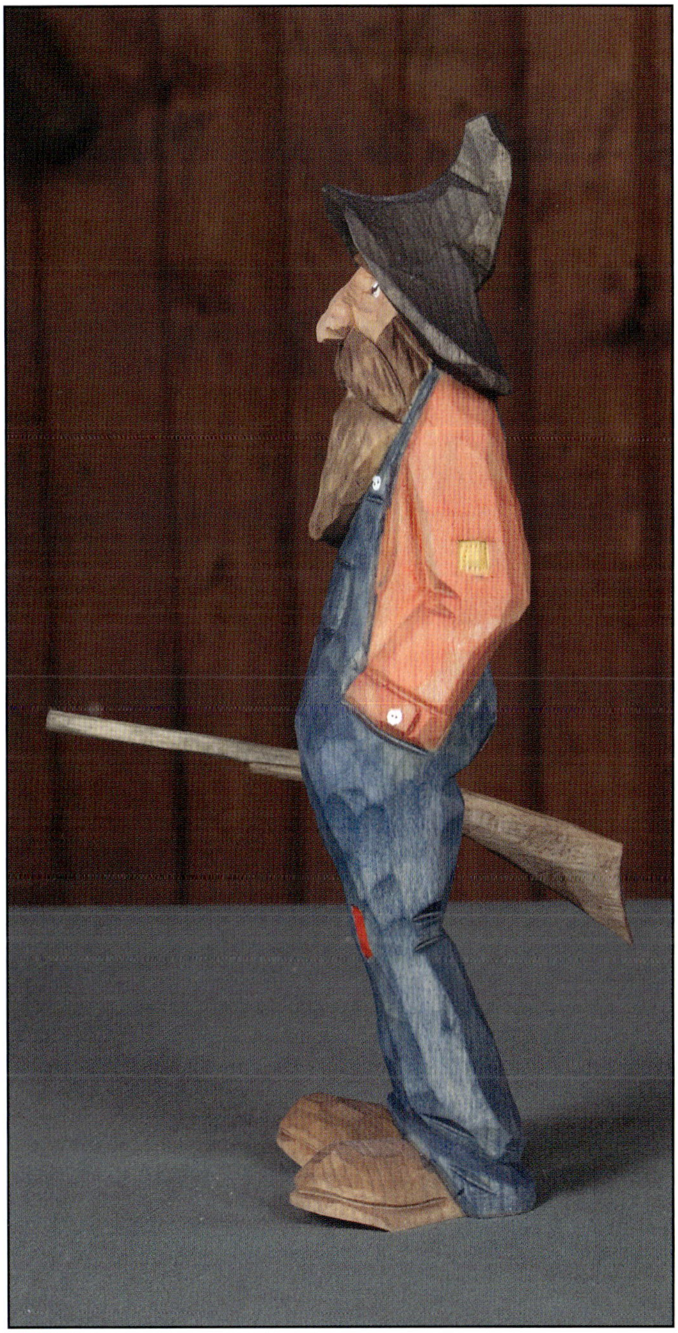

Frank could hold a jug instead of the gun. The hand is drilled with a ⅛" bit, and the gun and the hole in the hand are adjusted to fit. The gun just slides into the hand, barrel end first. Note that no hair is showing in the back. The hat comes down and rests on the top of the back and shoulders.

Enlarge pattern 120%

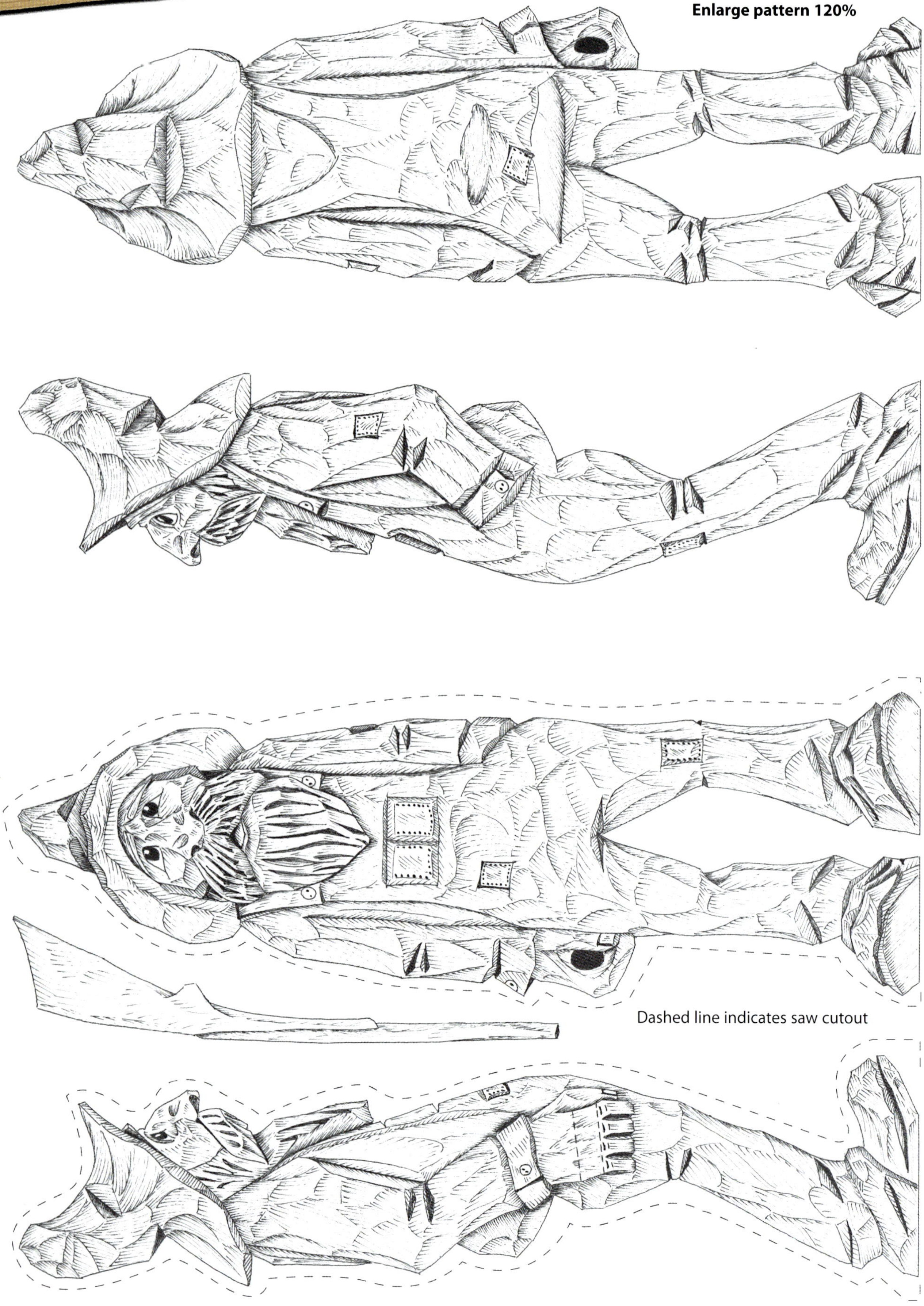

Acrylic paints:

White
Coffee bean brown
Flesh
Black
Christmas red
Navy blue
Burnt umber
Various colors (for patches)

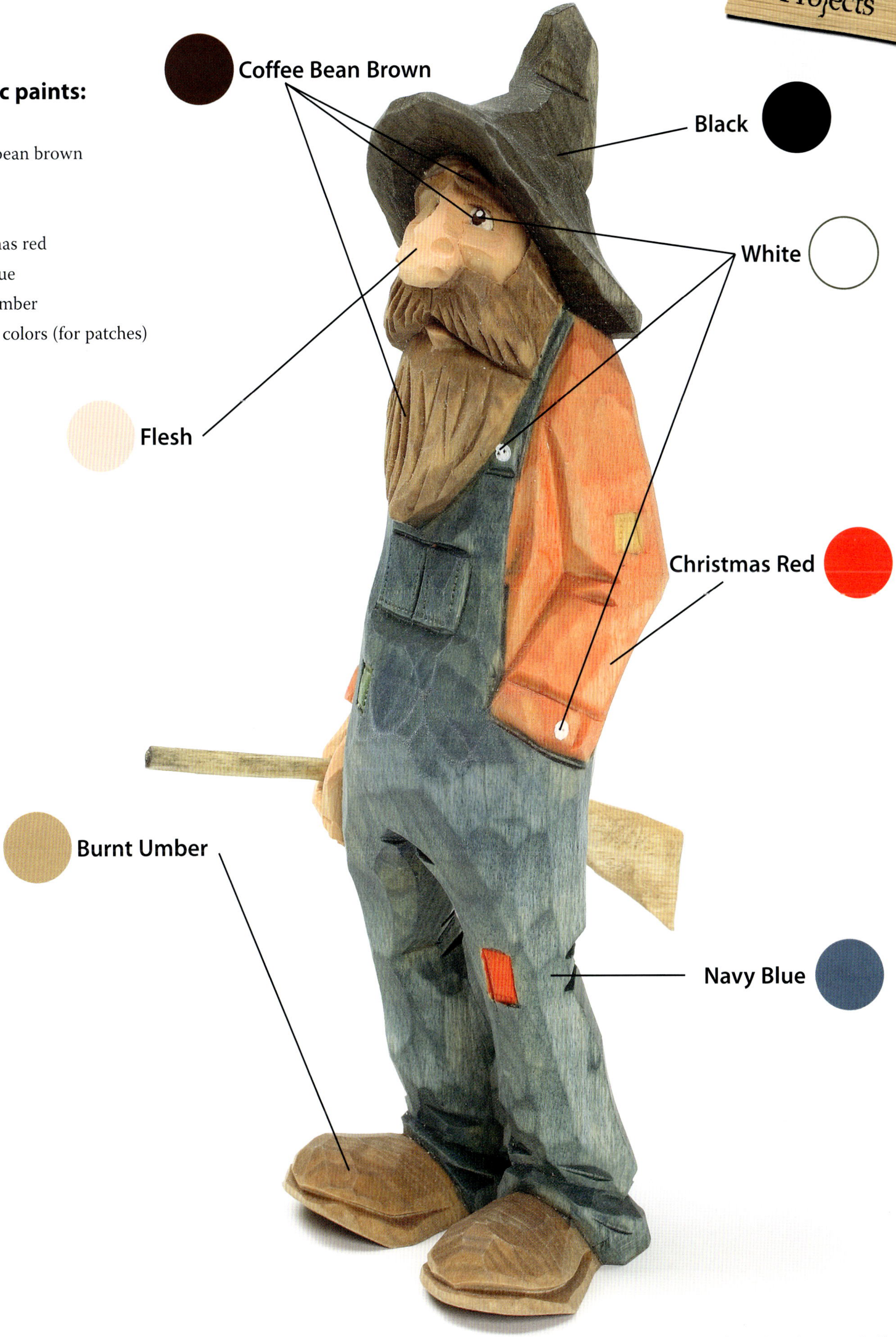

Beau

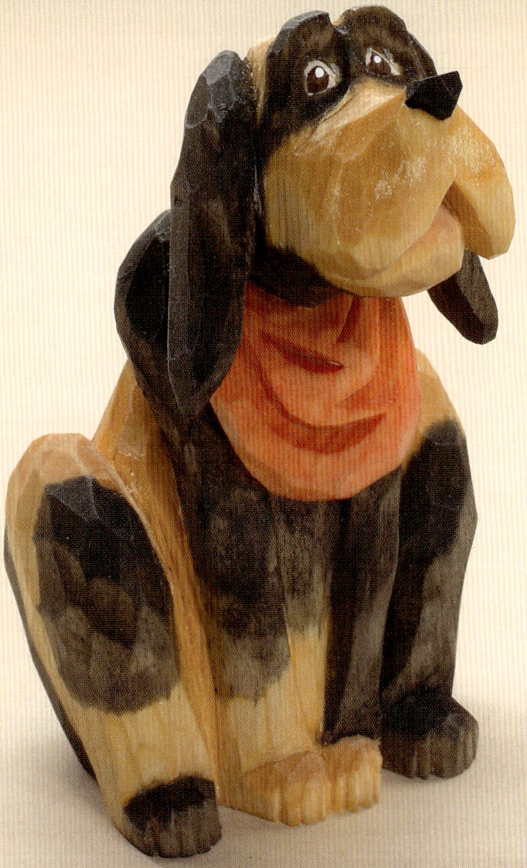

Most people don't think a hound dog is very smart, but don't let that droopy, dumb look fool you. Old Beau here is the best coon dog around. He's so good all you have to do is show him the hide stretching board, and he'll go out and get a coon to match the board.

I had a hound named Beau, and he made me look foolish more than once. One night, I parked the truck and turned Beau loose. Beau loved to hunt, and he took off on what promised to be a good one. When I was about a mile from the truck, it started to rain. I got under a cedar tree for some shelter from the rain and waited for Beau to check in with me. Beau didn't check in, so I headed for the truck. About three hours after I started out and being pretty much soaked, I made it back to the truck. Now I was really getting worried about my trusty dog, Beau, until I looked in the back. There Beau was, fast asleep. He was smart enough to know when to call it quits. I learned never to underestimate what was going on behind those droopy hound dog eyes.

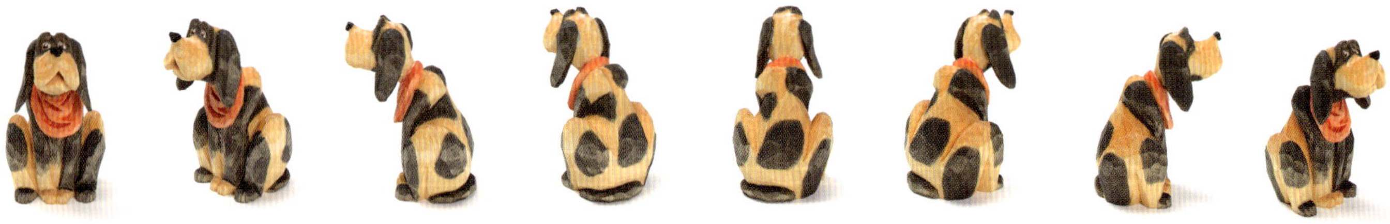

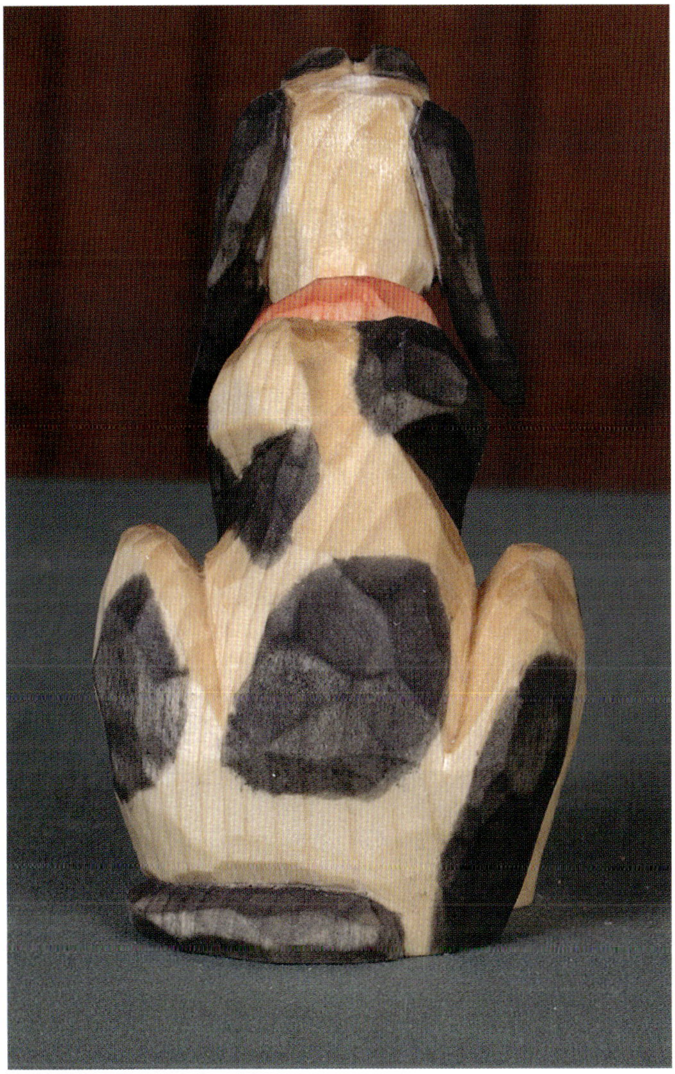

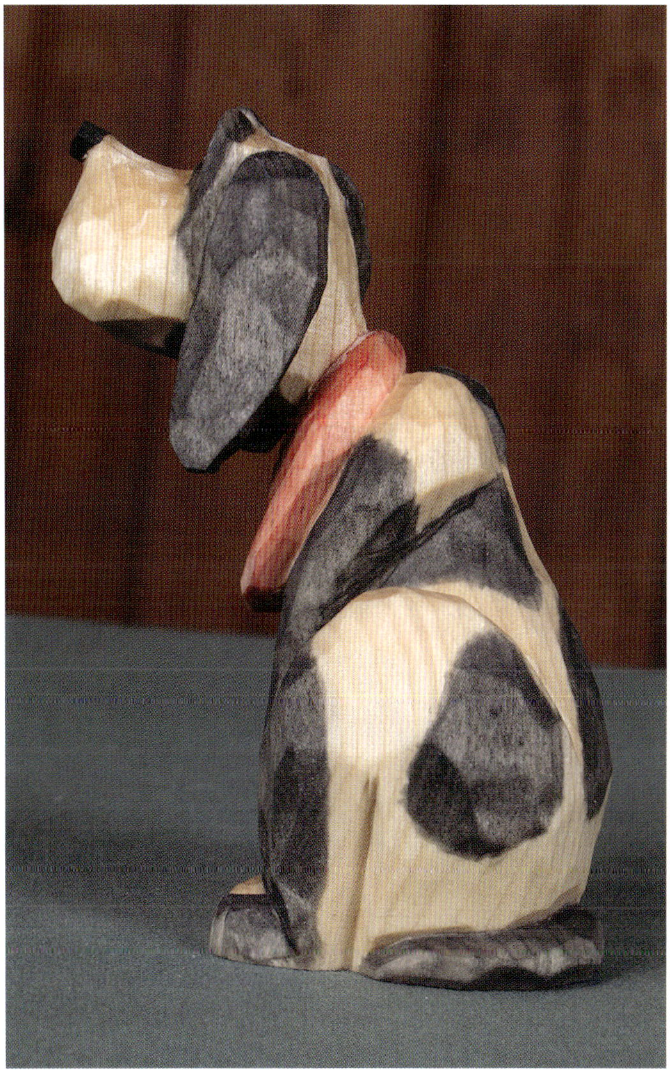

Beau can be painted any way you like. I painted the spots black and his bandana red. I left the rest natural. The stain colored the remaining areas.

Beau

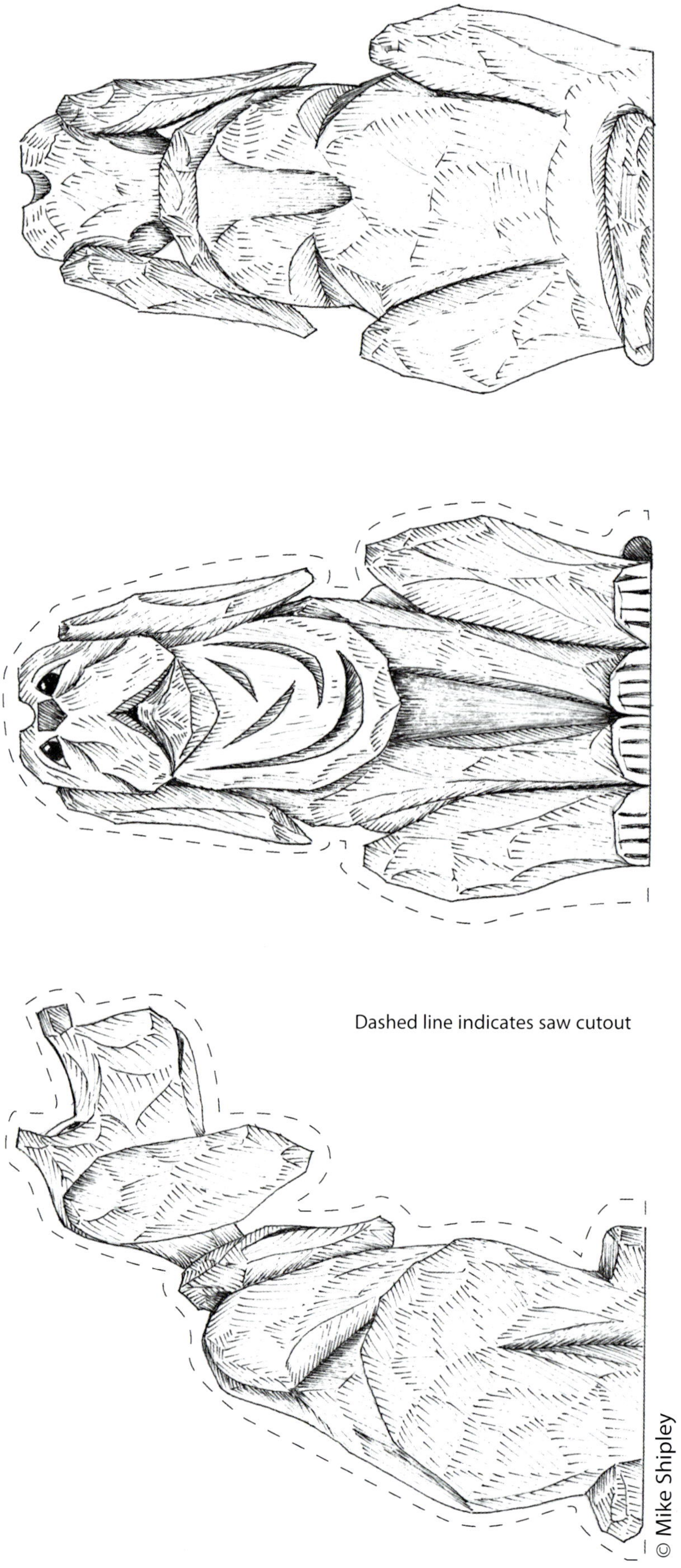

Acrylic paints:

White
Coffee bean brown
Black
Christmas red

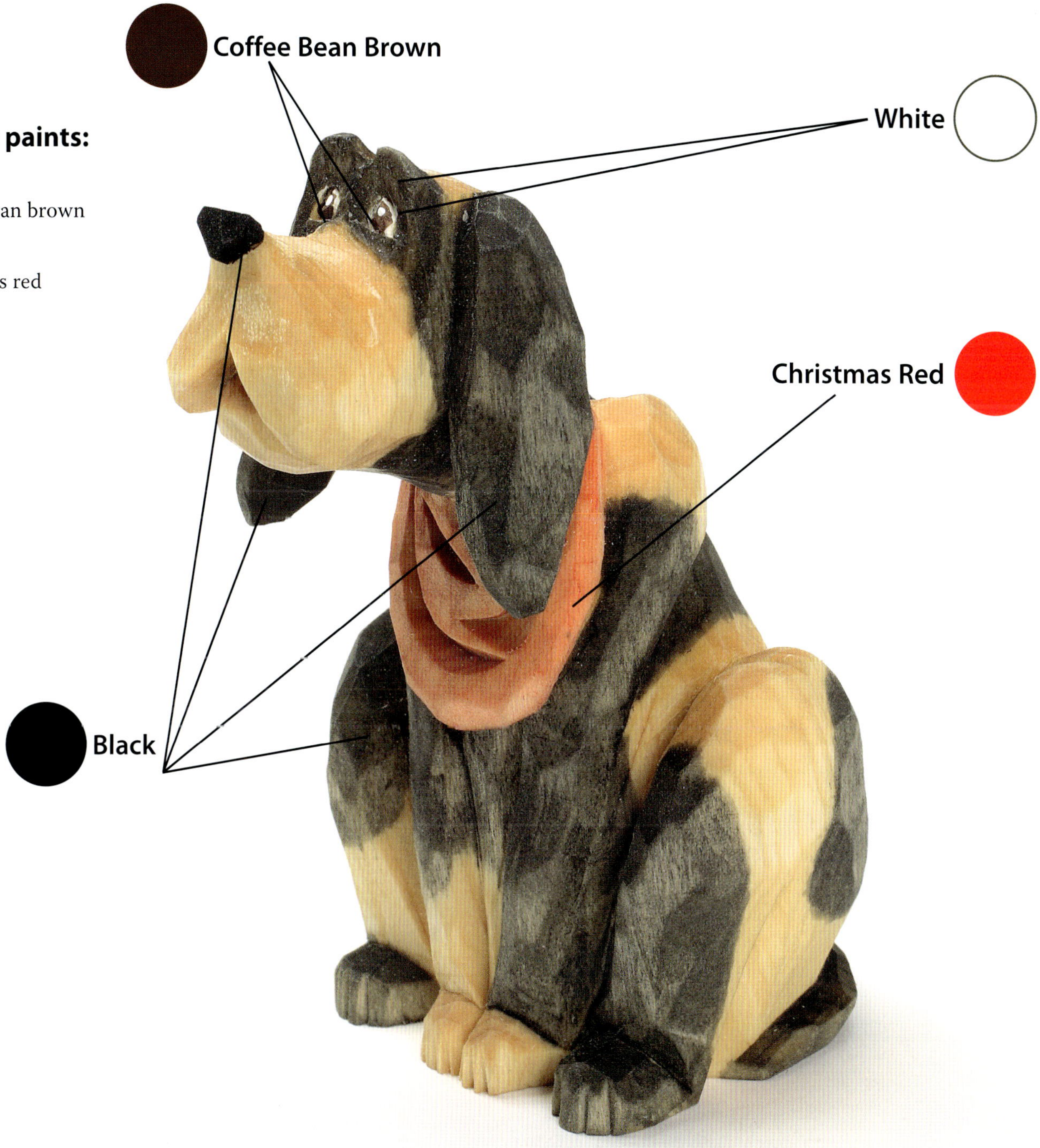

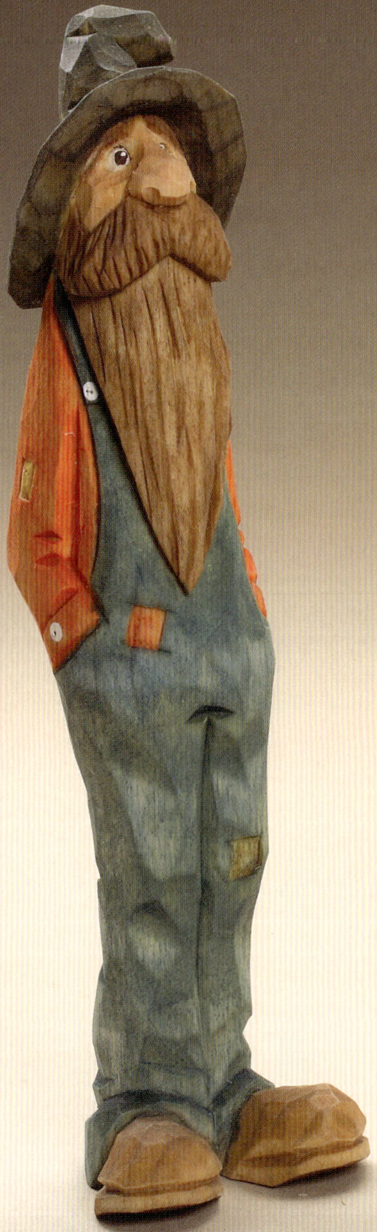

Skinny Lenny

Skinny Lenny is Delmer's little brother, but Lenny doesn't have the love of hunting that Delmer and Frank do, especially since Delmer tried to use Lenny as a poking stick in a holler (hollow) tree one night. You see, Skinny Lenny is so skinny that he worked better than a straight hickory sprout. After Granny heard of this episode, she used a hickory sprout on Delmer, and now she's doing her best to fatten Lenny up so the guys will stop picking on him.

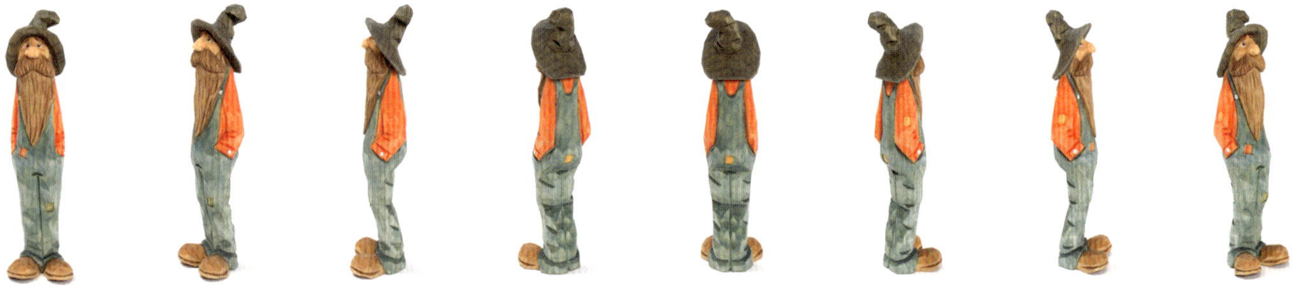

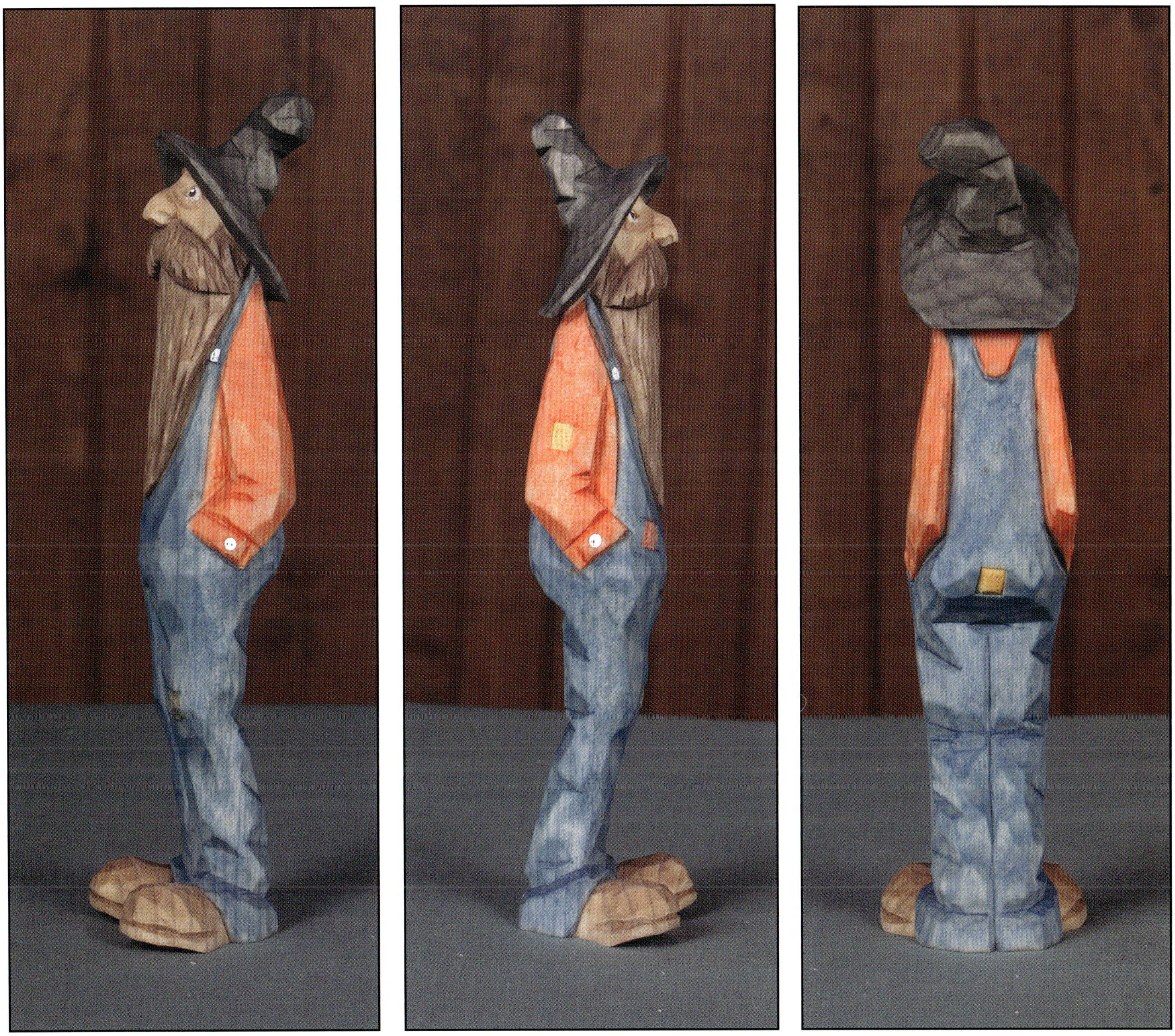

Carving Lenny is similar to carving Delmer. Lenny's mouth is covered by his mustache, and his arms are close to his body. You'll only need a V-tool cut to bring out the arms.

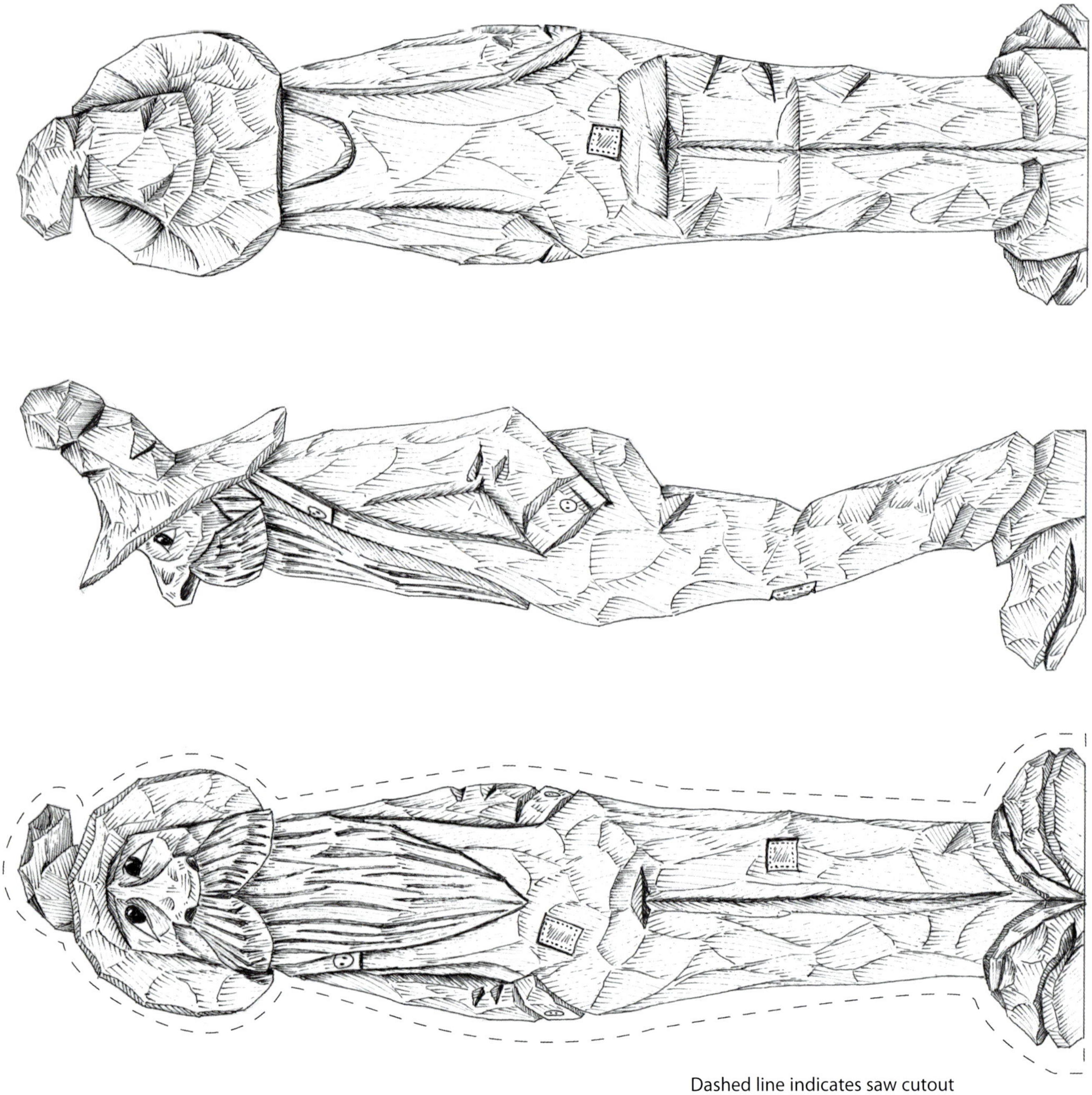

Dashed line indicates saw cutout

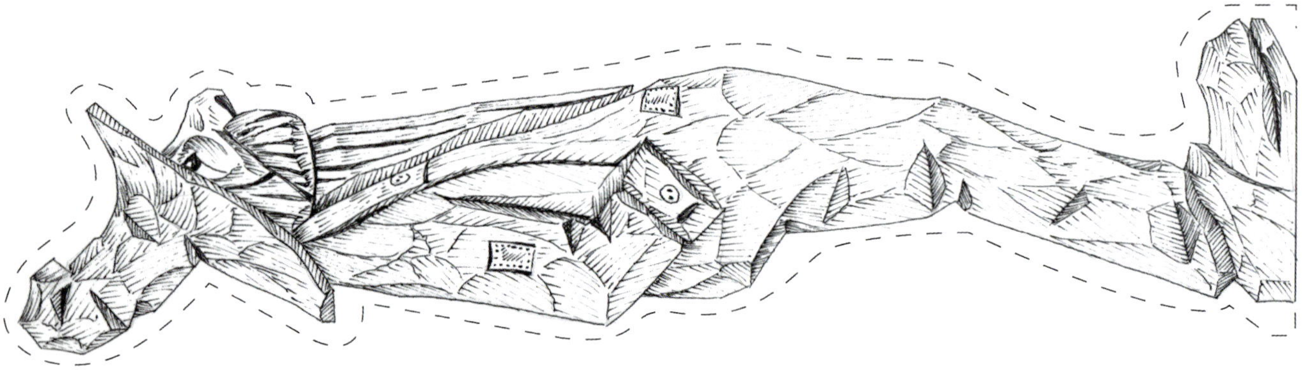

Acrylic paints:

White
Coffee bean brown
Flesh
Black
Christmas red
Navy blue
Burnt umber
Various colors (for patches)

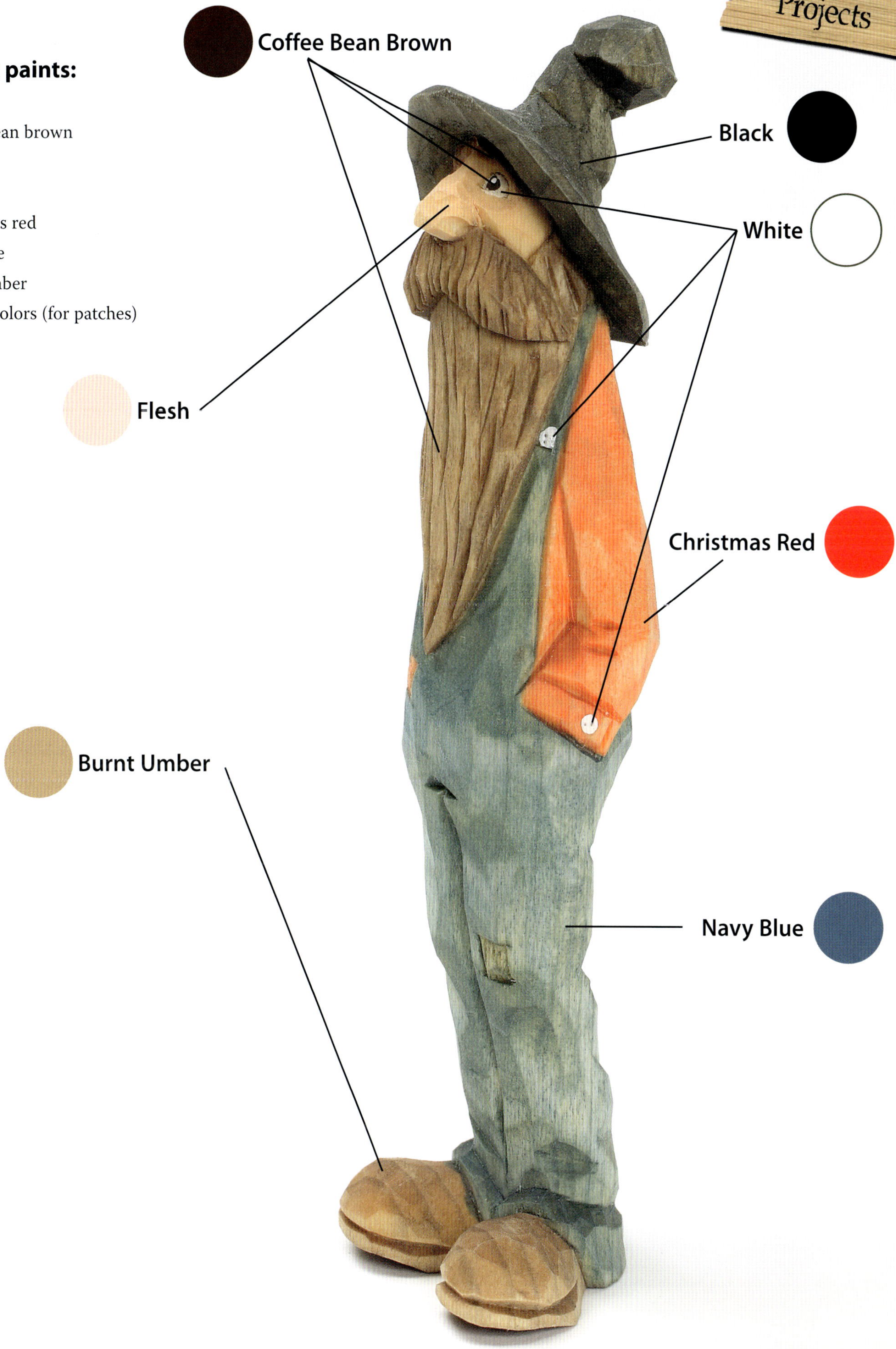

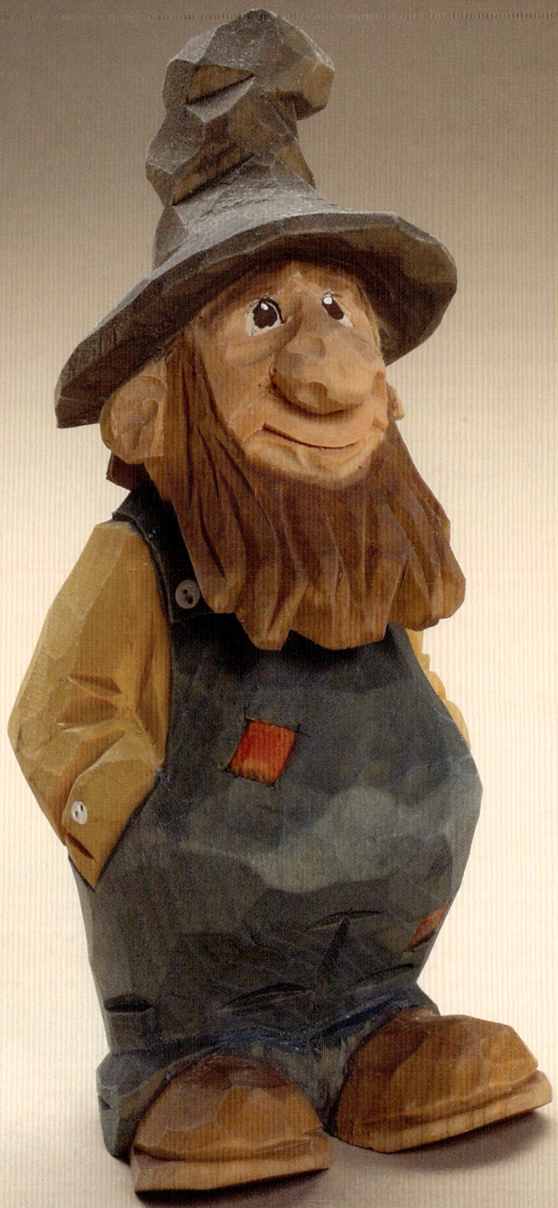

Willie

Willie, Benny, and Odie are identical triplets. No, I'm not kidding. Now that's not too hard to believe with Willie and Benny, but Odie I'm not too sure about, since their ma ran off with that pot-and-pan salesman. Everybody just called them family even though they couldn't really tell them apart. But they've done alright for themselves. Benny still puts a little change in their pockets, and Granny keeps them in cornbread.

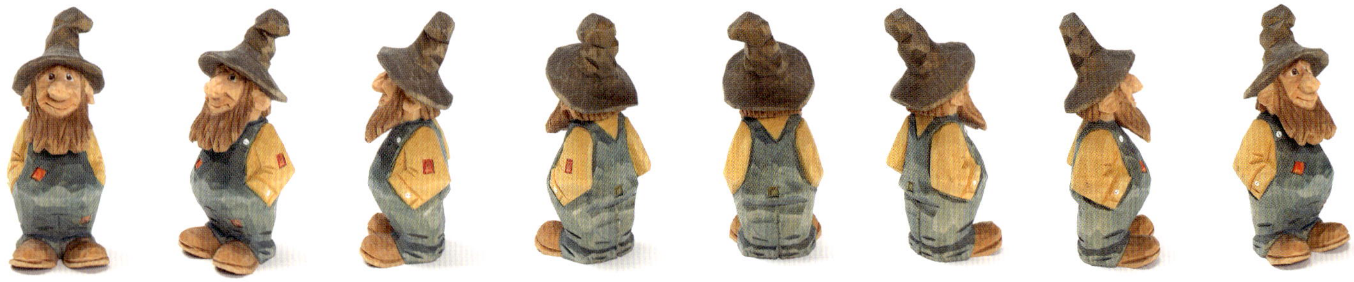

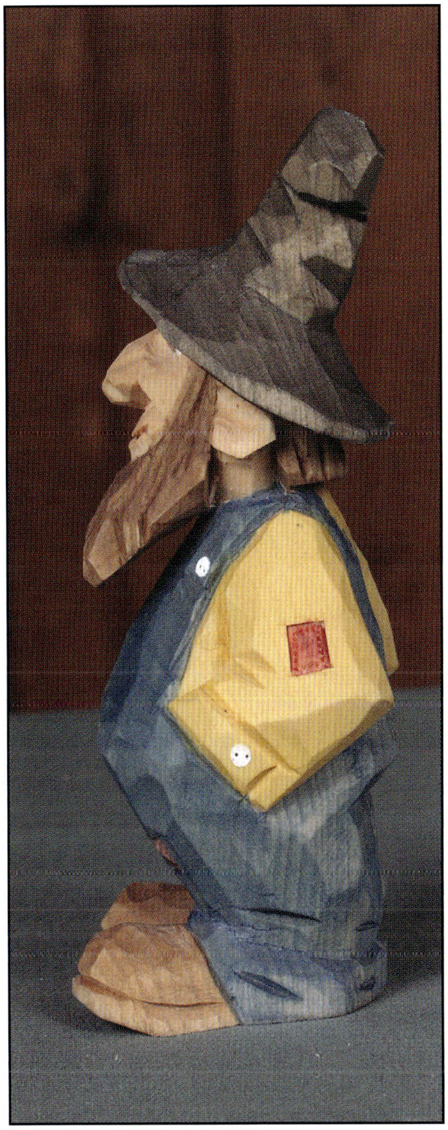

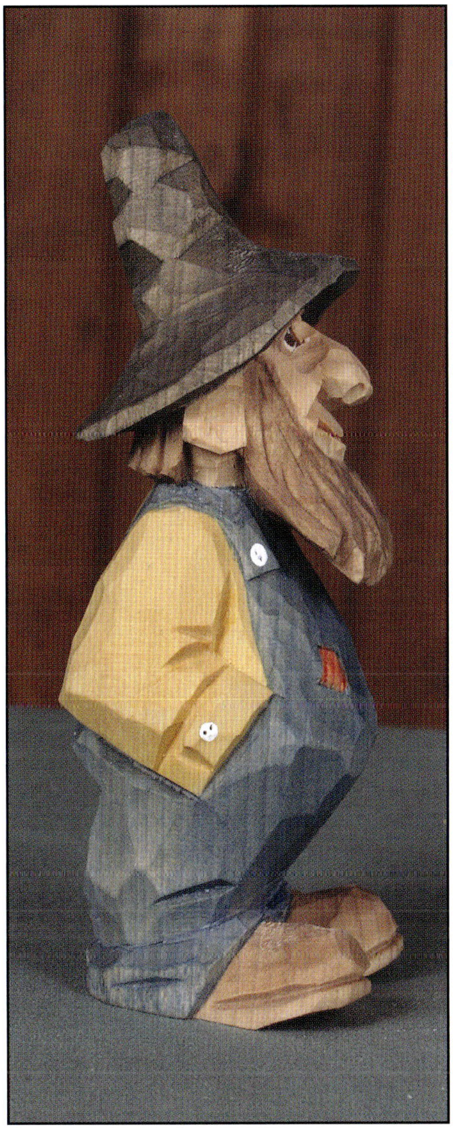

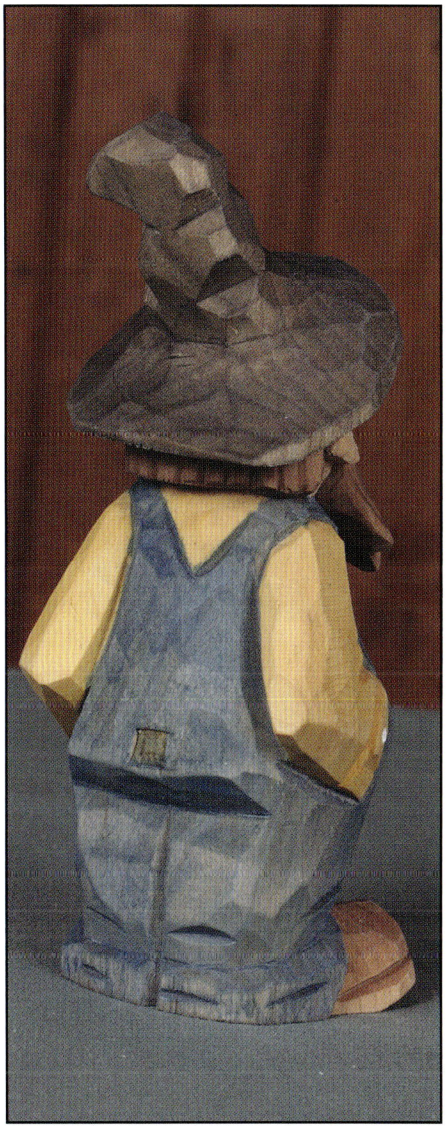

As you can see, Willie is pretty compact. He is also a change of pace because he has no mustache. Instead, his smiling mouth is showing. Use a small detail knife to work the area between the ear and the shoulder. Make deep cuts where the corners of the nose and the cheeks meet. Clean out the deep cut, but leave the mouth area raised with the mouth corners deeper. Notice that the mouth area is a raised mound—this helps to eliminate a flat, plain look in the mouth area.

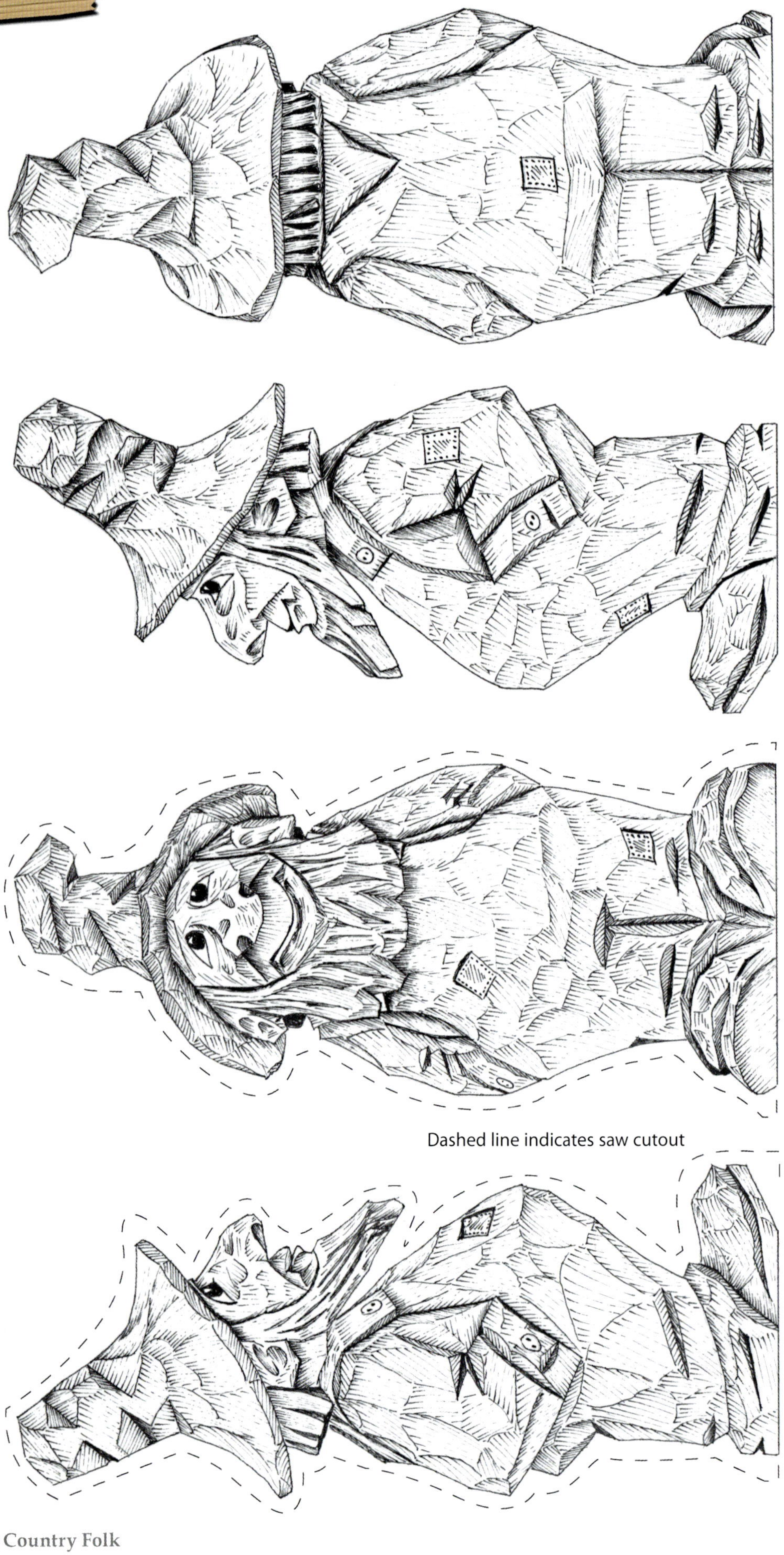

Dashed line indicates saw cutout

Acrylic paints:

White
Coffee bean brown
Flesh
Black
Straw
Navy blue
Burnt umber
Various colors (for patches)

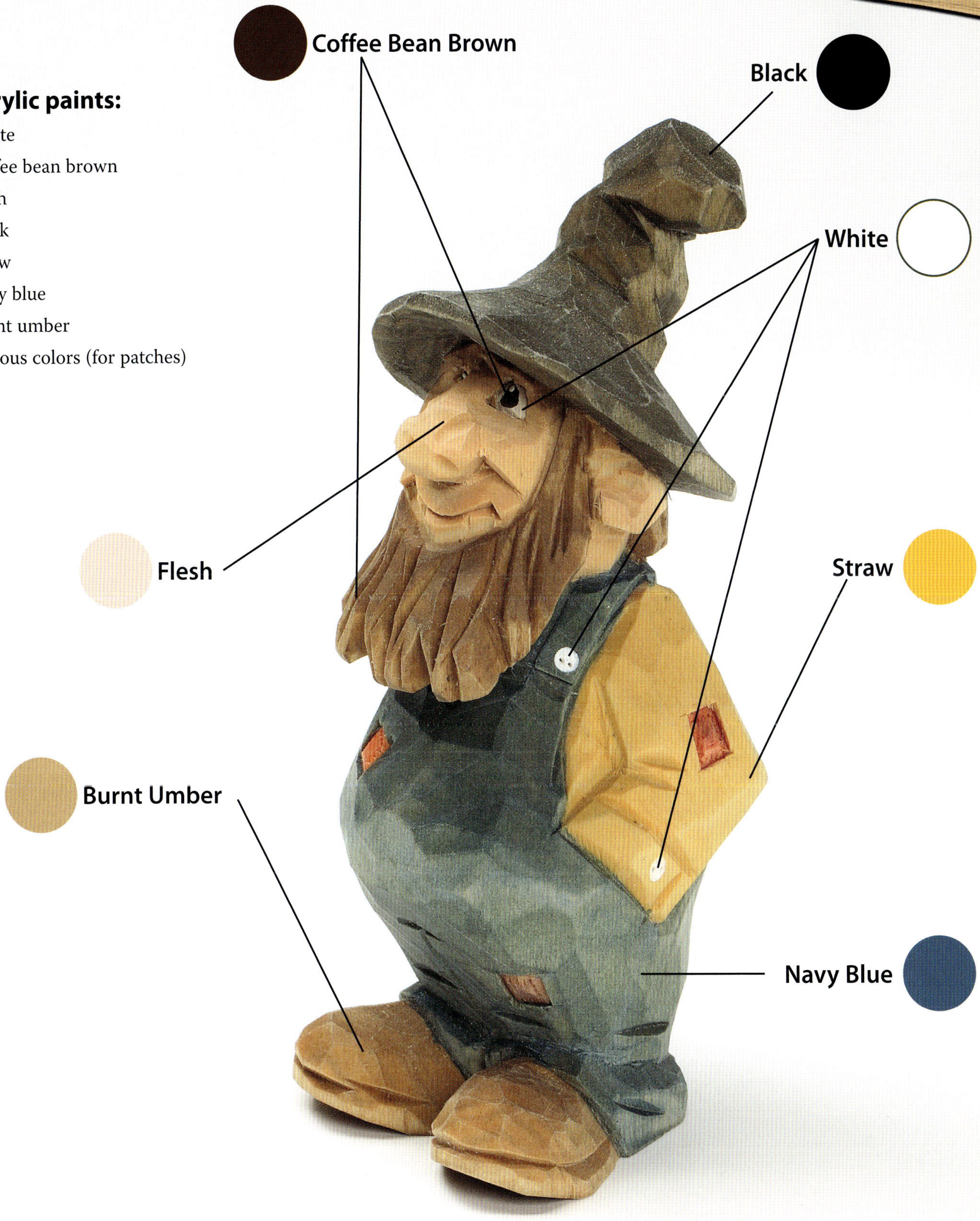

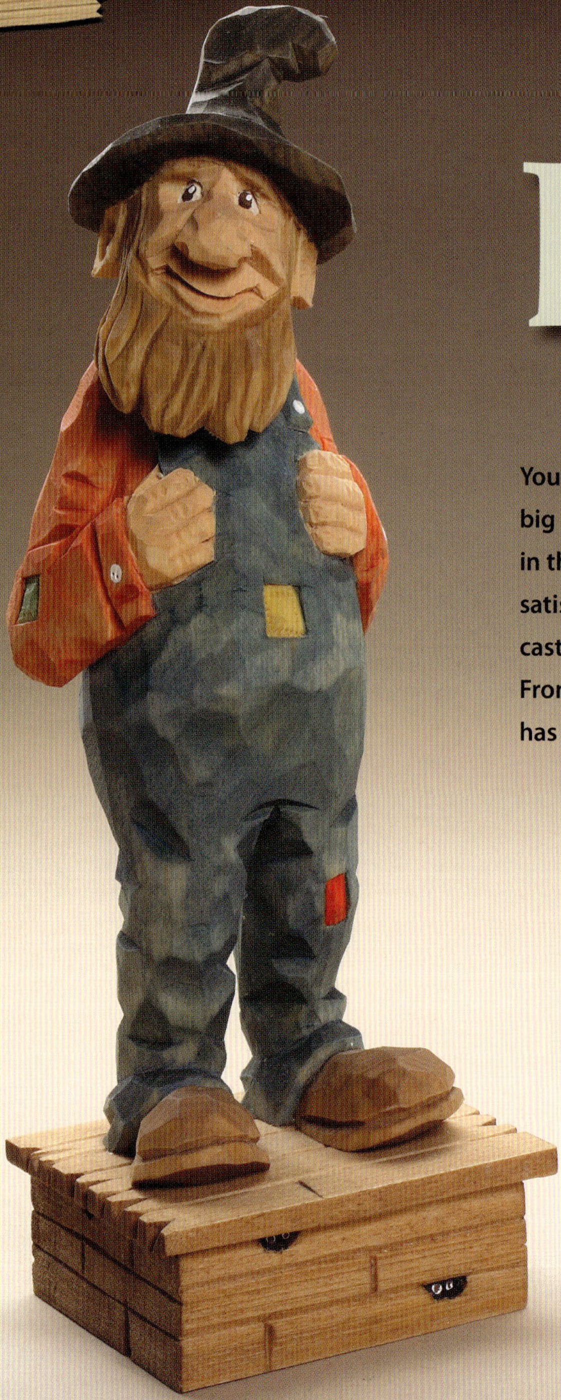

Ezra

You've heard the old saying that if you can't run with the big dogs, then stay on the porch. Old Ezra is a firm believer in that. He tried running with the big dogs, but now he's satisfied with just staying on the porch. Ezra's porch is his castle, and he's always willing to share it with a few friends. From the looks of all those little varmint eyes, I think Ezra has friends that he's not aware of.

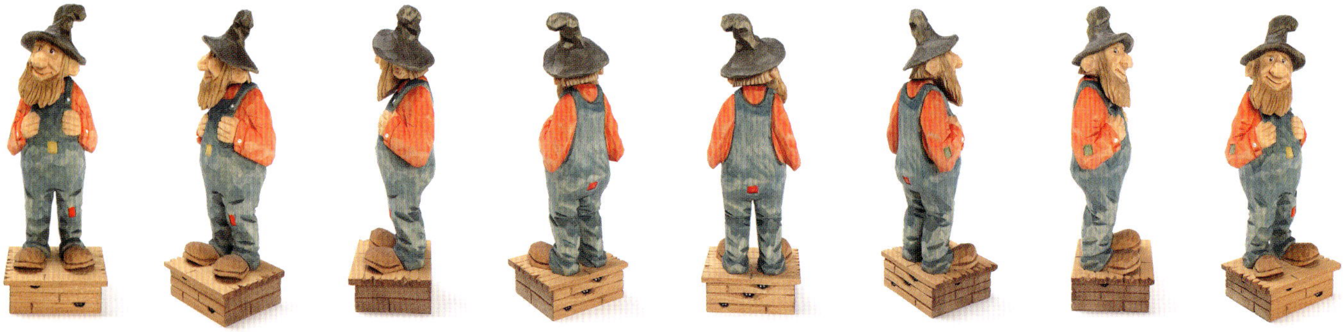

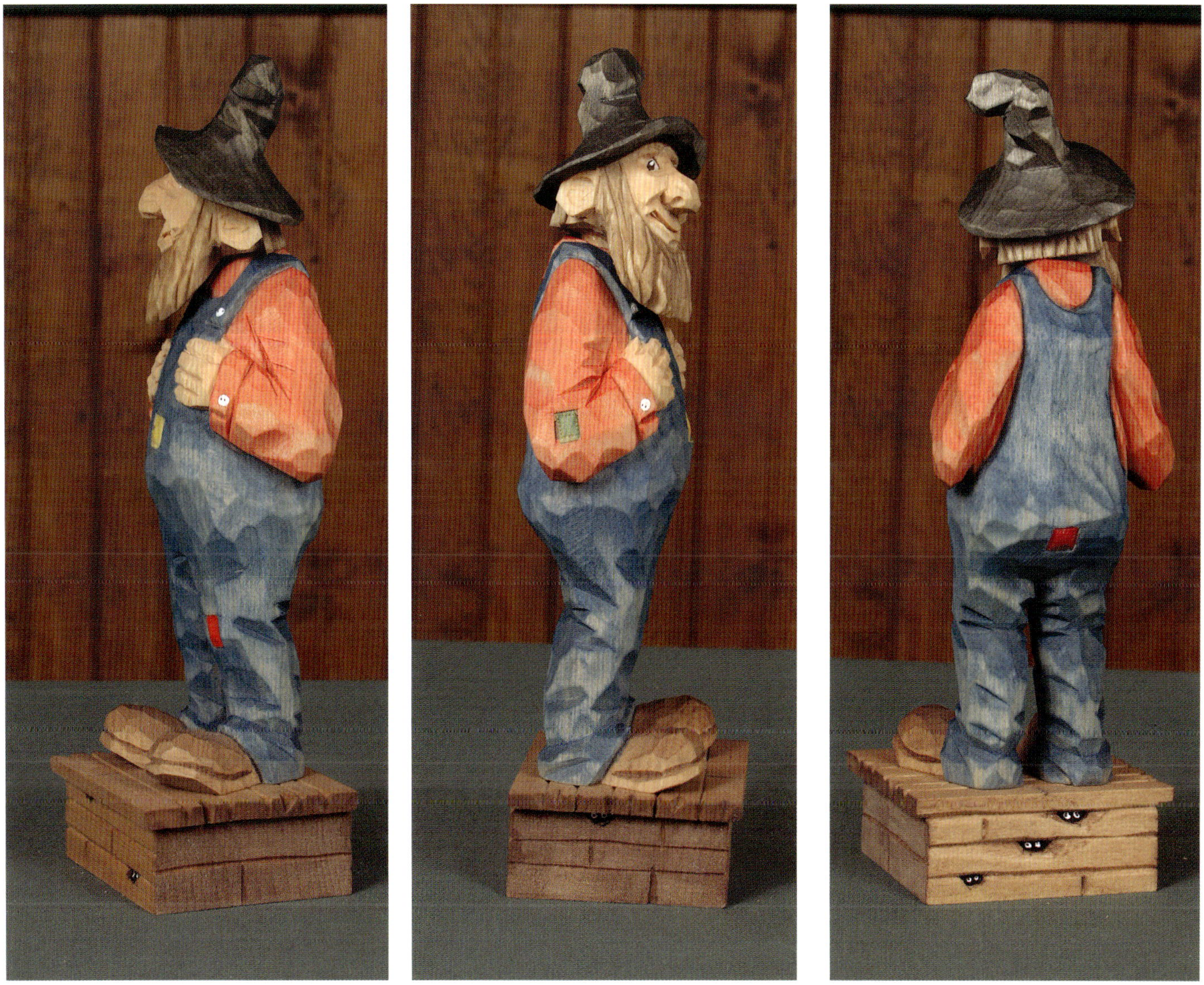

The slight turn of the head give Ezra a lot of character. The little varmint eyes in Ezra's base also add character and are fun to make—just carve out a little half-moon hole. Paint the hole with black straight from the bottle, dot on the white eyes, and then place a tiny dot of coffee bean brown on each white eye. Note that Ezra is carved separately from the base. Glue him on the base, after painting, with good-quality wood glue, but let the glue dry 24 hours before staining. Use burnt umber to paint the base. The hands are a little bit of a challenge: Notice the thumbs are tucked under the overall suspenders.

Dashed line indicates saw cutout

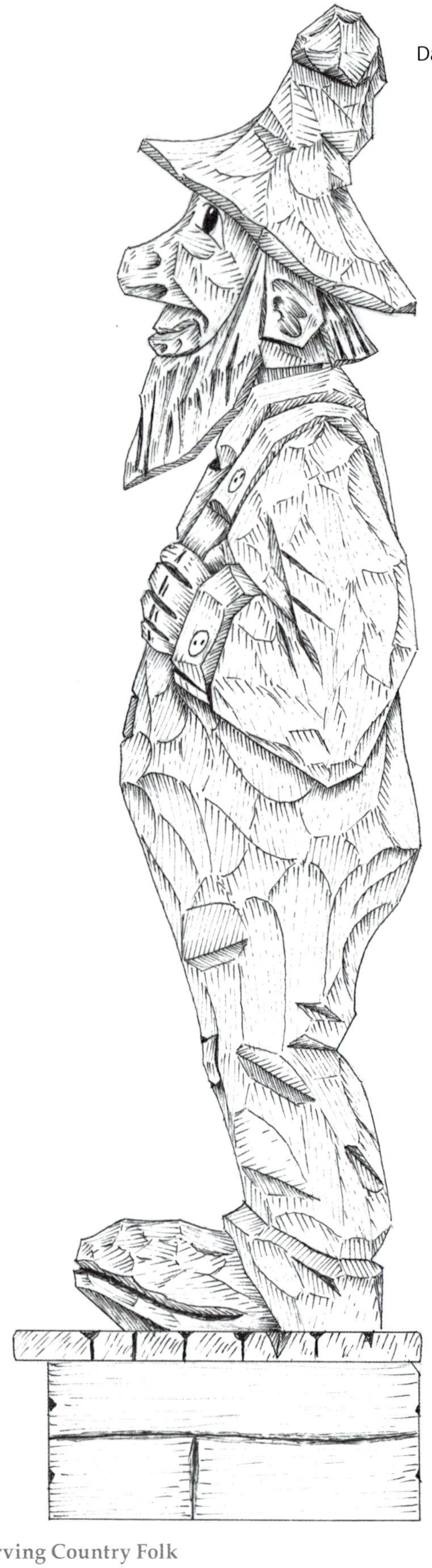

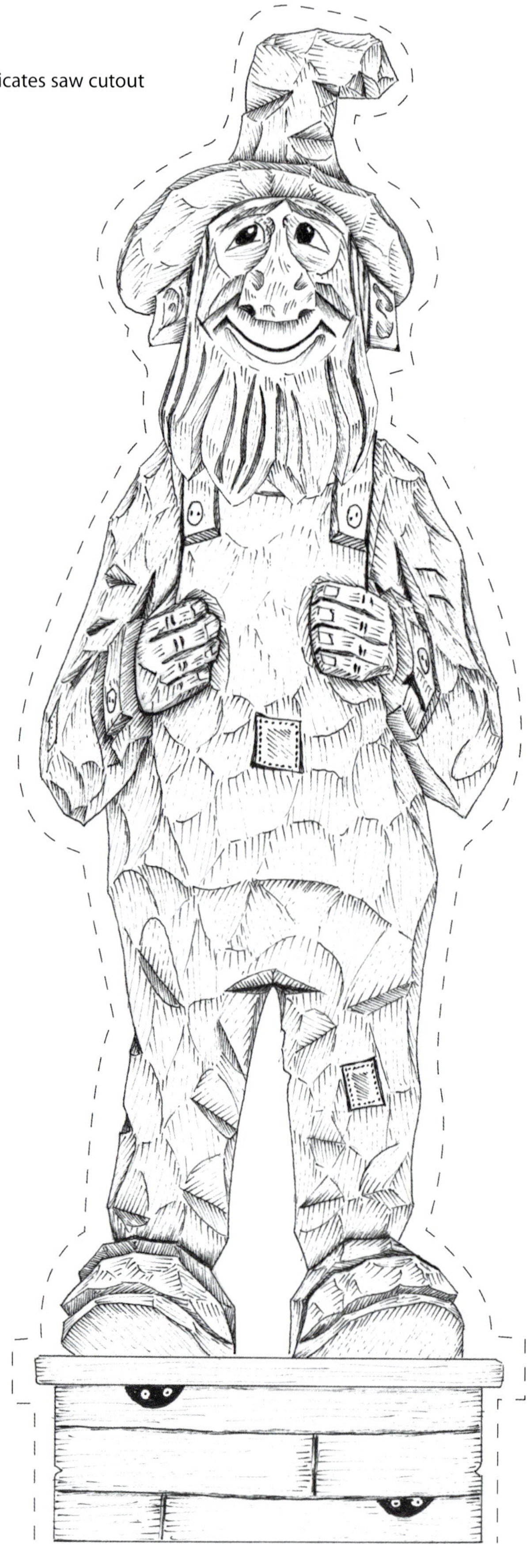

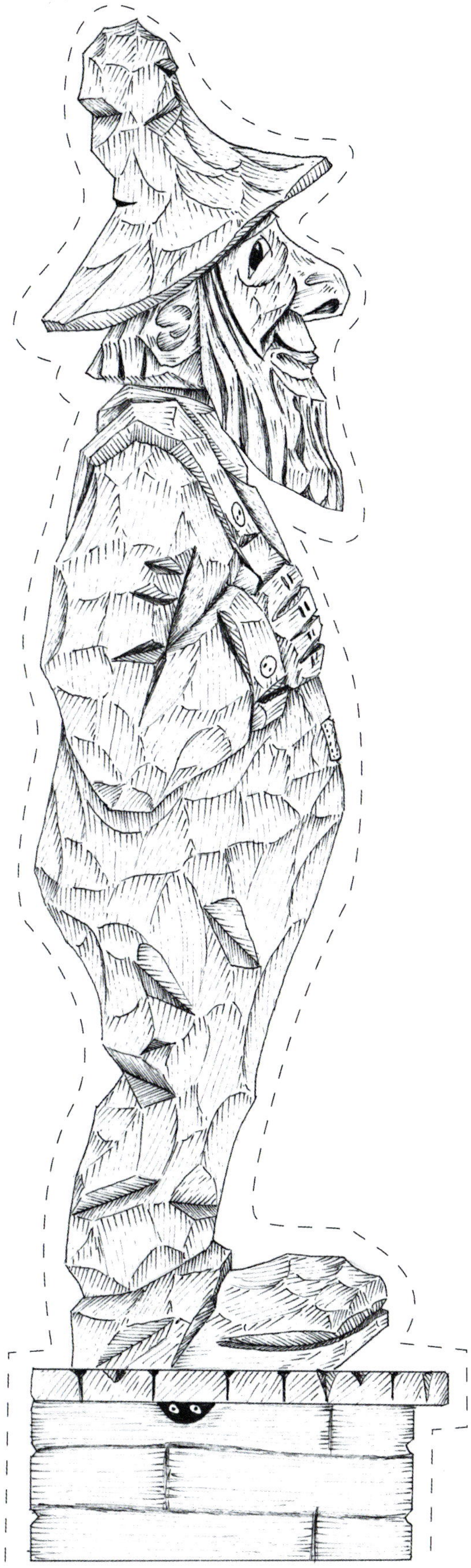

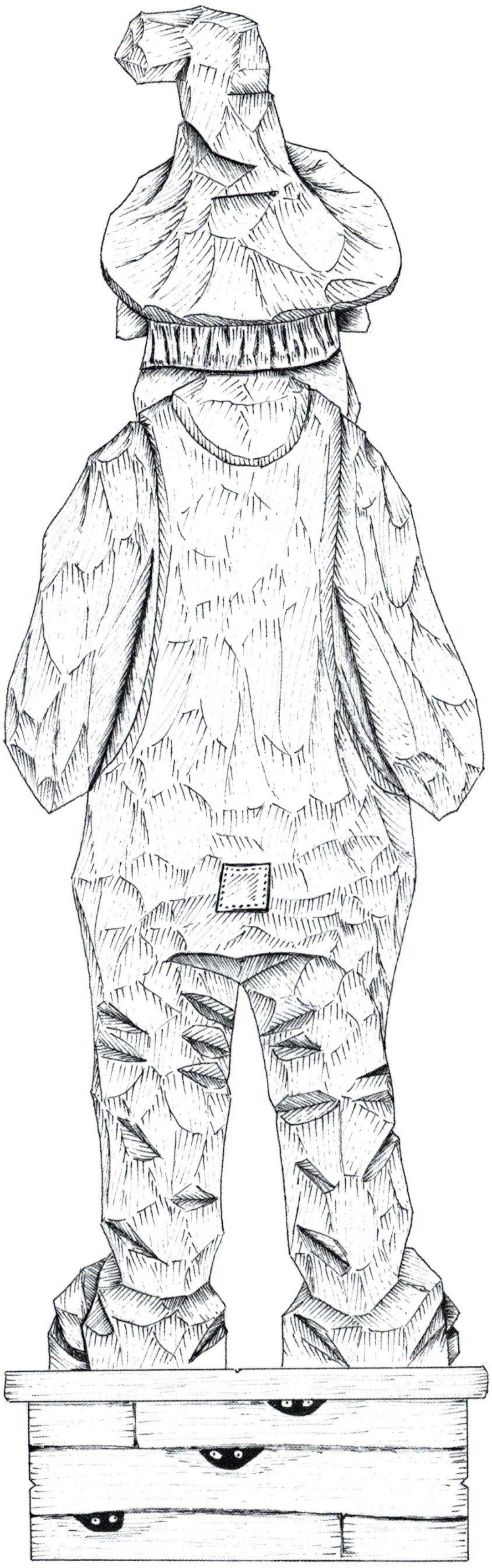

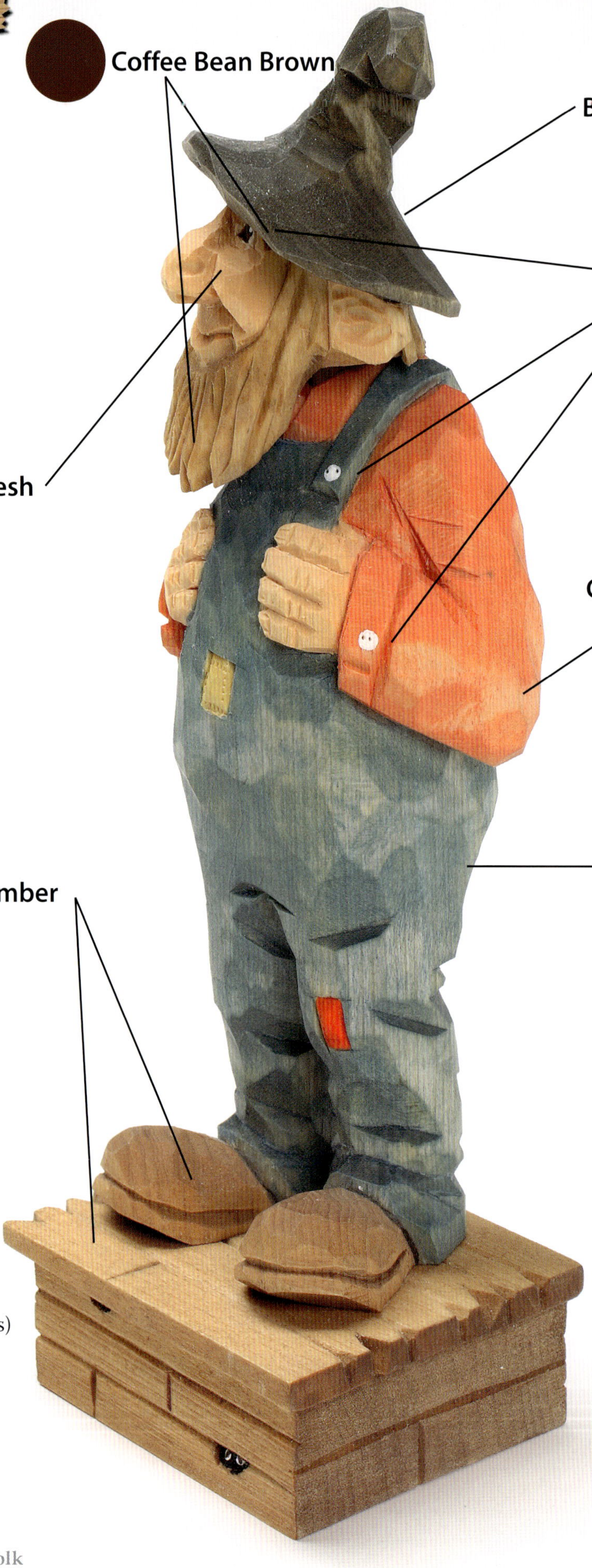

Acrylic paints:

White
Coffee bean brown
Flesh
Black
Christmas red
Navy blue
Burnt umber
Various colors (for patches)

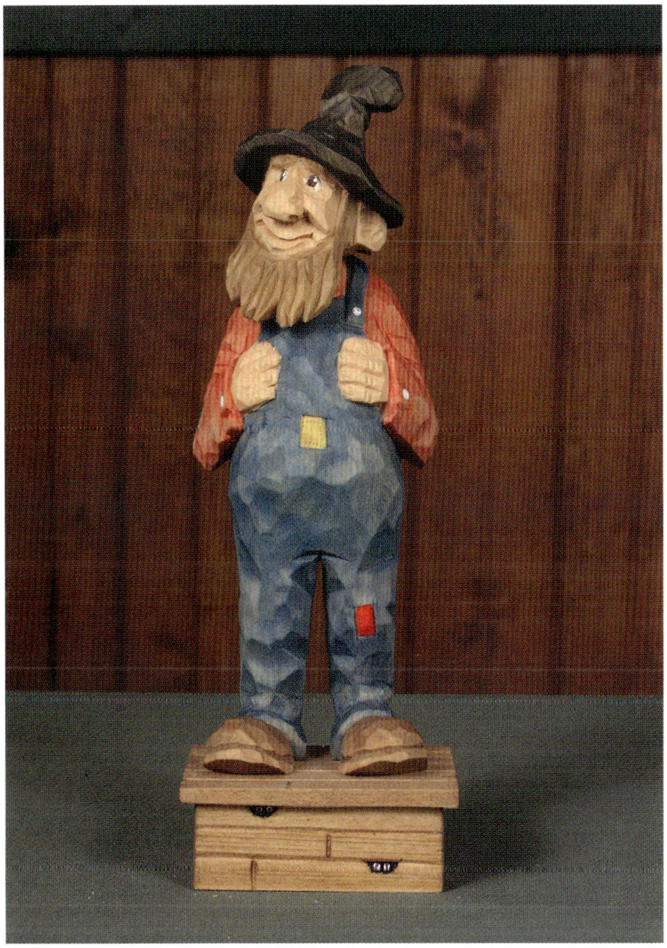

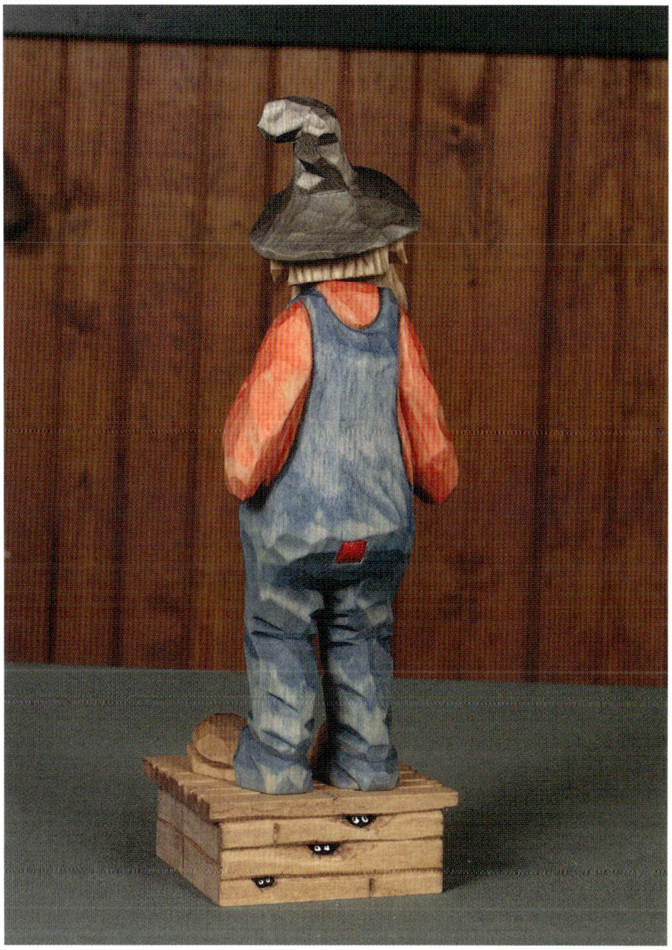

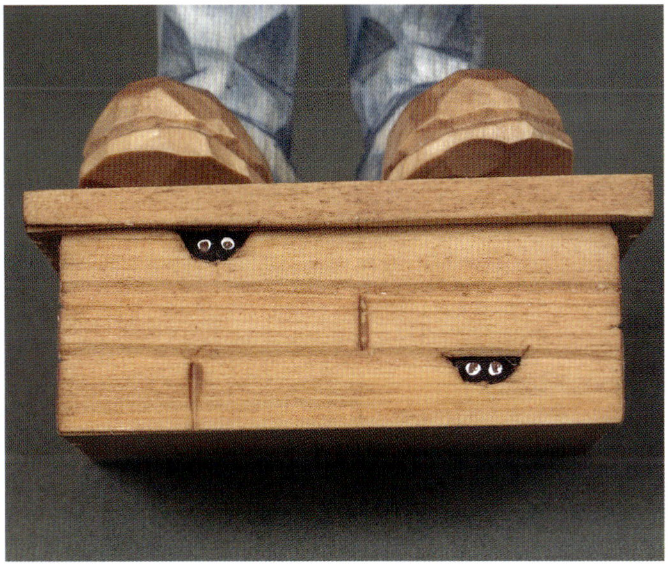

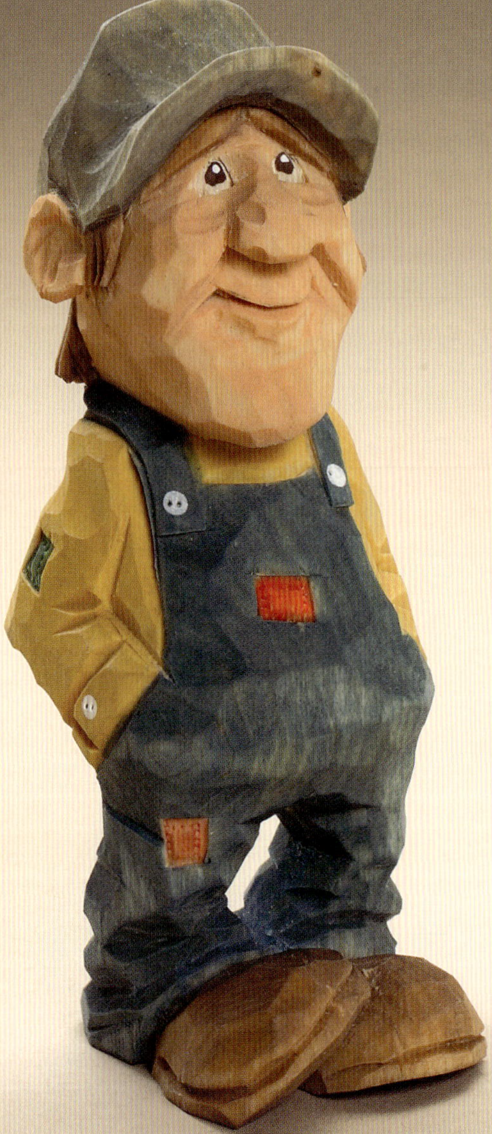

Bobby Ray

Bobby Ray is kind of the oddball of the family. You see, he's probably a ninth or tenth cousin to the rest of the bunch. And besides, he lives out on the flats, so he's not 100% hillbilly. His roots can be traced right back to the hills though, so he's always welcomed back for a visit anytime.

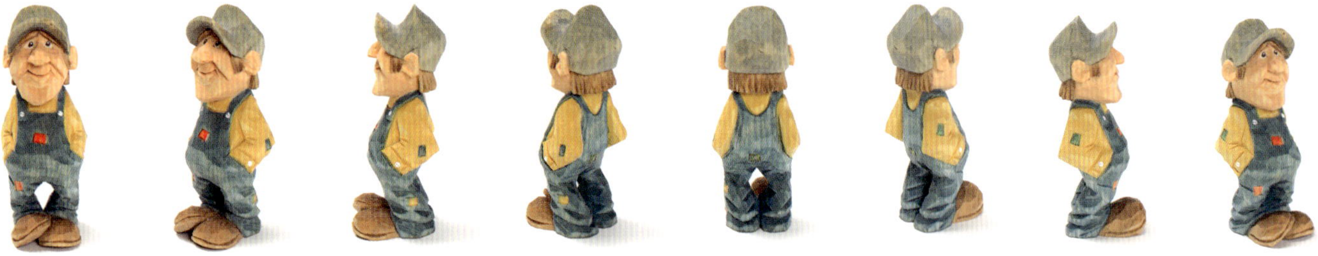

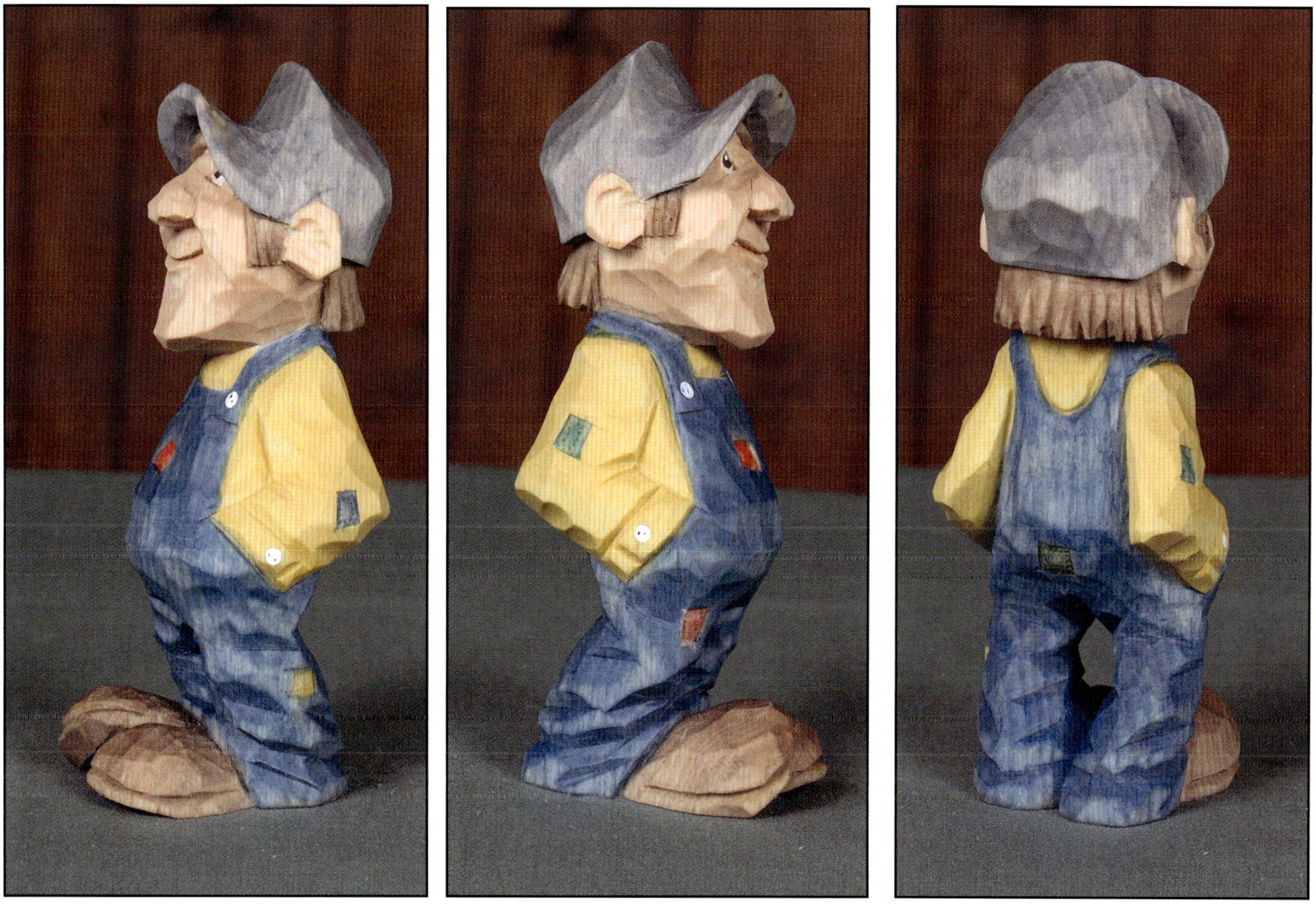

Bobby Ray is a change of pace from carving the rest of his family. He likes to wear a different hat from the rest of the kinfolk. (Fellow woodcarver Denny Neubauer shared this pattern with me; I altered it just enough to fit my style. Thanks, Denny, for a nice pattern.) Notice the ears extend out and slightly above the hat line.

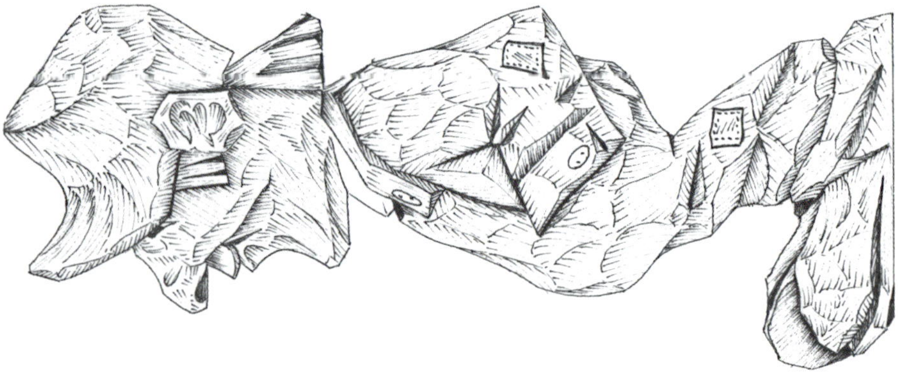

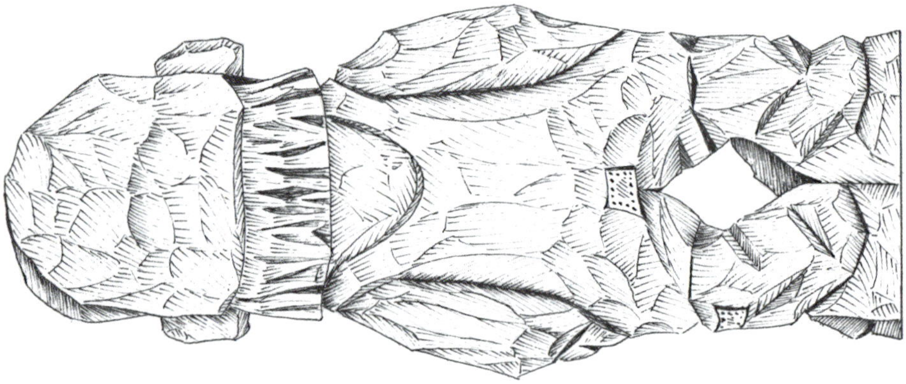

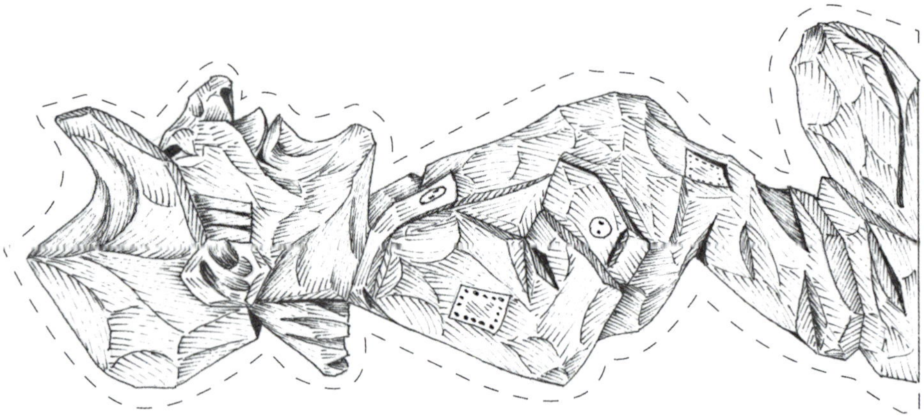

Dashed line indicates saw cutout

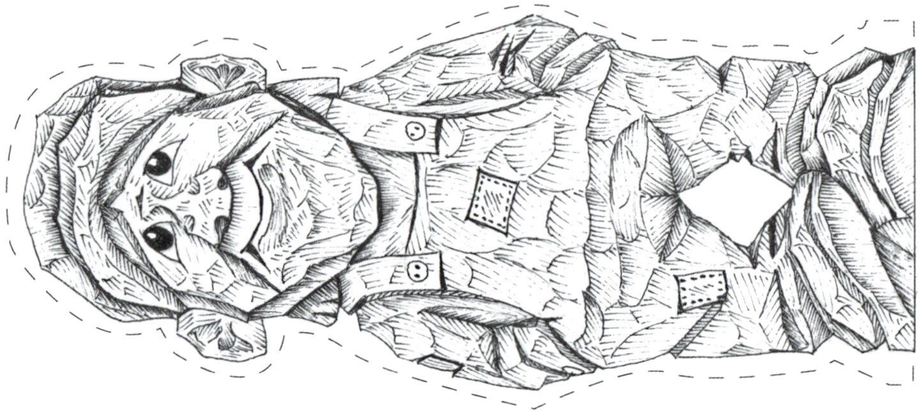

Acrylic paints:

White
Coffee bean brown
Flesh
Straw
Navy blue
Burnt umber
Uniform blue
Various colors (for patches)

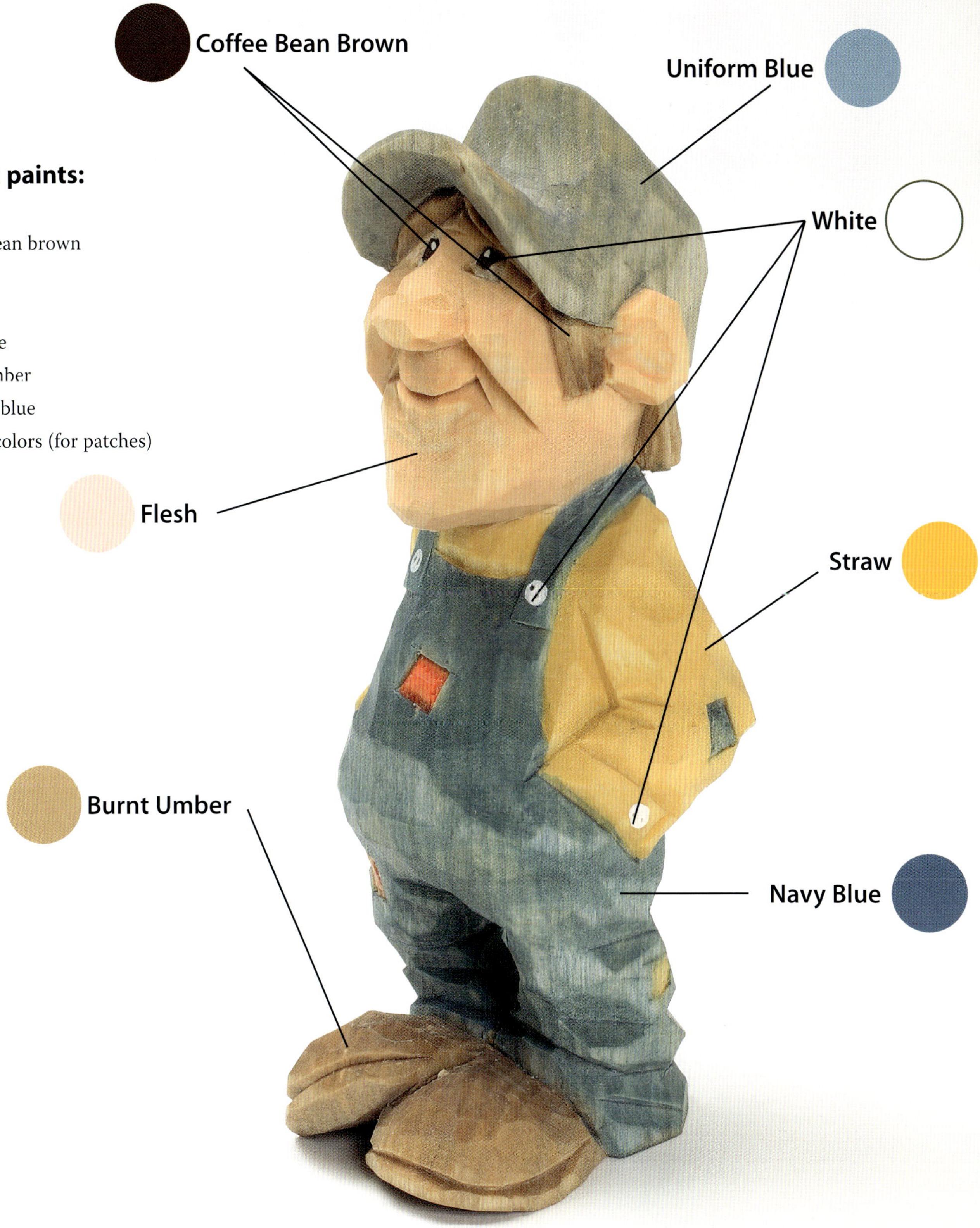

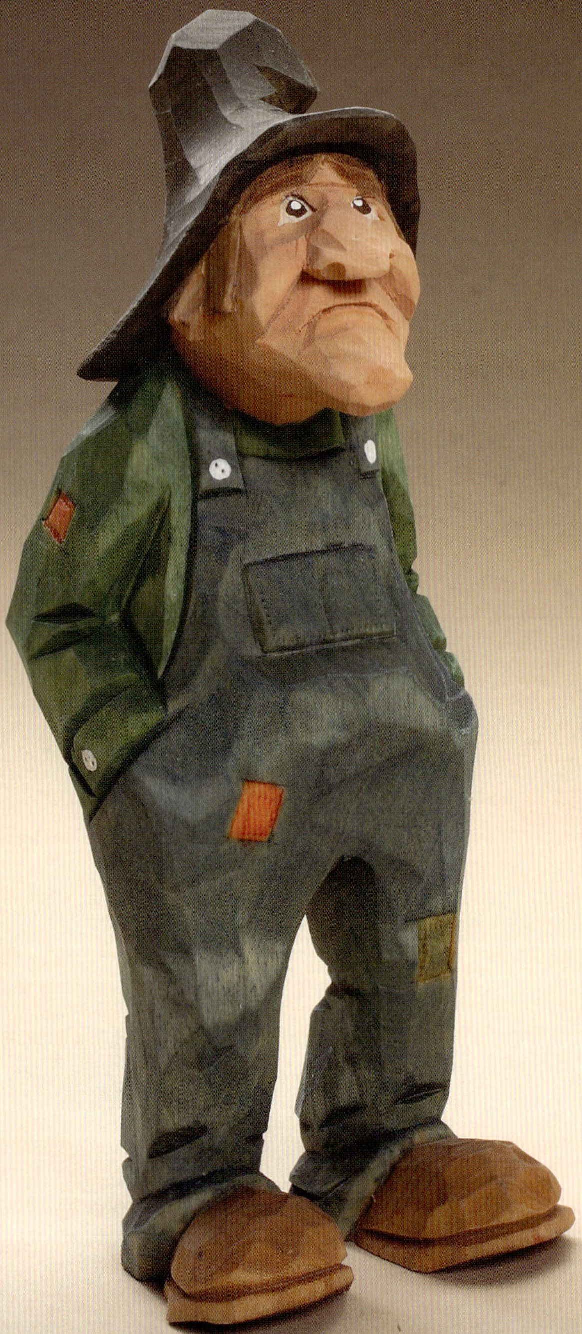

Arlo

Arlo's looks pretty much tell the story. He lives off down in Portwood Holler. Arlo is so grouchy that all the neighbors moved up to the ridge. Arlo is so grouchy that when he was born, the doctor spanked his ma. He is so grouchy that he has to sneak up on the water bucket to get a drink. Arlo is so grouchy he could scare off a hornet's nest. Well, you get the picture. Arlo is pretty hard to live with, but he is part of the family.

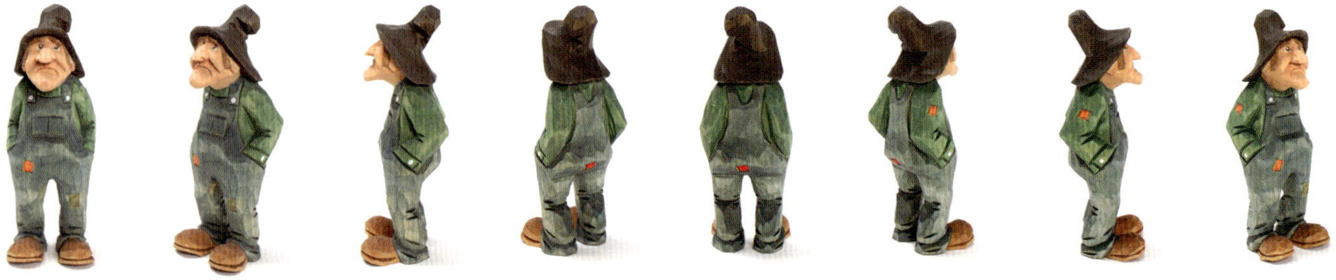

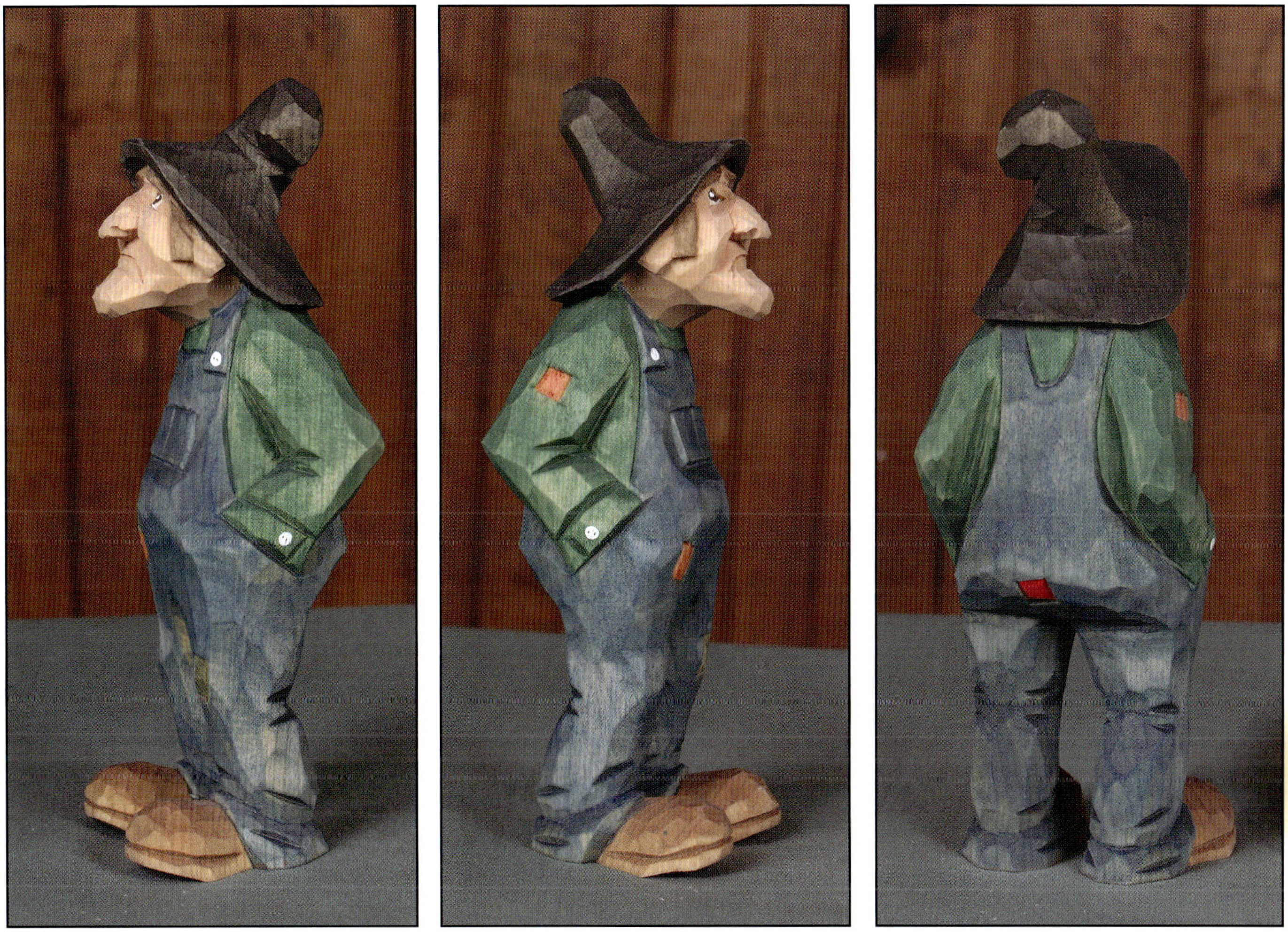

The chin and the overall hunched look give Arlo some character and add to his grumpiness. There's no hair showing anywhere except the sideburns; the hat rests on the top of the shoulders.

Enlarge pattern 110%

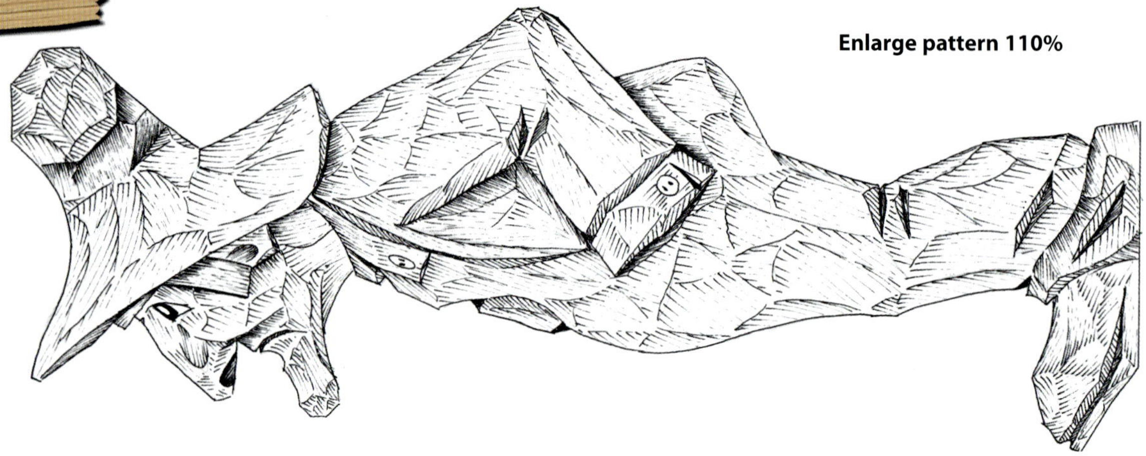

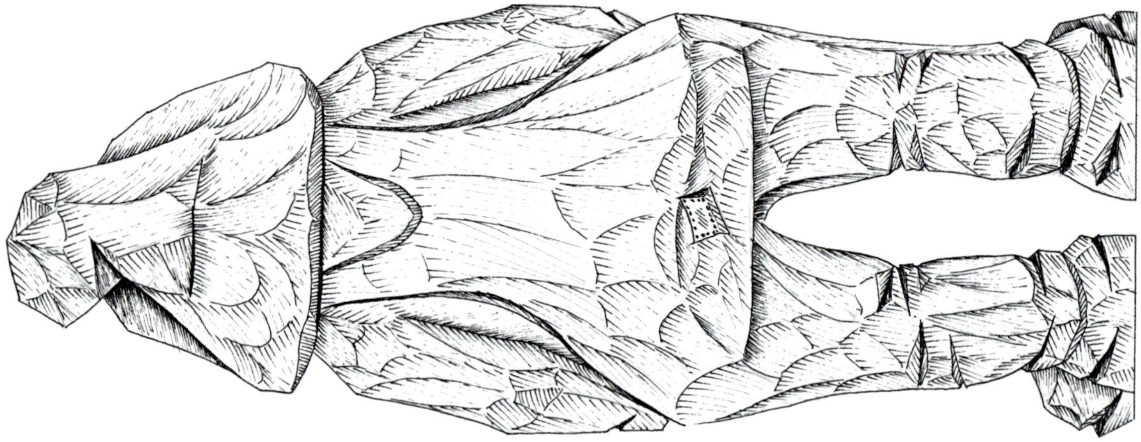

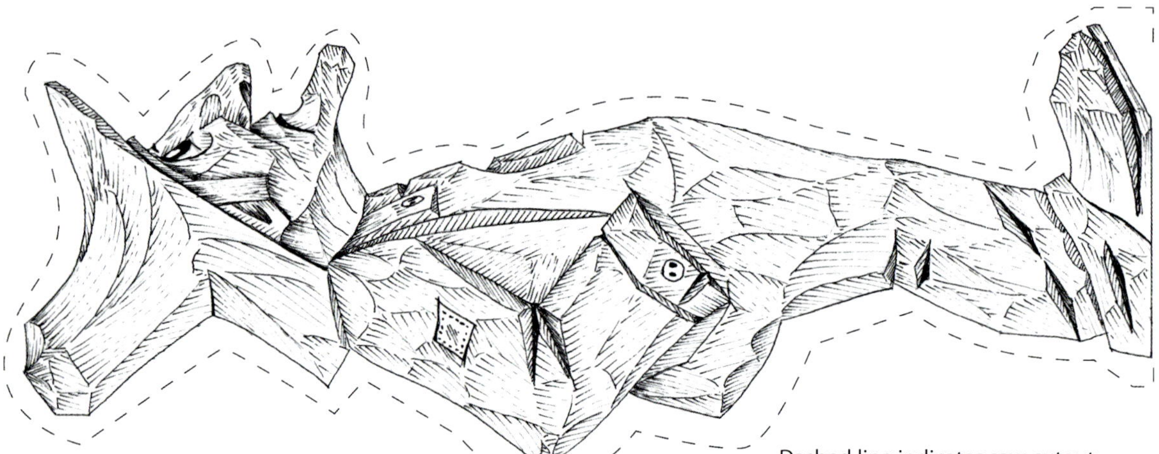

Dashed line indicates saw cutout

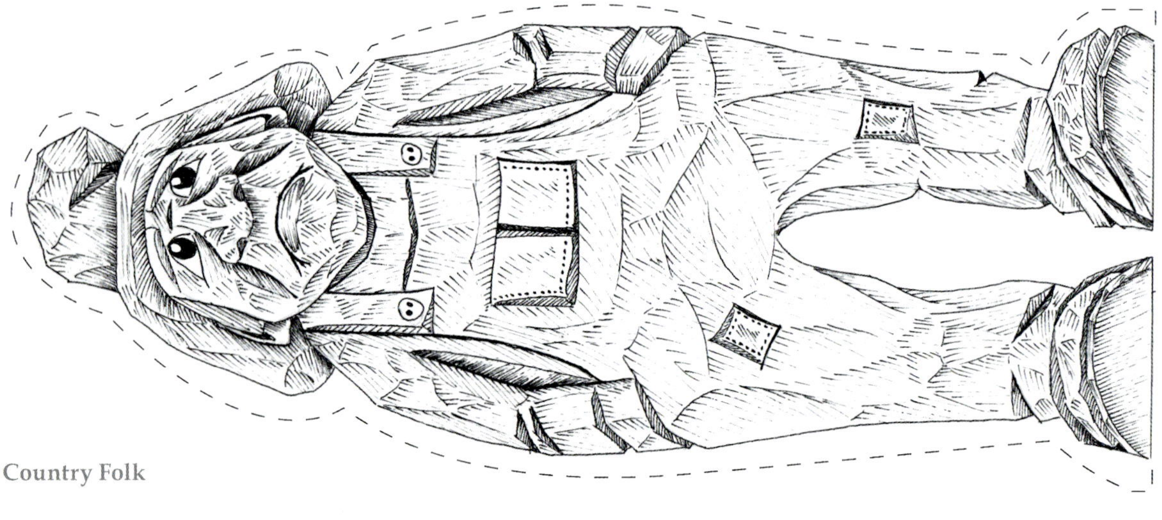

Acrylic paints:

White
Coffee bean brown
Flesh
Black
Hunter Green
Navy blue
Burnt umber
Various colors (for patches)

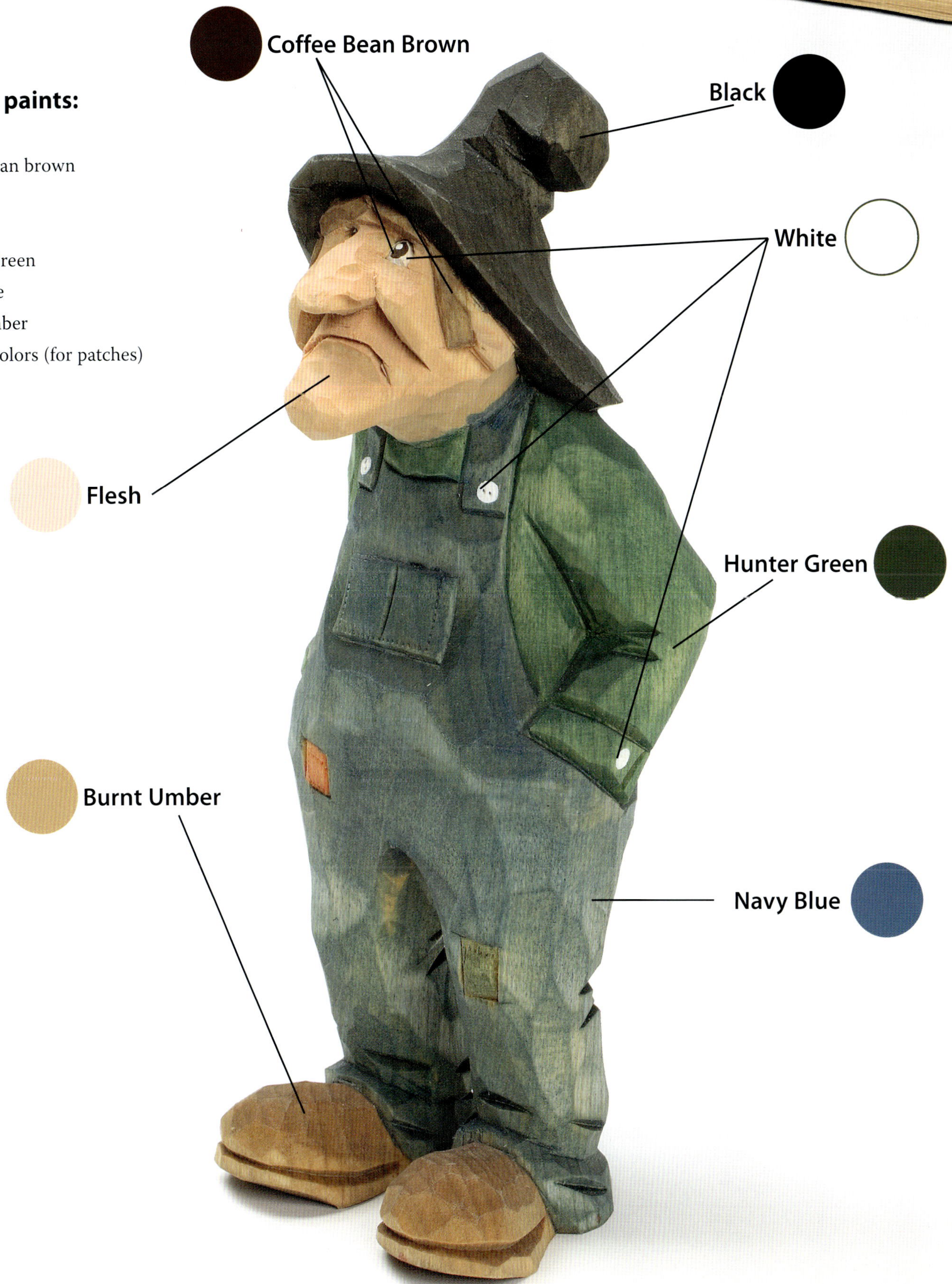

Benny

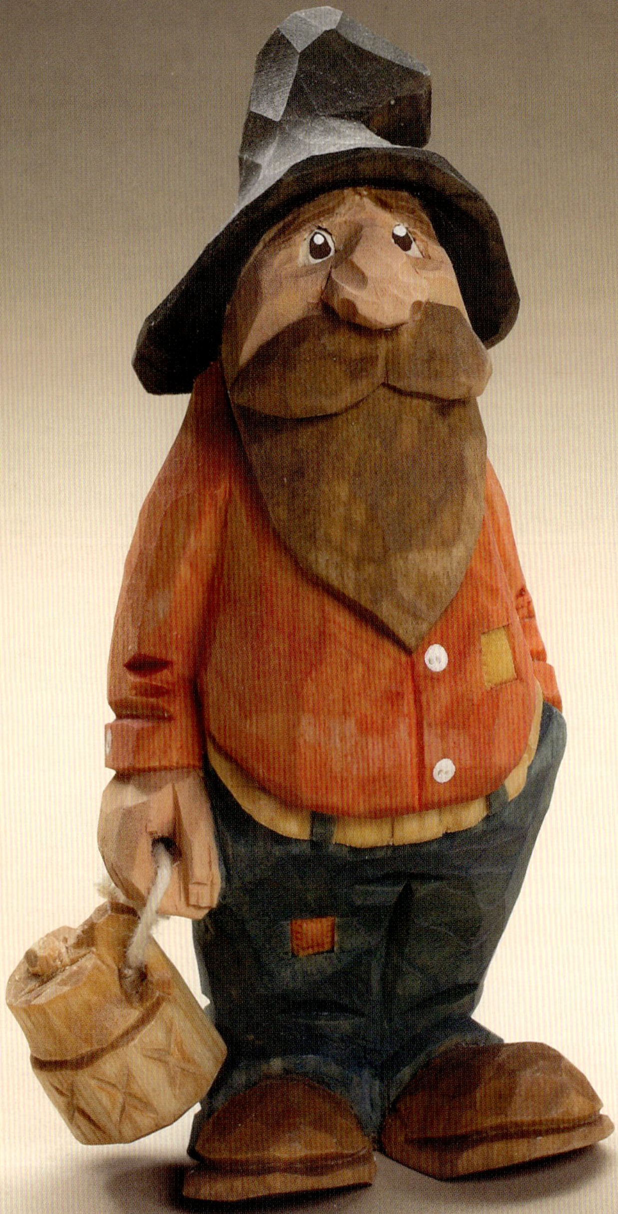

Benny is in the moonshine business with his brothers, Willie and Odie, and Benny is the brains of the business. That's why they call him "Benny the Brain." Benny built the business from scratch at the age of three when his ma ran off with that salesman, and he's been makin' shine and taking care of his brothers ever since.

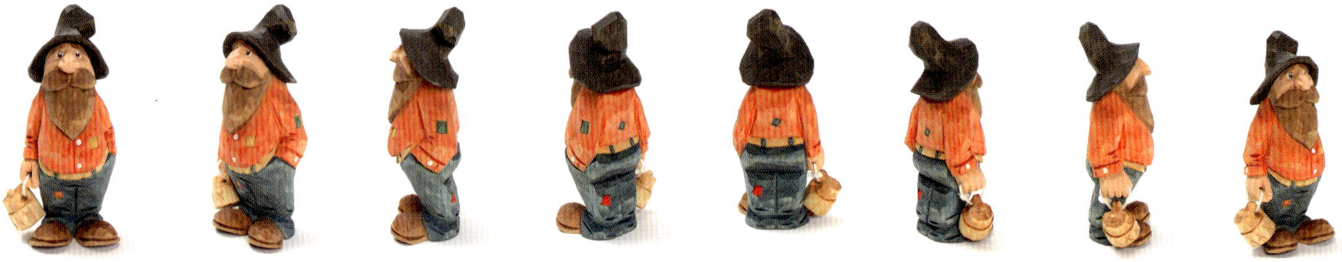

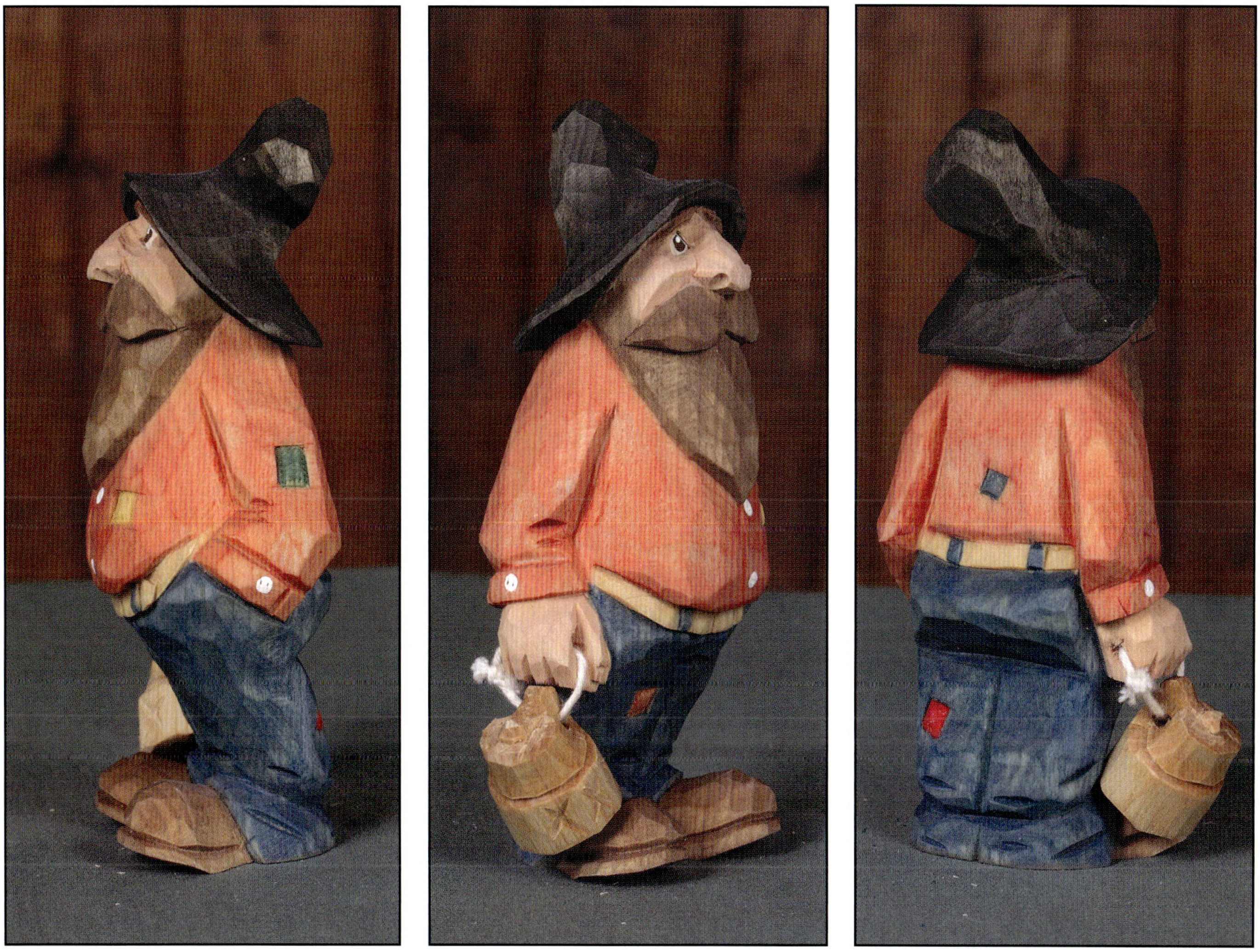

Looks like we've caught old Benny on the way to the still to refill that jug. The hand is drilled with a ⅛" bit, and the jug is carved from a ¾" square block. I don't use a pattern. The jug handle has a ⅛" hole. Carve some Xs on the jug.

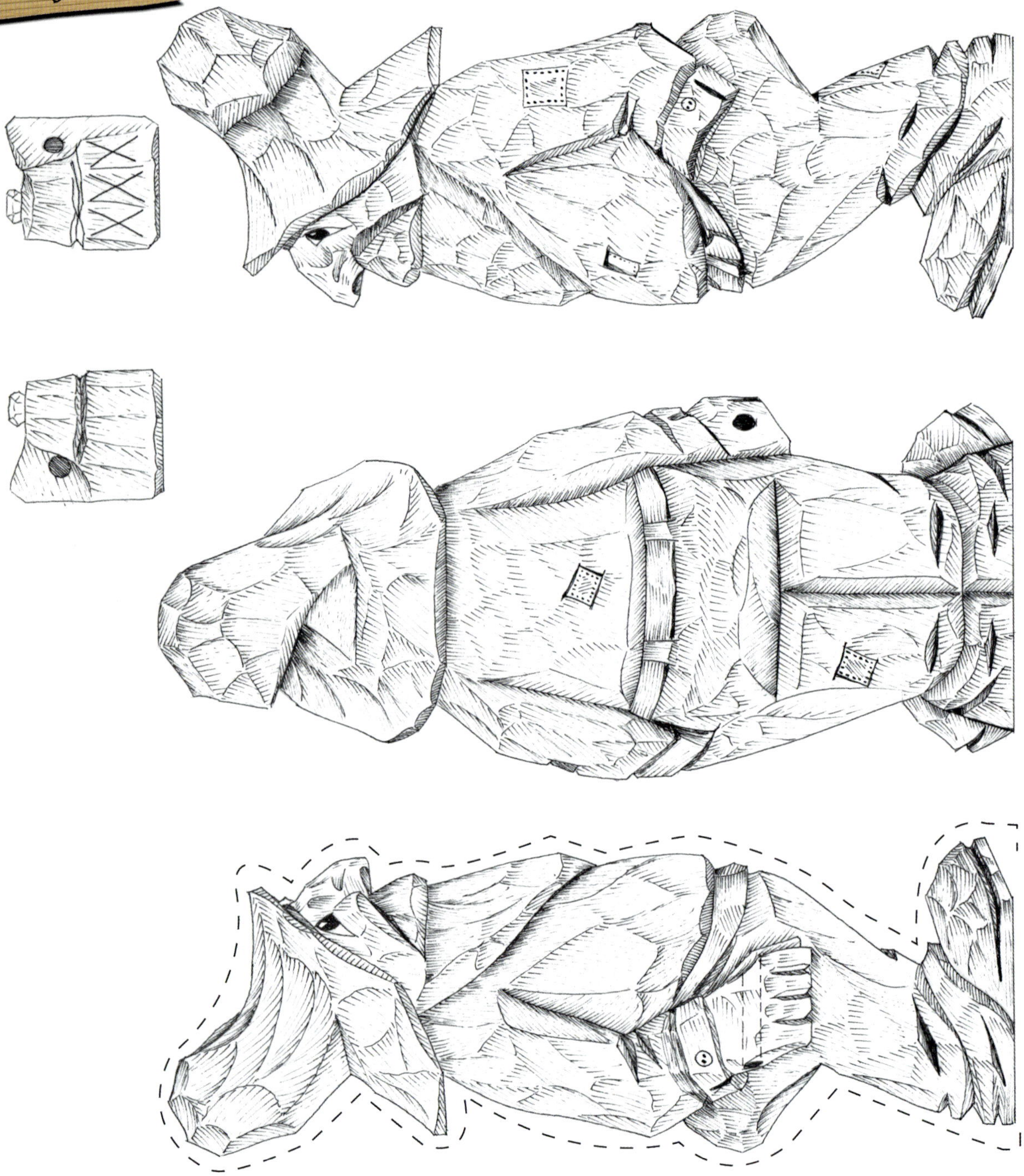

Dashed line indicates saw cutout

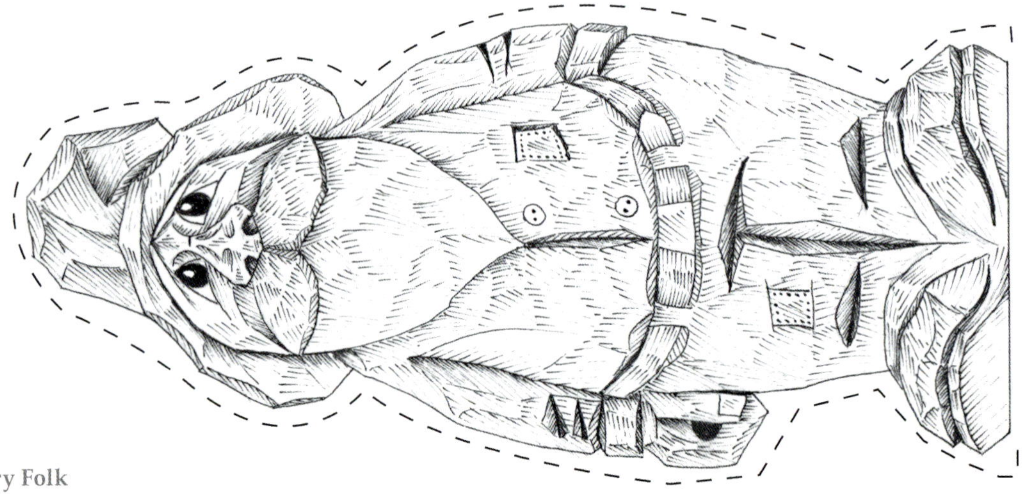

Acrylic paints:

White
Coffee bean brown
Flesh
Black
Orange
Navy blue
Burnt umber
Various colors (for patches)

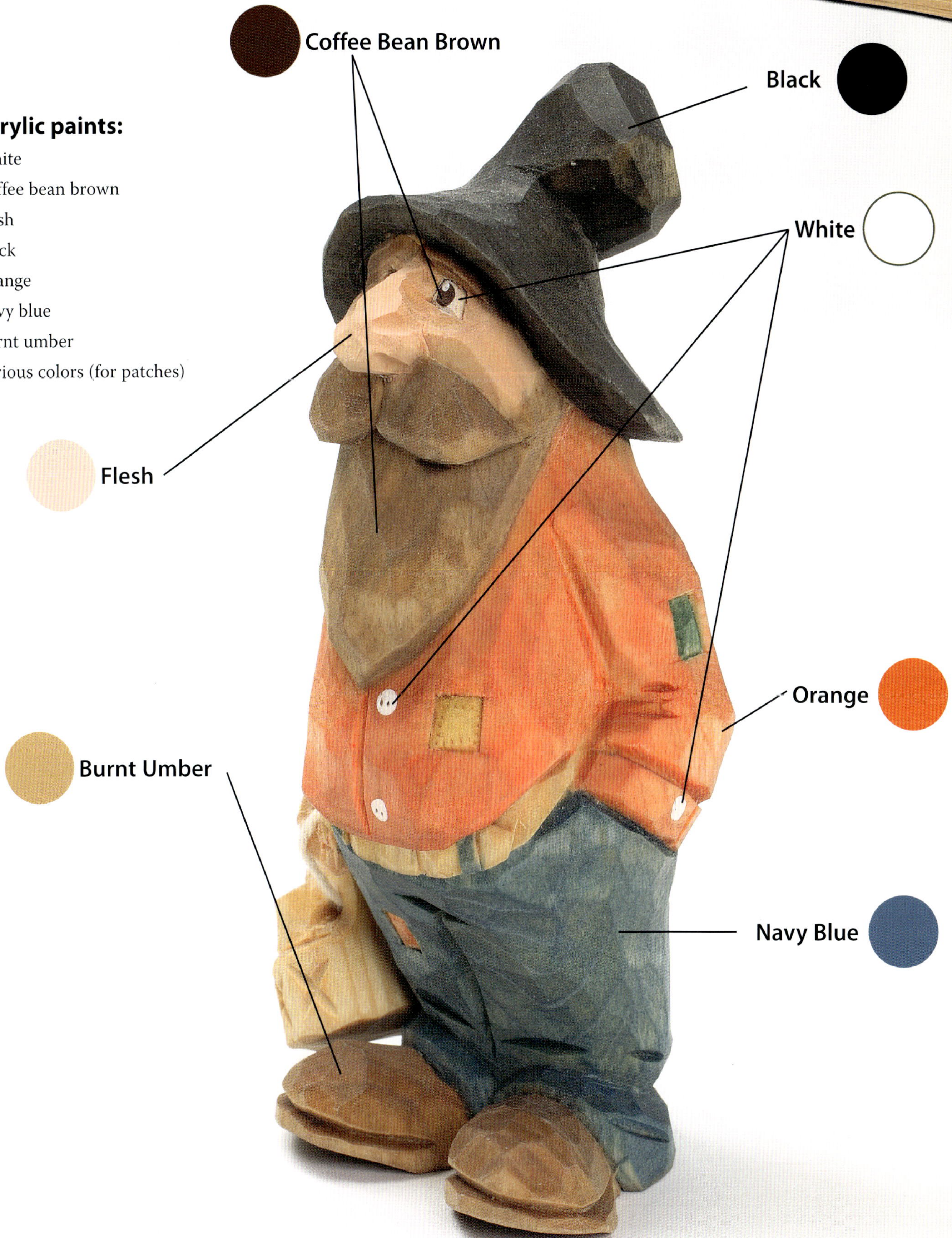

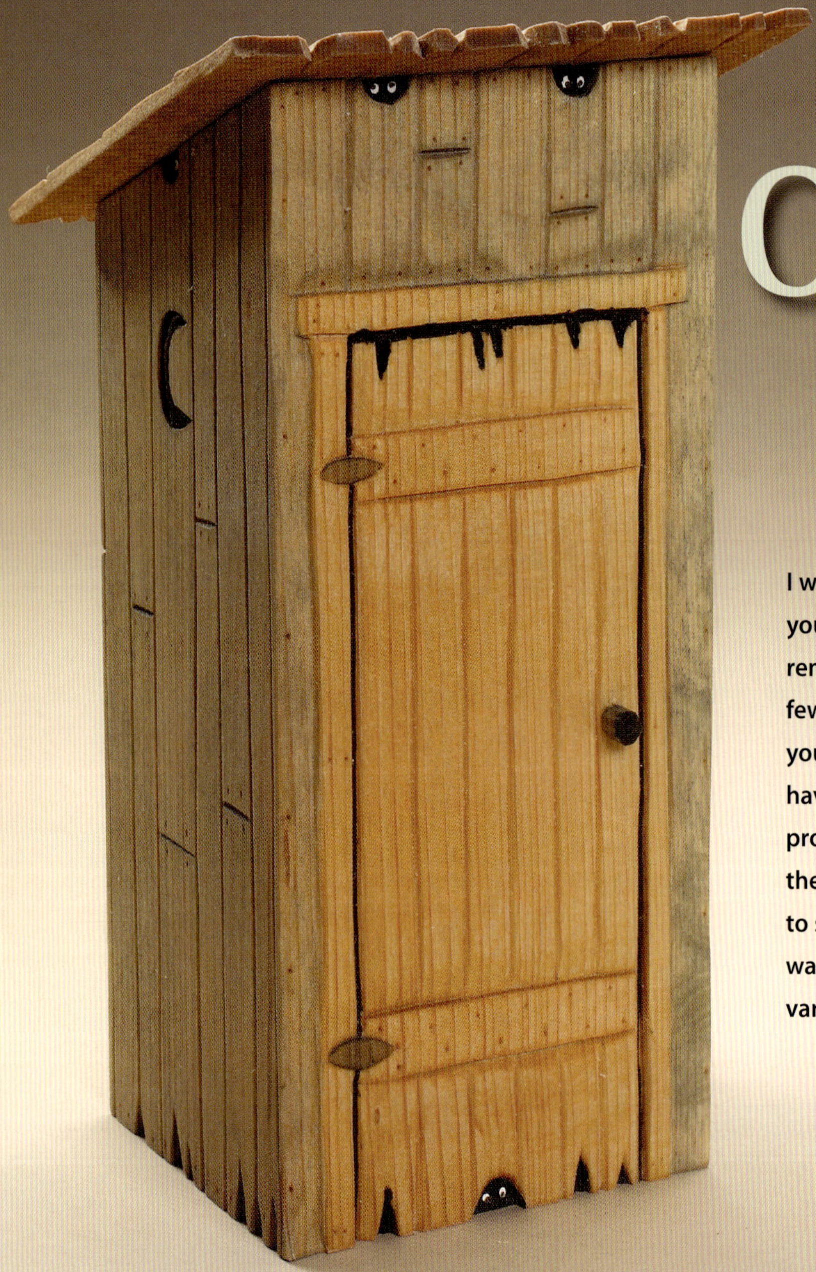

Outhouse

I want to see a show of hands: How many of you remember using the old outhouse? I can remember it very well, and I can show you a few that are still standing tall. For those of you who do remember, I'll bet you would all have stories to tell. Most of the stories would probably be pretty similar—like wasps and the occasional black snake. Nobody wanted to spend much time in the outhouse, so there wasn't any need for reading material. Even the varmints didn't like it much.

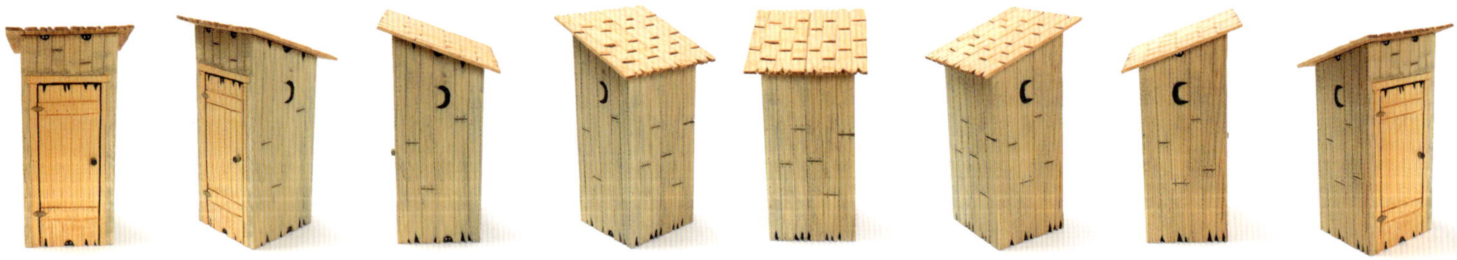

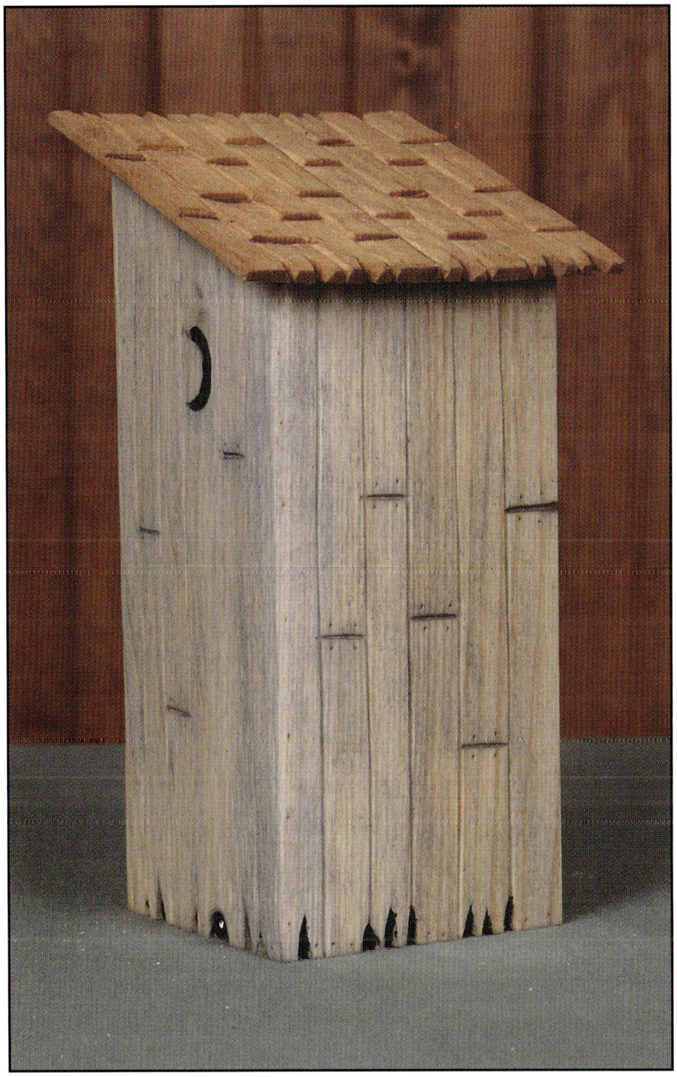

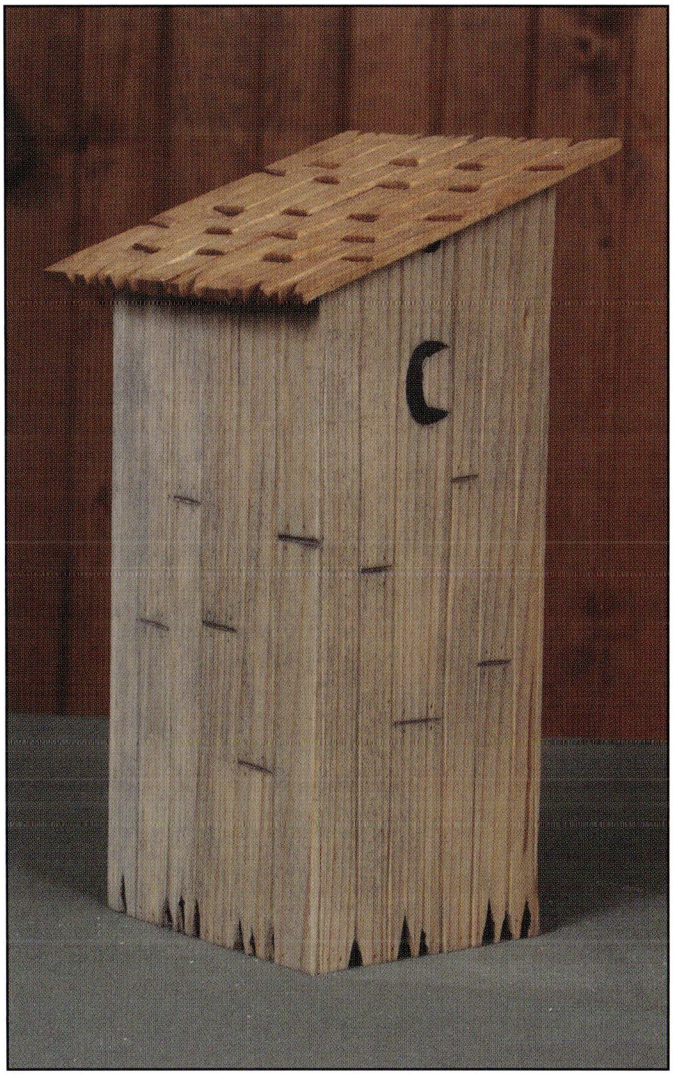

The outhouse can be any size; the slope for the roof should be pretty steep. The roof is carved separately and then glued on. The outhouse is a solid piece of wood with the details carved on. The cracks are just simple V-tool cuts. The cracks, holes, and moon are all shallow and carved with the knife tip and a small V-tool. Paint these areas with black straight from the bottle. Dot the eyeballs with straight white; then, dot the white with straight coffee bean brown.

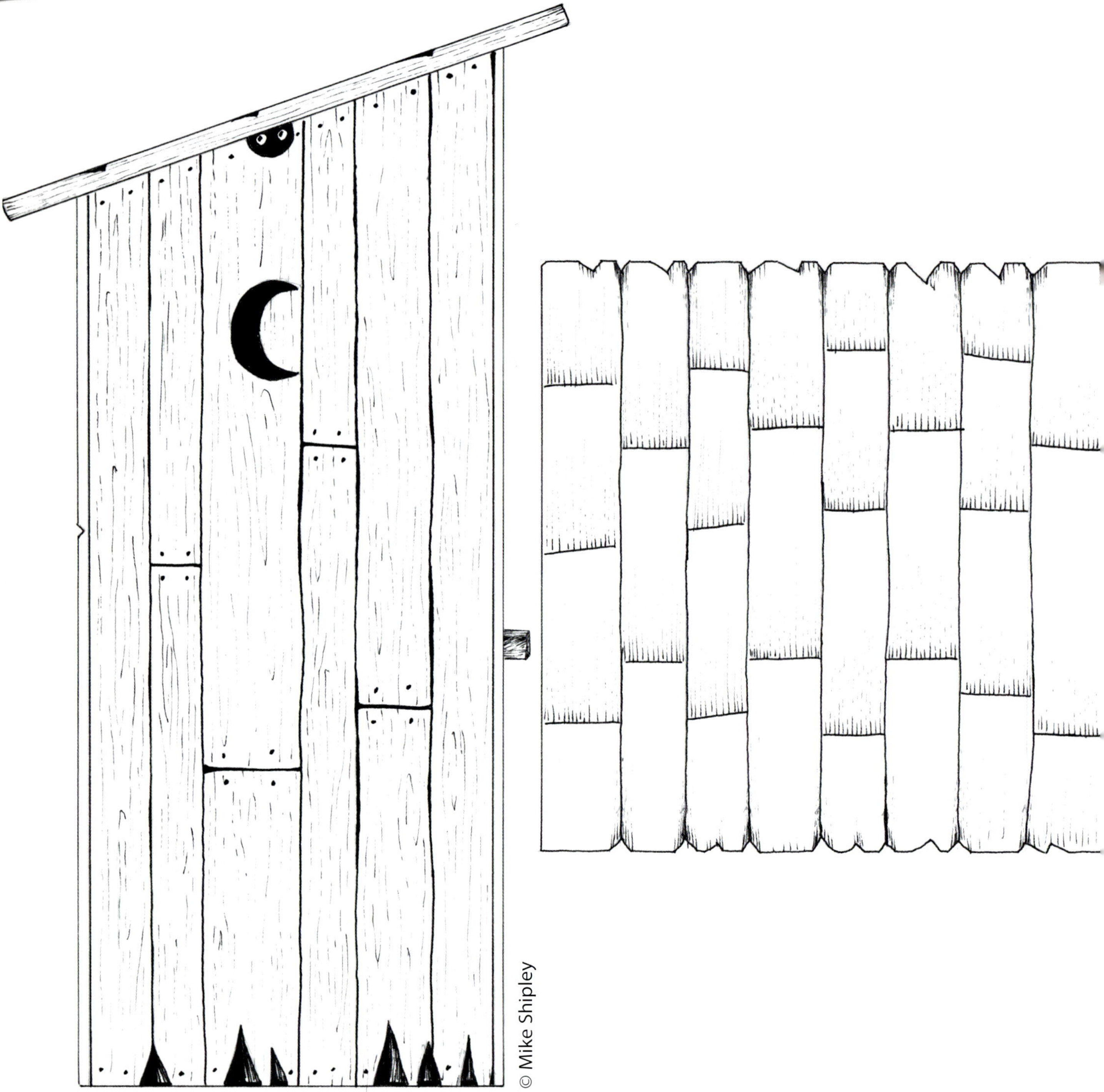

© Mike Shipley

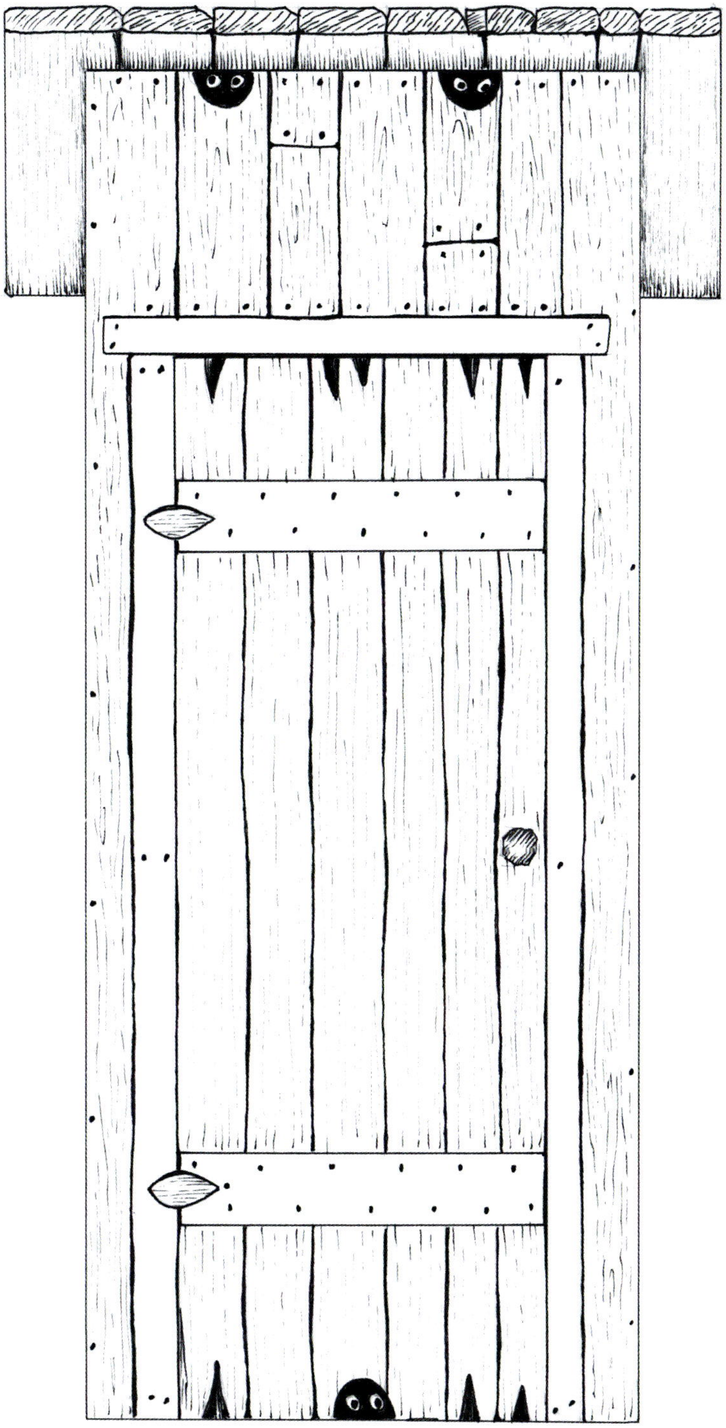

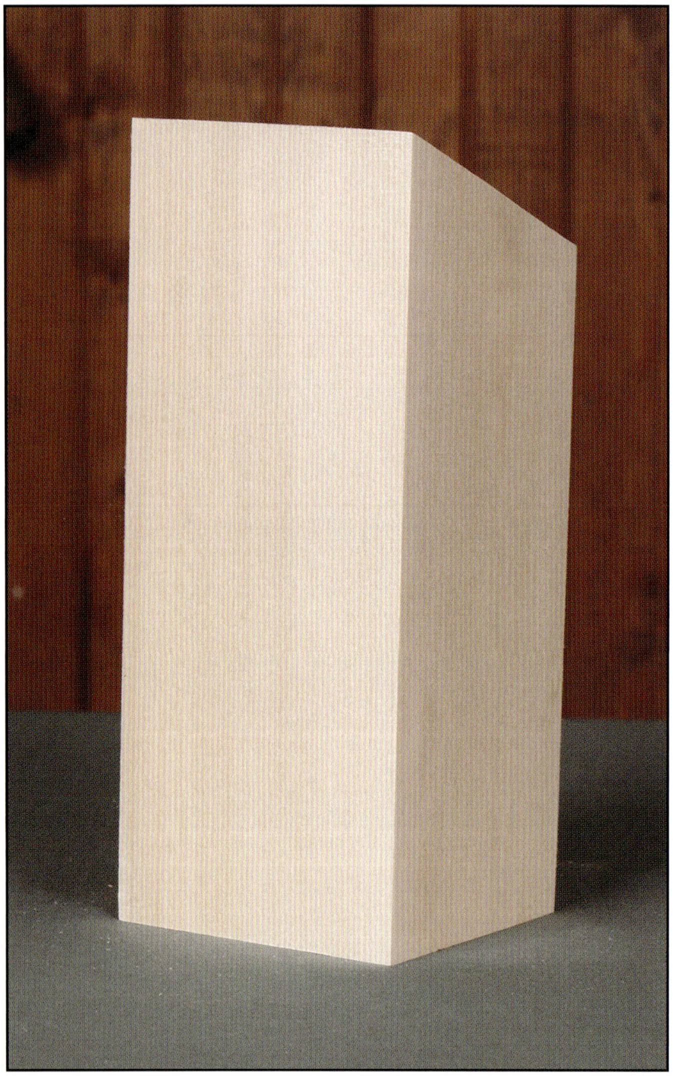

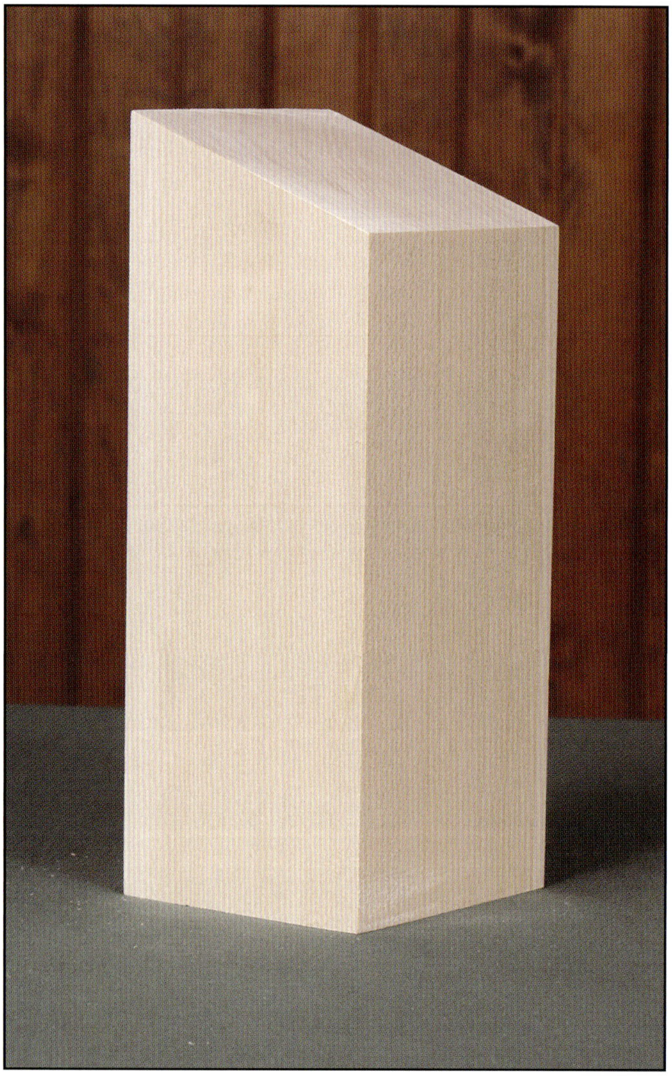

Acrylic paints:

White
Coffee bean brown
Black
Uniform Blue
Burnt umber

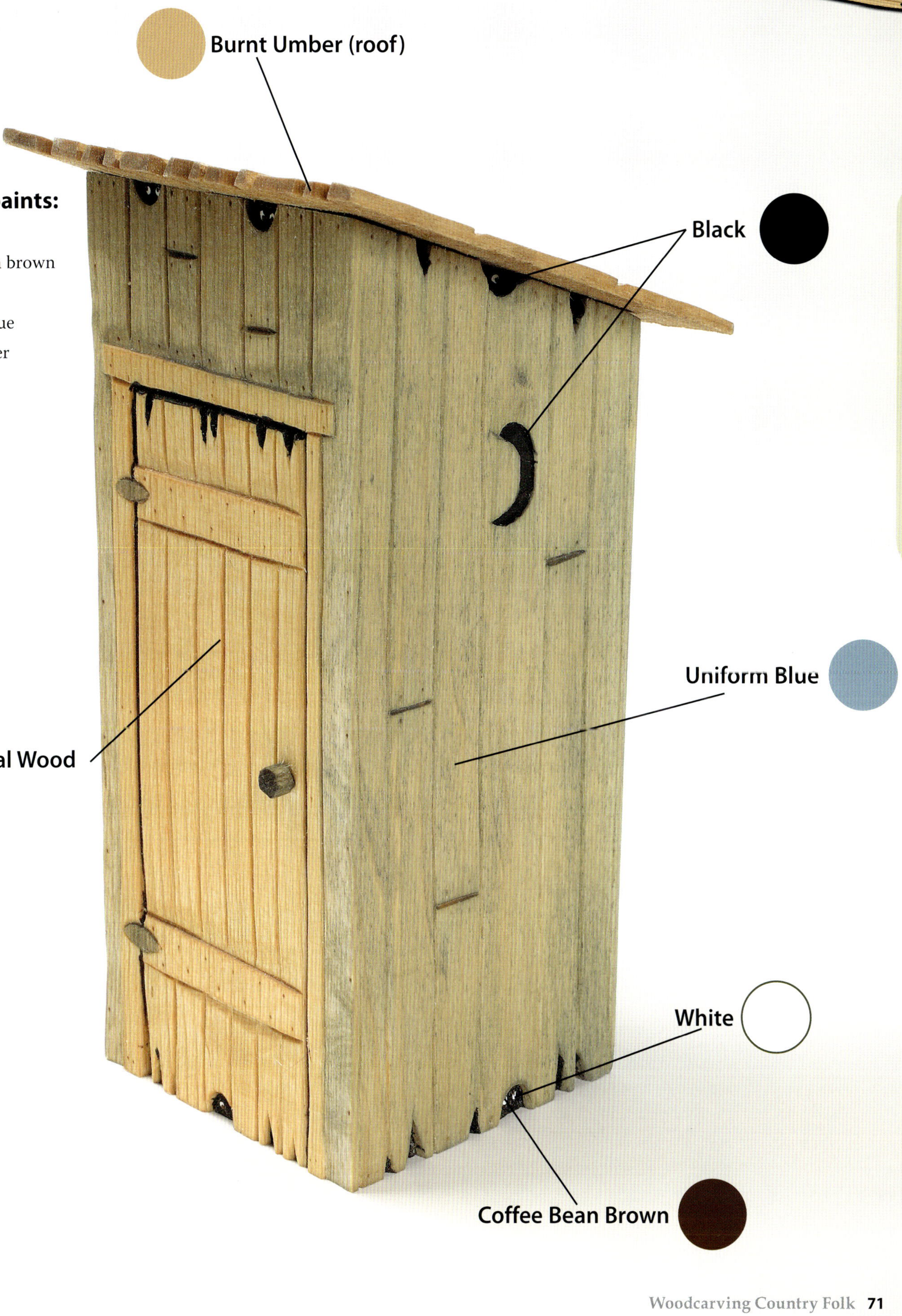

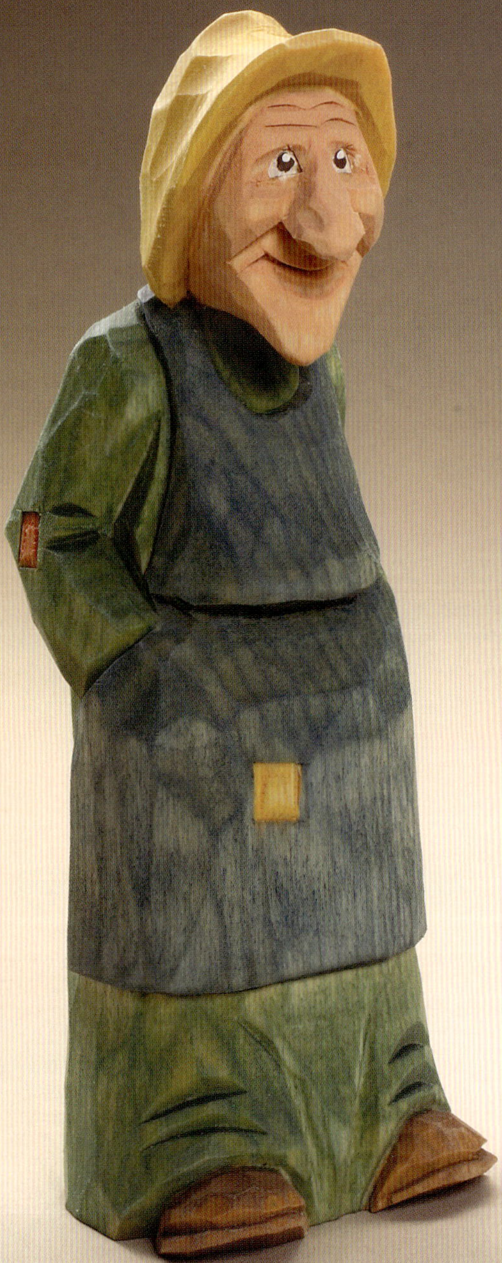

Granny

Most everybody can remember and relate to Granny. No matter what you called her, I'll bet you can remember Granny. I remember a grandma that was pretty stern when she needed to be, and even when she didn't need to be. But I can see now that she always had a soft spot for a group of boys that always seemed to wind up at her house just about every day. Granny has an awful time keeping this bunch in line, but if anybody can do it, Granny can.

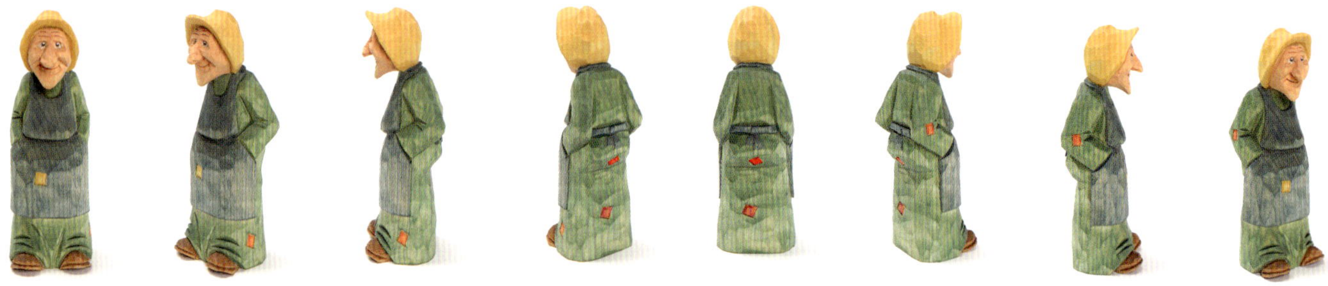

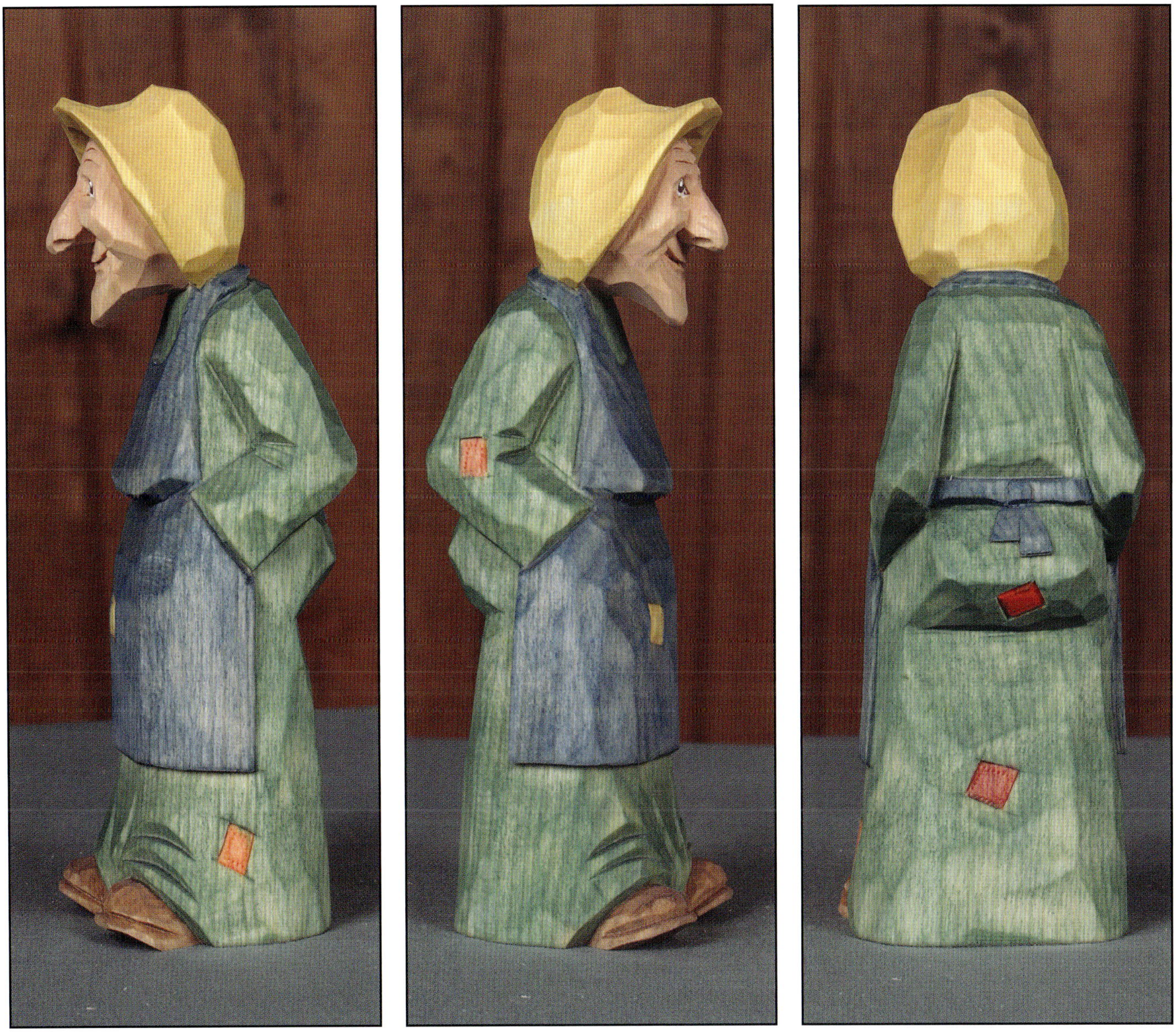

Notice that Granny has the same body shape as Arlo. I designed them using the same pattern.

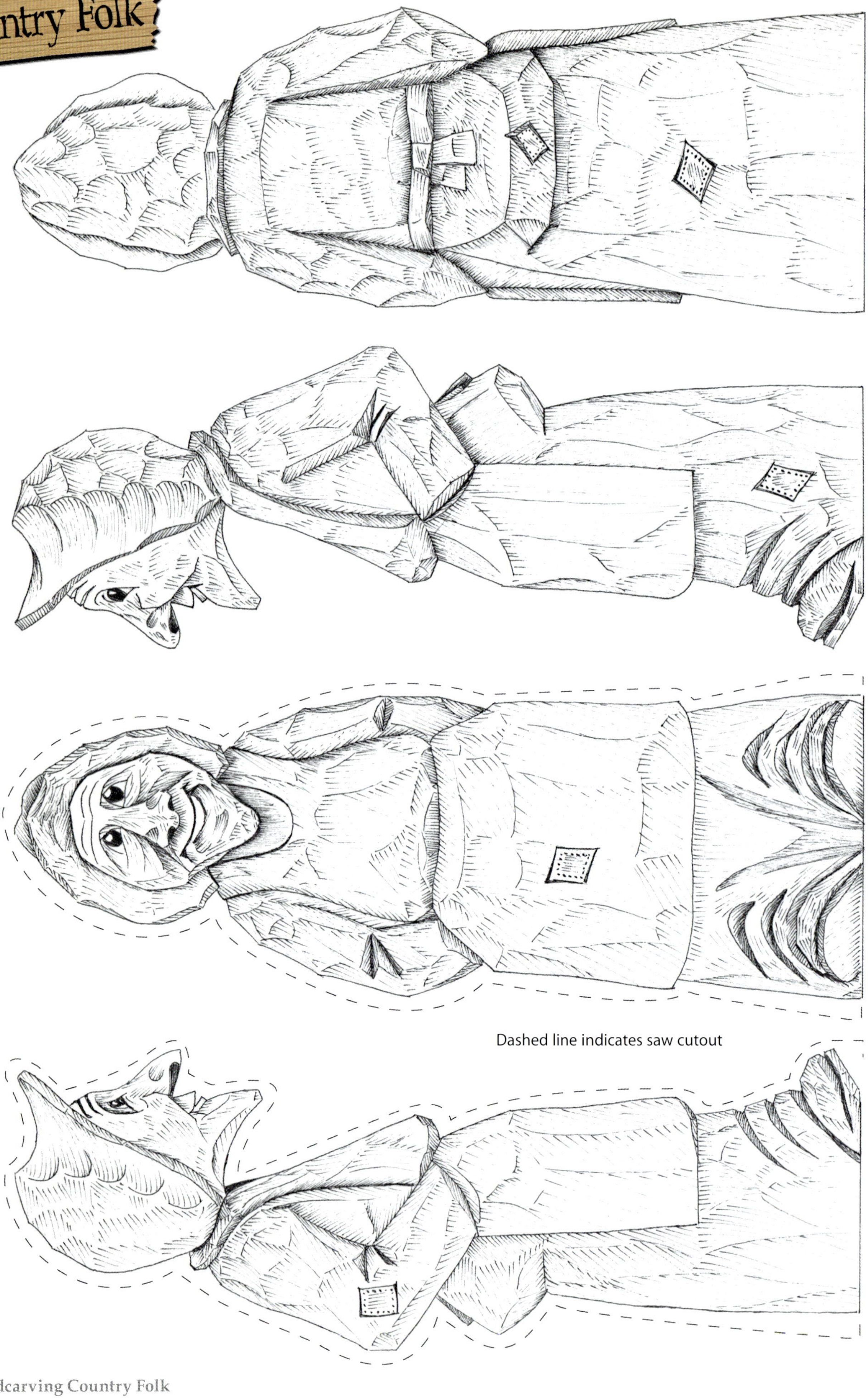

Dashed line indicates saw cutout

Acrylic paints:

White
Coffee bean brown
Flesh
Straw
Hunter green
Navy blue
Burnt umber
Various colors (for patches)

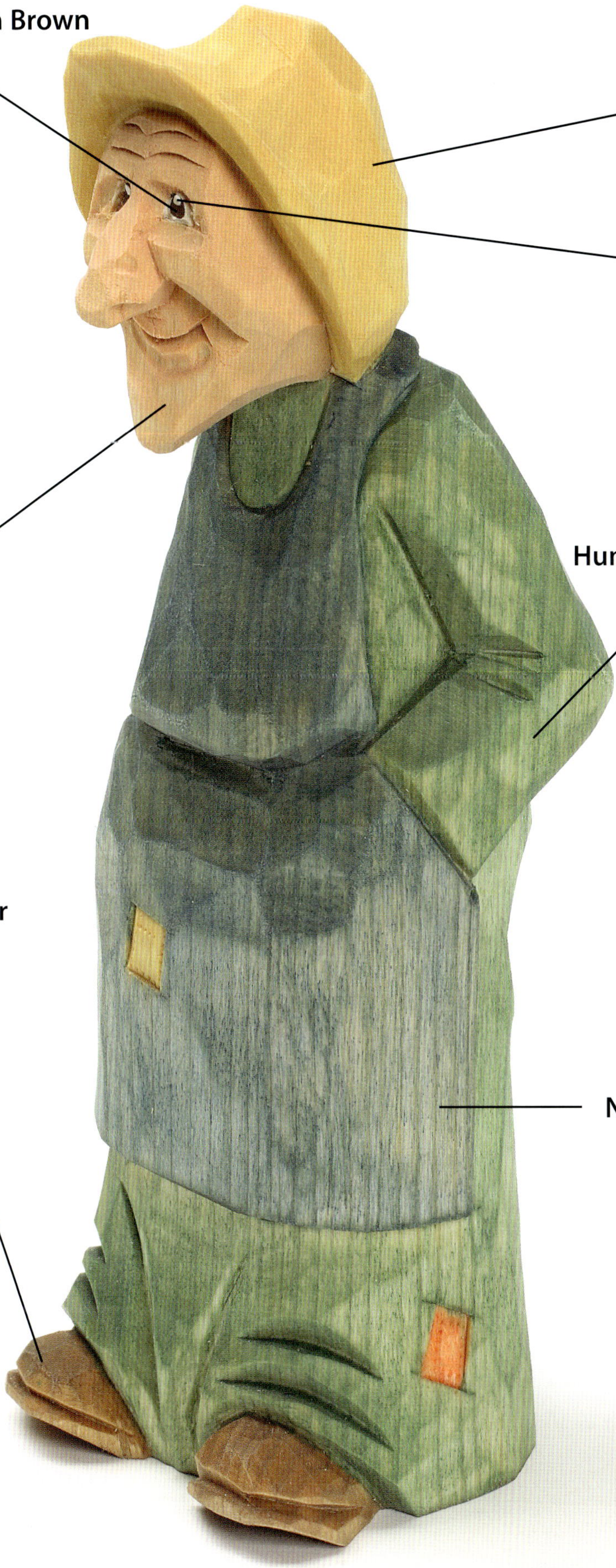

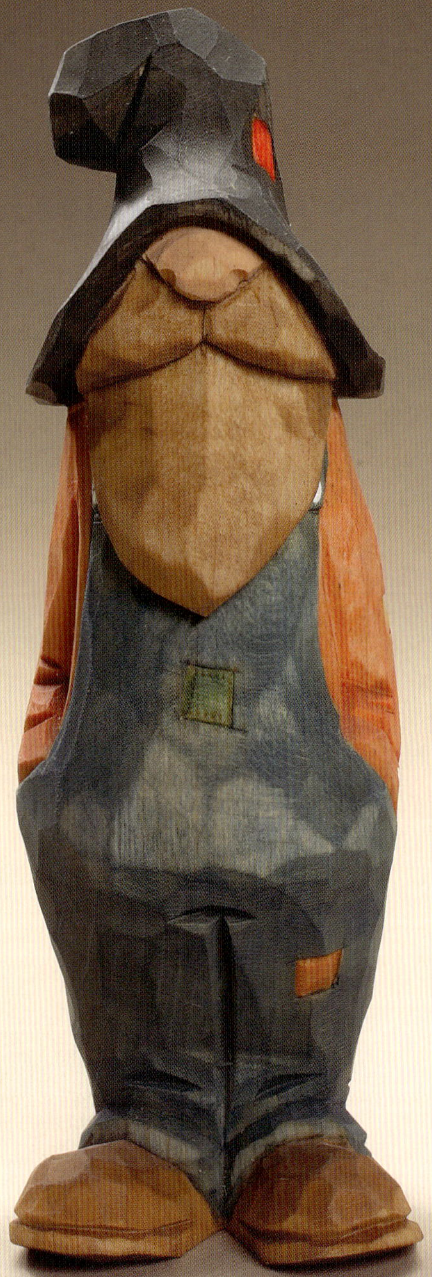

Odie

Now, if you remember, Odie is one of the identical triplets who had to pull themselves up by their diaper straps at the age of three. Odie may be bigger than his brothers, but in the pecking order of the brothers, Odie comes in dead last. Benny does the thinking, and Willie sees to it that Odie does all of the work. Odie does alright—as long as you keep him busy and keep him fed.

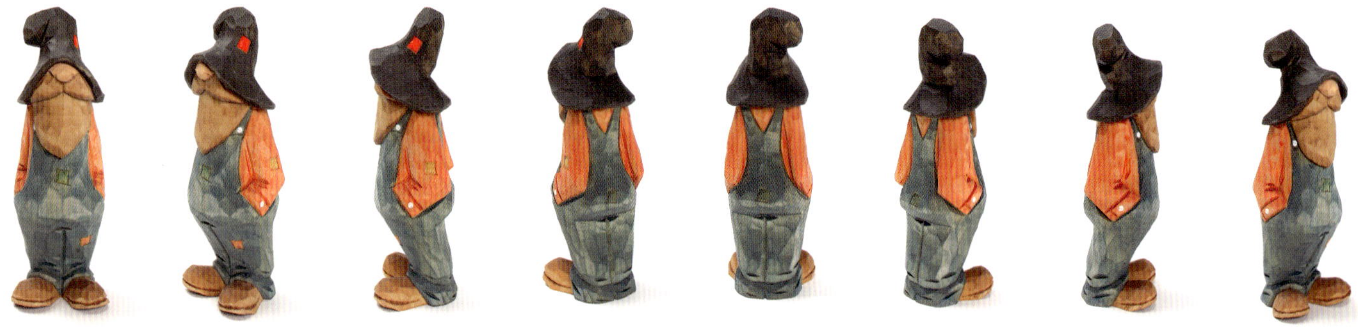

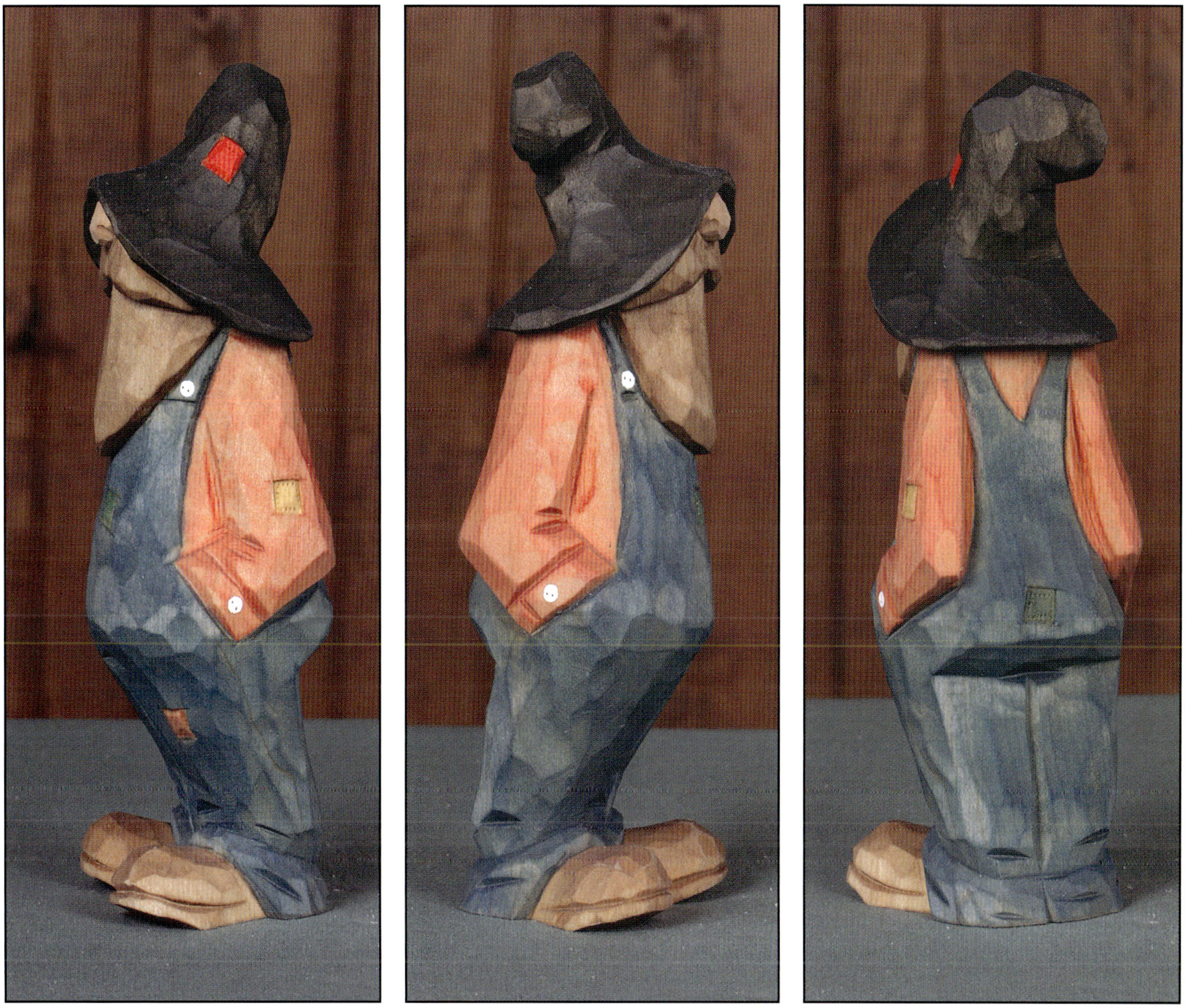

Odie is designed to be simple—no eyes, no hands, no mouth. Although this is a very simple piece, the droopy hat gives him some needed character.

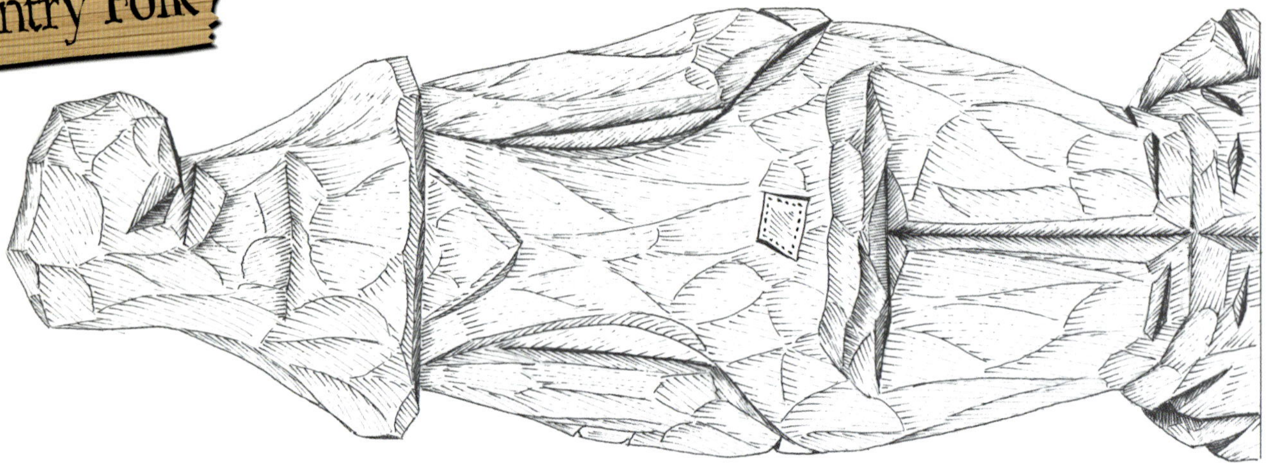

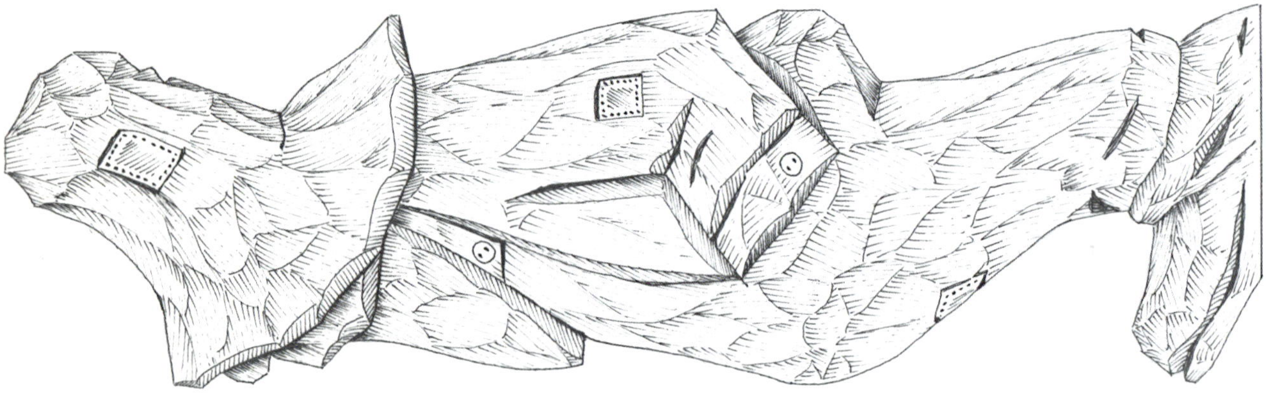

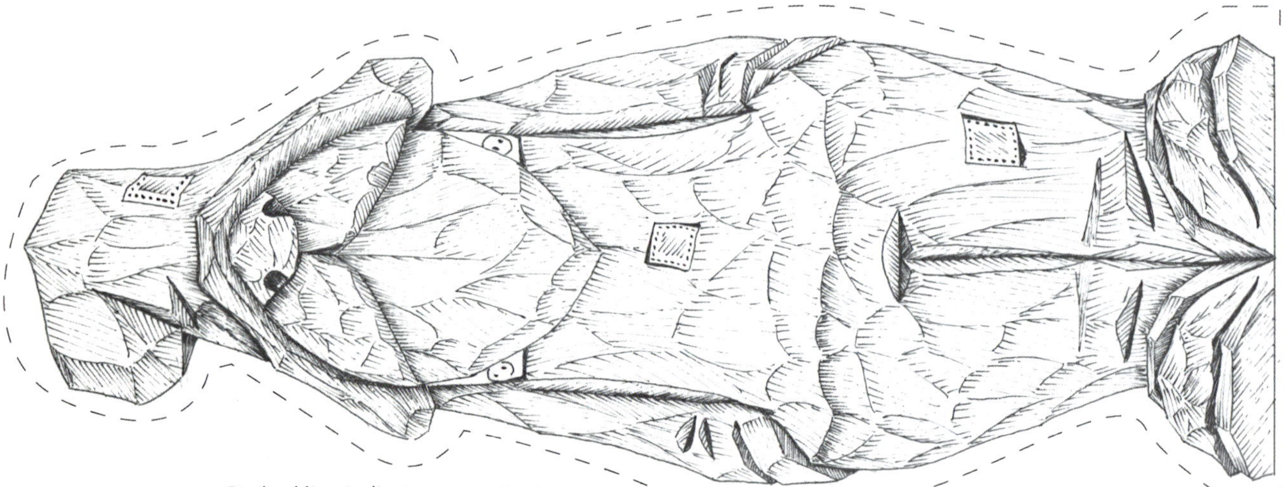

Dashed line indicates saw cutout

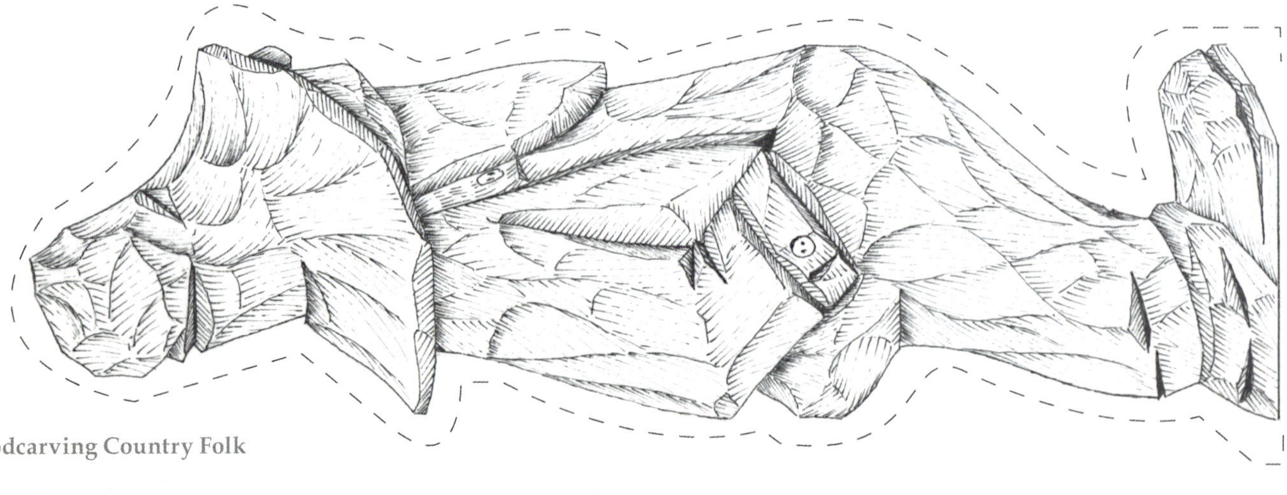

Acrylic paints:

White
Coffee bean brown
Flesh
Black
Orange
Navy blue
Burnt umber
Various colors (for patches)

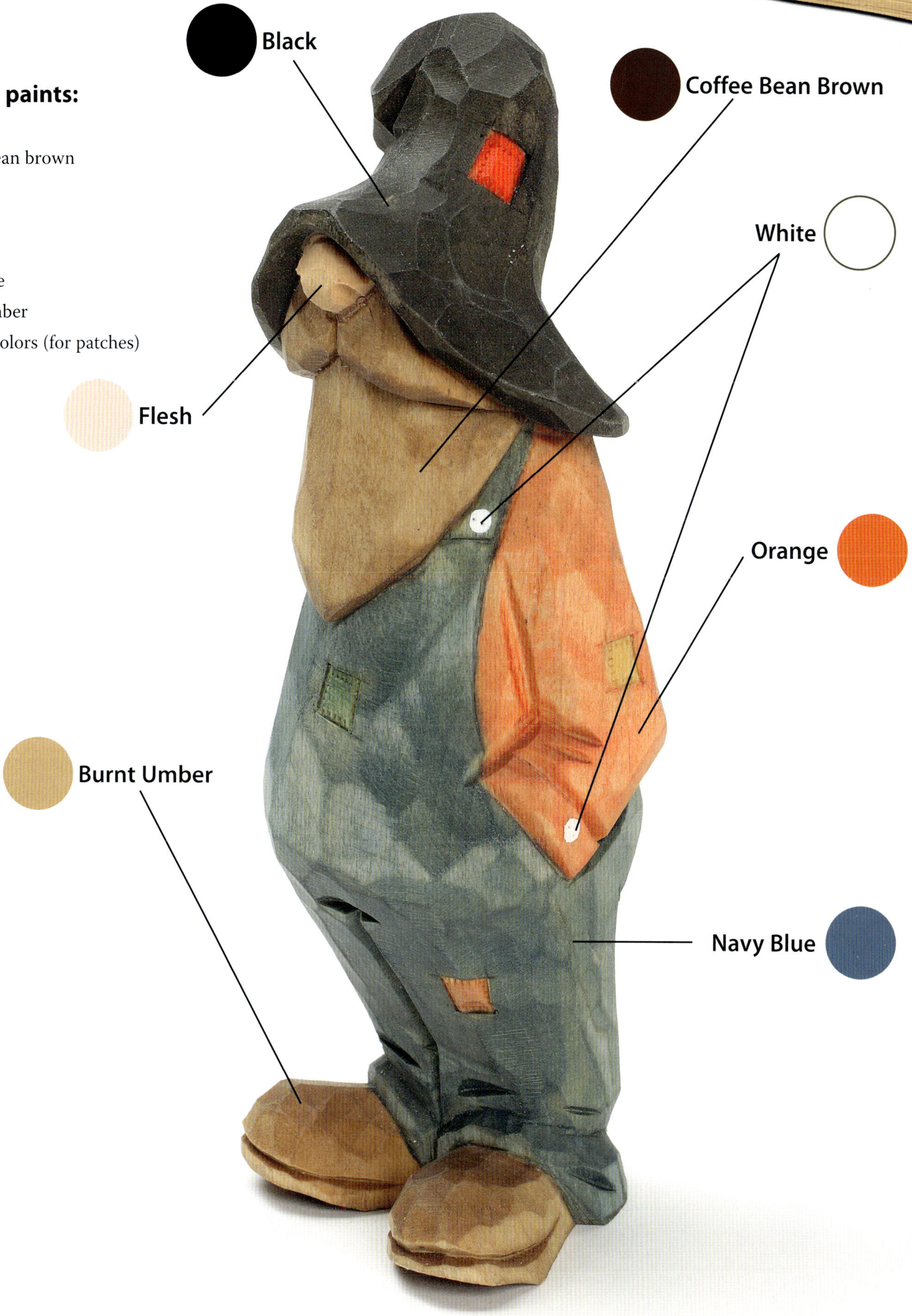